Mary Lou & John Tanton:

A Journey into American Conservation

MARY LOU & JOHN TANTON:
A JOURNEY INTO AMERICAN CONSERVATION

JOHN F. ROHE
FAIR HORIZON PRESS™ Washington, DC

Copyright © 2002 by John F. Rohe

All rights reserved. No part of this book may be reproduced or transmitted in any form or by any means, electronic or mechanical, including photocopying, recording, or by any information storage and retrieval system, without permission in writing from the publisher.

Published by FAIR Horizon Press™
1666 Connecticut Ave. NW, Suite 400
Washington, D.C. 20009

Publisher's Cataloging-in-Publication Data
Rohe, John F.
    Mary Lou and John Tanton: a Journey into American Conservation / John F. Rohe. — Washington, D.C.: FAIR Horizon Press™, 2002.

       p. ill. cm.
    Includes bibliographical references and index.
    ISBN 0-9710079-0-X
    1. Tanton, John. 2. Tanton, Mary Lou. 3. Conservationists—United States—Biography. 4. Conservation of natural resources—United States—Biography. 5. Immigration. 6. FAIR. I. Title.

S926,T368 R64	2002	2001090188
333/72/0973	—dc21	CIP

Editor's Note:
In the name of consistency and current copy-editing practices, minor changes have been made to the previously published appendices; the substantive content of the articles has not been altered.

Cover photo courtesy of Gary Williams
Cover design by Kelli Leader

06 05 04 03 02 • 6 5 4 3 2 1

Printed in the United States of America

To Debbie,
for the privilege of a shared life.

Contents

Foreword by Governor Richard D. Lamm ix
Preface xv

1. Heretics and Prophets 1
2. Something in Common 5
3. The Curiosity of a Child 11
4. Foresight and Myopia 27
5. A Darwinian Casualty 33
6. Prophecy and Charity 37
7. Striking a Balance 41
8. "Unto the Breach" 45
9. Confrontation or Cooperation? 51
10. Human Interest and Population Advocacy 55
11. "Of Grass and Grassroots" 65
12. Practice on Loan 77
13. Nation of a Billion 87
14. The Great American Paradox 99
15. A Good Thing 103
16. Mondays with John 107
17. Frames of Reference 113
18. Litter on a Stick 117
19. The Road to Ruin 123

20.	Ability or Agility	129
21.	Addition and Division	133
22.	A Barrel of Ink	139
23.	Bell of Freedom	143
24.	A Crash Course on Population	151
25.	Do You Know the Type?	157
26.	The Last Word	165

Epilogue: Random Events in a Safe
Refuge for Civility 171

Scrapbook of Memories 179

Appendix A: The Mitchell Prize: International
Migration 1975 by John H. Tanton 185

Appendix B: End of the Migration Epoch?
by John H. Tanton 201

Appendix C: Mary Lou Tanton's Viewpoint
on Abortion 231

Appendix D: Social Contract Themes
during John H. Tanton's Editorship 235

Appendix E: Nothing More Can Be Done . . .
A Fable for Our Times by John H. Tanton 251

Appendix F: Mary Lou Tanton's Twenty-Five
Most Influential Books 257

Appendix G: John H. Tanton's Twenty-Five
Most Influential Books 259

Appendix H: "Cast Down Your Bucket Where
You Are" by John H. Tanton 261

Endnotes 265

Index 269

About the Author 275

Acknowledgments 277

Foreword

by Governor Richard D. Lamm

THIS IS MUCH MORE THAN A BOOK ABOUT TWO VERY TALENTED people. It is also a book that articulately illustrates two powerful themes. First, it is an insight into how new viewpoints gain a foothold in the world of ideas (perhaps more specifically it is about the emergence of new and heretical ideas). Second, it is a lesson on how people from even remote parts of America can assert their ideas by the power of their message, the wisdom of their strategies, and the strength of their personalities.

The world of ideas is always in flux, but occasionally certain old, deeply established ideas are in need of revolution. "In every age there is a turning-point, a new way of seeing and asserting the coherence of the world," says Bronowski in *The Ascent of Man*. Copernicus caused a revolution in how humankind saw the universe, Darwin in how we viewed the human place in the natural order, Freud in how we think about the unconscious, and Betty Friedan in the way we view women's roles in modern society. All these individuals and many more were branded heretics. But John Rohe wisely reminds us of George Bernard Shaw's statement that "All great truths begin as blasphemies" when referring to the work of Mary Lou and John Tanton.

Giving birth to a new vision is one of the great challenges of history. These new ways of "asserting the coherence in the world," however logical, do not come easy. Reformers always face entrenched opposition from the status quo and more than a few have lost their lives trying to assert a new coherence. The status quo is always protected by an army of conformists blocking the door. James Joyce observed that "It's as painful to be awakened from a vision as to be born."

This is not true in the world of innovation or technology. Technological change usually forces itself on a competitive society. Technology does not wait for a consensus. It diffuses speedily through competition and the marketplace. Miss the latest technological advance and you could be out of business. Alvin Toffler describes the results of this process: "Western society for the past 300 years has been caught up in a fire storm of change. This storm, far from abating, now appears to be gathering force. Change sweeps through the highly industrialized countries with waves of ever accelerating speed and unprecedented impact." Consequently we have a great imbalance between change in the real world and how tradition and public policy react to that change.

The Tantons often ask cosmic questions, forcing us to see the consequences of present change. I remember well when John pointed out that the original U.S. Census in 1790 found four million. John observed that meant in our short two-hundred-year history that we have had six doublings of that original number (4, 8, 16, etc.) and that with only two more doublings, we would be a nation of more than a billion people. He asked, is that what we wanted for our grandchildren?

All his listeners knew the movement had a new metaphor.

Typical of the type of questions the Tantons ask is "What is our nation's demographic destiny?" We define the world by the questions we ask and we have too few people like the Tantons asking long-range questions. These two creative minds saw twenty-five years ago that "how many" and "who" would soon become controversial issues in most of the world's nations. John, in his 1975 Mitchell Prize essay (Appendix A), recognized that these would be particularly painful questions in the United States, with its tradition of immigration. Yes, the United States could physically absorb more people, but what would that mean to our quality of life? Increasingly, citizens of this nation (and citizens of most states and regions) are asking the following questions: "Why do we want additional population growth?" "Who benefits?" "What public policy reasons are there to double the population of Michigan or Colorado?" "Why would America want to leave its grandchildren a nation of one billion people?"

The Tantons, years before most other environmentalists, saw that our nation's demographic future had shifted from an unalterable given to an alterable variable—from something we blindly inherited to something we consciously determine. Yes, earlier environmentalists had known that the world institutions atavistically promoted population growth and were starting to ask heretical questions about population limits. But most of us had not focused on how important immigration was to this challenge in the United States. Even today, most experts are uncomfortable about nation-specific population and look at population only from a worldwide viewpoint. In 1992, the U.S. Academy of Sciences and the Royal Society of London warned:

> *If the current predictions of population growth prove accurate and patterns of human activity on the planet remain unchanged, science and technology may not be able to prevent either irreversible degradation of the environment or continued poverty for much of the world.*

In the same year the Union of Concerned Scientists issued a "World Scientists Urgent Warning to Humanity," signed by 1,600 of the world's leading scientists, including 102 Nobel Prize winners. It stated that the continuation of destructive human activities . . .

> *. . . may so alter the living world that it will be unable to sustain life in the manner that we know. A great change in our stewardship of the earth and the life on it is required if vast human misery is to be avoided and our global home on this planet is not to be irretrievably mutilated.*

These are not ordinary public policy questions. They are life-and-death questions about the future of the globe. But does it require a question of life or death before a nation considers population a threat and attempts to set limits? Does a nation or a region have to let its demographic situation deteriorate to intolerable limits before it acts?

In one sense, human history can be seen as asserting control over factors once thought immutable. Children were a "gift from God" until humankind discovered the fertility cycle. We either lived or died until we discovered the "miracles" of medicine and public health. We were stuck in the same social class as our parents until our institutions reformed to allow social mobility. Human history is constantly redefining the unacceptable and changing what was thought to be unchangeable.

This is clearly true of world and national population growth. For most of human history, the question of how many people the world or a particular nation should have was never asked—never thought of. Population growth was an asset, and the more population increased, the more blessed a country considered itself: France and Russia gave medals for large families, pre-World War II Germany had a variety of pro-natalist policies to encourage population growth, and Mussolini turned off the lights in state-owned housing at 9:00 p.m. so people would go to bed and conceive new Italians. "Be fruitful and multiply and replenish the earth" had its counterpart in all the world's religions, and public policy followed. The larger a country's population, the stronger the country was thought to be militarily, economically, and geopolitically. Towns equated size with success. "Watch Us Grow" was once the literal or symbolic slogan outside most of the world's cities and towns.

These conflicting visions are being played out in the United States today. Growth versus no growth. New ideas versus old concepts. Essentially, the Tantons have been confronting the implications of finitude. They think about the world from a different, but emerging, viewpoint. They ask: "Is a given human pattern ecologically possible and sustainable? Is it consistent with the integrity of the world's biosystem?" I suggest that these might well prove to be the ultimate twenty-first-century questions.

Increasingly, the whole world has started to ask the type of questions the Tantons have been asking for thirty years. For instance, the 1994 report of the Cairo Conference on Population and Development stated:

> *Population-related goals and policies are integral parts of cultural, economic and social development, the principal aim of which is to improve the quality of life of all people.*

What should be the "population-related goals and policies" for America? Asking the question at this stage is more important than the answer. Politicians almost always confirm change after it has been brought about by others outside the political system. This is never more true than in contemporary America, where politicians base their campaigns on polls and focus groups and seldom take a very long lead from the safe second base of conventional wisdom.

That leads us to another virtue of this book. The only thing harder than changing the status quo is the attempt to change it from an obscure place. Universities, think tanks, and pressure groups all generate new ideas. Most people feel powerless to effect change, especially if they are not associated with one of the more conventional change agents.

Yet America often has found its leadership in obscure places. Dwight Eisenhower came from a small farm in Kansas, Harry Truman from a small town in Missouri, Ronald Reagan from an even smaller town in Iowa. Martin Luther King Jr. rose from a neighborhood church in Atlanta, Betty Friedan from the role of a frustrated homemaker with a wider vision. The challenge of any society is to be open enough to recognize talent and vision, even if they do not arise from the established order.

John Gardner, former secretary of the Department of Health and Human Services, stresses so well the need for excellence at the various levels of society:

> *Our society cannot achieve greatness unless individuals at many levels of ability accept the need for high standards of performance and strive to achieve those standards within the limits possible for them. We want the highest conceivable excellence, of course, in the activities crucial to our effectiveness and creativity as a society, but that isn't enough. If the man in the street says, "Those fellows at the top have to be good, but I'm*

just a slob and can act like one,"—then our days of greatness are behind us.

It is said that "Revolutions are started by one individual, but succeed through the efforts of many." So now it's our turn. Our turn to take the Tantons' creativity, passion, and sense of the future, and help give birth to a new world.

Preface

IN OUR TIME, CELEBRITY STATUS HAS BEEN DEVALUED. THE media brims with scandals and corruption. We harbor a numbing disdain for names and faces in the news. The search for eligible mentors has become altogether unrewarding. Self-absorbed glory-seekers actively compete for our attention on the celebrity pages, while worthy role models elude recognition.

Unsurprisingly, we live in cynical times.

The selfless still find themselves in a world they did not invent and seldom transcend. Even so, they remain tirelessly engaged in the business of trying to make this a better place, a more civil society, a safe refuge for dignity and compassion. They respond persistently to the call of the future. Their theater awaits tomorrow's audience. Meanwhile, they are easily overlooked on today's stage. They are not likely to be found in the videos, locker rooms, and corporate boardrooms spawning contemporary role models. Yet the future will search them out and so can we.

Our search will be advanced by looking in the still patriotic hearts of Americans, the neighbors who, in their quiet ways, touch our lives and provoke a thought, prompt an insight, and keep our sense of vulnerability and false security in perspective.

That's the justification for this biography in conservation: to restore an interest in identifying worthy mentors, the folks we can present to our children as good citizens and role models—the family up the hill, the neighbors who, in their quiet ways, have not been distracted. Through their fellowship, we establish more meaningful friendships. Through their kindness, others are empowered to bring out their best; through their insights, we understand that the tools with which we shape our surroundings will also shape us in the process.

Through Mary Lou's and John's writings about who we are today, a reflection of who we could be gazes back from the page. When they speak to us about the end of the nation's frontier on the land, we realize that the next frontier resides in our hearts and minds. Their land ethic enables us to appreciate how our well-being fades when the life light dims for endangered species.

By recognizing the neighbors up the hill, by peering through their wide-angle lens, we derive a better sense of place on our new frontier. While the conservation movement has capably focused on preserving valued habitats and biodiversity, our mentors have often been allowed to slip away. A biography in conservation enables the conservation community to preserve the history of its mentors.

If you seek a biography brimming with innuendo and gossip, proceed no further. You will be disappointed. If you expect a biography to expose secret, scandal-filled lives, the time spent with this book will be entirely unrewarding. If you hope to read a glowing account of unbounded success enjoyed by two people on the front lines of conservation, your excursion here may be unfruitful. But if you are satisfied to read a case study of conservation in action, if you still believe our humanity allows sufficient rewards for selfless charitable works in service of the future, and if an interesting biography does not, for you, require cynicism, then, kind reader, your time here will be well spent.

This manuscript was written to memorialize two lives while the facts are readily accessible. The author anticipated this book might see the light of day near the middle of the twenty-first century, when the effects of surging population pressures will increasingly bear upon our successors. The book might have become a posthumous tribute. If the hastened interest in publication causes the book to seemingly lack poignancy, then please set it aside for a few decades. History will be the final arbiter.

Welcome to this biography on conservationists Mary Lou and John Tanton.

John F. Rohe,
August 2001

Mary Lou & John Tanton:
A Journey into American Conservation

Chapter 1

Heretics and Prophets

> *All great truths begin as blasphemies.*
> ~ George Bernard Shaw

JR: Which of today's heretics do you believe will be recognized tomorrow as prophets?

JT: Only history will tell which were prescient. Keep in mind that the role of a prophet is not to *predict* the future, but to *project* where current behavior will lead, thereby convincing people to change their ways so the prophecy will *not* be realized.

MLT: I believe demographers citing below-replacement fertility in several countries will be recognized for prophesying notable changes in the future of those countries.

Heretics have never been in short supply.

The foundational principle in a democracy is this: No one really knows how to run a government. If someone did, then even dictatorships might prove satisfactory. Democracy involves the steady exploration of new concepts and ideals. It provides fertile soil for new ideas to take hold. Some do. Others perish on the vine by trial and error. Receptivity to new ideas, some deemed heretical, allows the experiment in self governance to continue for ourselves and for our successors.

Heretics are to be found in every age, but only some heretics are eventually recognized as prophets. Heretics probing the future often challenge the constraints of prevailing orthodoxy. They elude respected recognition in their day. Their restless souls must be content with posthumous rewards.

For example, Susan B. Anthony, Mary Wollstonecraft, and other heretics of the mid-1800s argued that women deserved a political voice. The first organized convention for women's suffrage was held in Seneca Falls, New York, in 1848, yet women were not given the right to vote until 1920. In 1859, Charles Darwin humbled his fellow human primates by unearthing their genesis in the fossil record, yet his discoveries are assailed still. We were unable to recognize Mendel's early insights in genetics until several decades after his death. Galileo epitomized the friction between conventional wisdom and heresy in the seventeenth century. At age sixty-nine, he was placed under house arrest and condemned to the gallows until his death nine years later. He defied prevailing dogma by gallantly denying that the earth was the center of the universe. When his oppressors were invited to peer into his telescope, they declined. He was forced to recant, but more than three hundred years later, his oppressors' successors recanted.

Similarly, many of our political ideals began as heretical notions. Thomas Jefferson and John Locke introduced the revolutionary notion of self-governance. Abraham Lincoln aspired to confer dignity upon those who were not considered part of humanity. In 1862 he stated: "As our case is new, we must think and act anew. We must disenthrall ourselves."

All were heretics in their time. They were mocked by the raging forces of their present. Their vision awaited the validating vision of history's long view. They became prophets only when vindicated by the future.

We know future prophets dwell among us now. But where? Will their great truths be masked for present observers? Orthodoxy inhibits our perceptions. Perhaps this is why Arthur Schopenhauer observed that "All truth passes through three stages: first, it is ridiculed. Second, it is violently opposed. Third it is accepted as being self-evident."

Among today's heretics, how might we distinguish those destined to become tomorrow's prophets? Who, today, possesses tomorrow's self-evident truths? Will they be found defending future interests today? Or will they be content to leave future interests to chance? How will they be known? Can we capture a glimpse through their eyes? How can we loosen the jaws of orthodoxy to release their "great truths"? Might we "disenthrall ourselves"?

By challenging the ordained wisdom, today's heretics are readily misconstrued and misunderstood. Thus, today's heretics will be judged by future standards. Meanwhile, they will be shrouded by controversy. Clairvoyance is best defined with the benefit of hindsight.

We make our deals with the future invisibly, unconsciously, and in its absence. The future will reflect on our transactions, just as we reflect upon the legacy of our forebears. Future historians will acquit only some of today's heretics.

Chapter 2

Something in Common

> *The Night is mother of the Day,*
> *The Winter of the Spring.*
> ~ John Greenleaf Whittier

JR: What should someone look for when selecting a mate for life these days?

MLT: Someone who meets the definition of good friend and shares common ethical, spiritual values and interests.

JT: Try to marry above yourself, as to strength, intelligence, and ethics. I did. (Presumably that means Mary Lou didn't!) A commonality of interests seems essential to me.

They both had better things to do that weeknight. It was a study night, so a social gathering held little promise.

Mary Lou was vice president of the Kappa Alpha Theta sorority and scholarship chair. By then she had outgrown the "Brownie" appellation and was known as "M.L." She quickly learned the best bridge players had the worst grades. Bridge M.L.? Probably not.

As a junior at Michigan State University, she took responsibilities to heart. She played clarinet and was involved in synchronized swimming. There was little time for a social life if she was to maintain her grade point average. She made time only for Friday night parties and an occasional pizza and beer at the Coral Gables in East Lansing. And there were still the obligatory sorority functions. As scholarship chair she assigned sorority members to study tables when their grades weren't up to par. They relied upon her regimen to keep up the Kappa Alpha Theta grade point average.

John was in his senior year, president of the Delta Upsilon fraternity and relieved to know that tonight would be his last exchange dessert. The protocol for an exchange dessert with a sorority involved the ritualistic greeting by house mothers, a round of desserts, small talk, and spirited chants of traditional house songs. He was preparing for medical school and preoccupied. Time was at a premium. Fraternity life was primarily a means of securing housing and a social life on campus. At times, however, social imperatives became a meddlesome infringement on school responsibilities.

Mary Lou and two of her study mates were hoping to dodge the obligatory social function on that springtime evening in 1956. They were discreetly tucked away in a back room studying for comprehensive exams. If successful, they could waive several course requirements, a priority of the first order. The sorority count, however, was three short for the evening's exchange dessert with the Delta Upsilon fraternity on Evergreen Road. Several fraternity members were waiters at her sorority. It was a familiar group. Any three members would fill the quota and high spirits were not essential, so M.L. and her two study mates would suffice to fit the bill.

M.L. was discontented and disgruntled. Even an evening's entertainment with John's fraternity brother Paul Stuckey was not a sufficient inducement to go. After all, Paul was a known underachiever whose grades were slipping (but that didn't keep him from eventually slipping into the billboard charts as Paul, of the Peter, Paul, & Mary trio).

The sorority was determined to make the count. Mary Lou had no alternative, so when the forty or so sorority sisters walked the block and a half to the Delta Upsilon house, she begrudgingly abandoned her nightly studies.

On this weeknight the sorority visited about thirty fraternity brothers in the downstairs living room of the Delta Upsilon house. Festivities started at 7:30 p.m. and continued for about two hours.

These were simpler times. Individual identities were less confrontational but still marked by fashionable distinctions. Bobby socks, saddle shoes, skirts, sweaters, and turtlenecks were the norm. For men, "casual attire" implied a blazer and an occasional tie. "Nifty," "groovy," "cool," "wow," and even "spiffy" were not yet common parlance. They used words such as "classy." It was pronounced "ca-lay-ah-see" and spoken with a distinctively haughty, cynical wince.

It was April 1956. The media was just beginning to notice a twenty-one-year-old truck-driving, guitar-picking upstart named Elvis. And M.L. was just beginning to notice the seemingly preoccupied, intriguing D.U. president. By any credible wager, both would likely become passing fancies.

Their eyes had never met. They had never spoken. Yet his was a familiar face. He was known through a friend, Carolyn Lintz, who was pinned to John's roommate, George Snyder.

Mary Lou had spotted him a few months earlier while sipping coffee with a friend, Donna Sandberg, at the Spudnut Shop in East Lansing. This was a convenient stop along the way to class. With a little extra time on their hands, they were taking a few frivolous courses: Family Finance, Floral Design, and Horseback Riding. M.L. considered this a form of fun. She periodically returned to the Spudnut Shop to discreetly view him from behind the window. While unsuspectingly ambling to class, he became a routine subject of conversation for M.L. and Donna.

She walked the block to the Kappa Alpha Theta-Delta Upsilon dessert exchange that night and arrived on time. He merely descended the stairs and was fashionably late. Her bobby socks were folded. His arms were crossed. She leaned inconspicuously against the wall. He mingled indeterminately. Both were decidedly intolerant of the trivial distractions from a scheduled night of study.

Although she never said it, the thought must have crossed her mind: Did anyone else in the room find these events equally meddlesome, boring, and dismal?

Ordinarily, obligatory attendance would diminish prospects for civility, but on this night civility mysteriously triumphed. Neither M.L. nor John were able to conceal their boredom, but that inured to their advantage. Languor imparted a strangely endearing quality to each. Their mutual distaste for the social tedium drew them together.

Common friendships were the topic of their initial, and surely awkward, conversation. One thing led to another, and soon Carolyn, George, M.L., and John were double-dating. On their first date they went to a movie near campus. The four maintained an enduring friendship. George eventually went to law school and assisted John in advancing the first claim under Michigan's Environmental Protection Act.

M.L. soon met John's family on the farm. Their warm welcome and her frequent visits fostered a comfortable relationship in the familiar farm setting. By May 1956, she was spending weekends there and her other suitors were abruptly consigned to the sphere of past friendships. Similar backgrounds, common interests, shared methods of structuring priorities, and like-minded values sealed the promise that this would become more than a passing association for the hopelessly bored. In Mary Lou's words, the relationship proceeded "deliberately, but fairly rapidly." She continued to visit the farm even after John graduated from MSU and began attending medical school at the University of Michigan.

Mary Lou was raised in the glacially carved, gently sloping region known as the Irish Hills in south-central Michigan. John's family farm was flat bottomland in Michigan's "thumb." Several thousand years ago this region was submerged beneath what would become the Great Lakes. The flat character of the land required a conscious adjustment for Mary Lou. It is a habit she has retained: She develops a consuming sense of place by making a conscious effort to understand her surroundings. Natural history and the imprints of ancestors become a tangible part of the surrounding landscape for Mary Lou.

On June 15, 1958, Mary Lou and John tied the knot, two years after their cheerless, yet memorable, first meeting. As their joined lives began, they forged a union of principles. They did not just stumble upon a life of good works. Their conservation ethic was no accident. There is a trail of causation. Even in a world of infinite variability, general patterns emerge. Their patterns began with the curiosity that set the stage for their future works.

CHAPTER 3

The Curiosity of a Child

Old farmers, like old soldiers, never die.
They stamp a piece of land with an indomitable spirit.
~ GENE LOGSDON, YOU CAN GO HOME AGAIN, 1998

JR: At what age, if ever, in your life was the die cast?

MLT: Accompanying my grandfather to the mill to grind our grain, listening to my grandmother tell of her childhood on the farm; also helping with the garden, pets, and farm animals, riding my pony around the farm, and "practicing" for school are vivid early childhood memories.

JT: I was a slow starter . . . couldn't read very well until the sixth grade. I knew all four of my grandparents—a great advantage in the intergenerational relay race we call life. Our children had the same advantage. I still feel quite flexible—I don't think the die is finally cast at any particular age—or ever.

THERE WAS A TIME WHEN NATURE'S PERSISTENT CYCLES resonated clearly, when formations in the night sky kept time with planting and harvesting sequences, and dwelling in the near-term carried a long-term price. There was a time when the line between success and failure was not drawn by imaginary fears. The harvest was the only safeguard that preserved the basicness of subsistence farm life from the bitterness of a bank's foreclosure. Life's vicissitudes were not determined by frenzied abstractions of the stock market. There was a time when rain was patiently awaited in the blistering sun, when the same disciplined patience sought a reprieve from floods after a drenching downpour. Understanding the land required uncommon sensitivity to crop rotation and fertilizers.

In the haze of recollection, there was a time when learning, thinking, and caring were not optional, when the exercise in self-sufficiency of a family farm became a lesson in nature's delicate balance. It was a pastoral time, when the morning sun illuminated a soft fog in the meadow, and bees, our now forgotten pollinators, busily stirred in the blossoms.

It was a time when a child's sense of wonder was coaxed by the diversity of life's fascinations. Trees were not just rigid structures; they were a moment in life's endless cycle, part of a ceaselessly changing past and an indeterminable future. The land informed as it transformed. The freedom to succeed implied the freedom to fail, and the tenuous thread of each individual in life's complex web was palpable. It was a simple time, when dreams were fulfilled with a warm meal in the comfort of the family home on the farm. Human effort was meaningful because feeding the chickens and putting up the hay were matters of survival.

Satisfaction from humble activities may seem quaint in an urban culture, yet today there are fewer opportunities for constructive and meaningful activities for our urbanized children.

In Mary Lou's and John's time, rain glancing off the rooftop nourished thoughts even as it soaked and softened seed beds. The deliberate pace of agricultural growth satisfied the quest of childhood wonder. Winter's leaf buds, poised to receive spring's carefully timed signal, burst forth and inspired the hopes and aspirations of youth. Harmony and balance with nature's rhythm were not just topics of pride, but the mainstays of life.

There was a time when Harry S. Truman was up in the White House and Mary Lou and John were down on the farm. Time was momentarily frozen as they worked hand in hand with two other generations husbanding land homesteaded by ancestors. They defined themselves through the perils of farm life. Pets were accidentally killed, and hazards loomed with every chore. Every deed was dependent upon weather conditions and seasonal cycles. Like a branding iron, patience scorched a discipline.

Shaped by the rigors of subsistence farming and schooled by seemingly humble tasks, the skills and habits of thought they acquired helped them withstand the blows when they were swept into the center of a divisive national controversy.

Mary Lou Brown was born at the local hospital in Hillsdale, Michigan, on November 25, 1935, during a blizzard. Keith, her only sibling, was three years her senior.

Her mother's maiden name was DeGraff (quickly assimilated from LaGraff when the family fled to Holland during the French Revolution). Her great-great grandfather accompanied another Dutchman, Mr. Steketee (the great-great grandfather of a later figure in this biography), on a boat to America. The two settled in the Grand Rapids area.

Mary Lou's maternal grandparents were educators in Berlin, a southwest Michigan town. Because World War I engendered animosity toward Germany, the hometown name was changed to Marne (a less recognizable German name). The family still speaks of grandfather's distress as an educator when German books were burned in the town square during World War I. Her maternal grandmother's name was Bowmaster. She was also a teacher.

Mary Lou's maternal grandparents moved from Grand Rapids to Owendale, in Michigan's thumb, in 1911. Her grandfather, Martin M. DeGraff, became a superintendent of Owendale schools, where his name can be seen today on the school cornerstone. Coincidentally, Owendale lies within ten miles of Sebewaing, where John was raised.

Mary Lou's ancestors were predominantly farmers in southeast Michigan. Israel Buck (1807-1886), her great-great grandfather, homesteaded near Jonesville in Moscow Township, Hillsdale County, in 1835. This was just two years before Michigan statehood. Born in Peru, New York, Israel was orphaned at age nine. He made a career of farming and the ambition for more land drew him to Michigan. His parchment deed for the family's two hundred acres was signed by

President Van Buren in exchange for $1.25 per acre. Eventually, he traded forty acres for a team of horses. Mary Lou was raised here, and the land remains in the family as a "Centennial Farm" (state recognition for having been held by the same family for at least one hundred years).

Israel married Jane Green (1808-1882) from Dutchess County, New York, in 1828. With hard labor clearing the fields, he developed a productive farm. Grain was hauled to a mill in Adrian, thirty-five miles away. Round trips with a team of horses often required three days. Neighbor accompanied neighbor to provide protection against hazards along the way.

Israel and his youngest son, Albert (1847-1897), became lamb and cattle feeders. In the year of Albert's birth, a timber frame house replaced the log home on the property. They raised registered livestock, including Hampshire sheep, Duroc and pol, Percheron horses, and Holstein cattle. In 1919, a Western Electric farm lighting plant was installed, but by 1937, Consumers Power extended lines up to and beyond the farm, calling it the "Brown Extension."

After the farm passed through the hands of several family members, including Mary Lou's parents, her brother, Keith Brown, acquired it in 1970. The family maintains a dairy herd of up to 350 animals and has increased the original 200 acres to 665. Keith's sons, Vern and Dwight, are likely to maintain the family's agrarian heritage.

Mary Lou was not the first woman in her family to carry an activist's torch. Her mother summed up her own life's philosophy as follows: "The best of life is the joy of service and the way we serve is the test of human worth." She was a schoolteacher (in 1927 in Jackson, Michigan, she taught the first class of individualized education in Michigan), a 4-H Club leader, president of Jonesville Woman's Club, president of Hillsdale County Federation of Women's Club, American Red Cross chair for Moscow Township, American Cancer Society chair for Moscow Township, Polio Foundation chair for Moscow Township, Needlework Guild of America board of directors member, Community Concert Association township representative, president of Hillsdale County Association Order of Eastern Star, a Sunday school teacher for forty years, primary superintendent for twenty years, active in a variety of other organizations, and also "Mom."

For Mary Lou, life on the family farm seven miles from town involved active participation in household chores. She helped her mother and her paternal grandmother, who resided with them, in canning, cooking, sewing, flower gardening, feeding the chickens, gathering the eggs, and the other activities expected of young girls. Riding a horse for pleasure was permissible, but showing it in the 4-H Club was taboo for females of her time. Fond childhood memories include poking around back on the lane, visiting the farm's lake, and horseback riding with Dad. Outdoor activities were a "special treat." She even looked forward to cleaning the barn stalls for a change of pace.

The neighbor across the road was affectionately known as Grandma Denning. After completing the day's work, Grandma Denning's memorable homemade bread and apple butter became a cherished treat. Childhood images persist.

Grandma Denning's granddaughter, Nancy, was one year older than Mary Lou and lived half a mile up the road. This friendship born in days spent riding ponies, playing clarinets, and engaging in 4-H Club activities continues today.

Mary Lou usually rode the school bus, but because her father's insurance business was just across the city park from the school, she occasionally hitched a ride with him. Her father also transported her to Hillsdale for piano lessons, which she attended from third grade through high school.

Before freezers and televisions, there was a wooden ice box on the back porch and a radio in the home. Ice would be hauled from the lake and swaddled in sawdust. The radios were hand-crafted floor models. "Mr. Keene, Tracer of Lost Persons" was on Thursday night radio. Huddled around the set with her brother, friends, snacks, school books, and hopeless prospects for homework, Private Investigator Keene captured her imagination.

When Mary Lou reflects on her childhood, she vividly recalls transporting bags of grain to the mill in North Adams with her "grandpa" Brown, spinning the handle on a corn sheller, carrying the swill pail, and grandmother's tales of deer running through the ol' woebegone log cabin.

Recycling wasn't just a trendy thing to do in those days; it was a family tradition. Everything was reused. Wax paper, foil, and paper bags survived multiple uses. Nothing escaped her father's fix-it imperative. Grandma was equally compulsive about conservation. For decades, she pressed her full weight upon rubber rings to reuse and seal the same fruit jars. On a self-sufficient family farm with pigs, chickens, rabbits, dairy cows, sheep, and beef cattle, the family worked close to the land. Three family generations occupied the same household. They were governed by the admonition to "waste not, want not."

Mary Lou describes herself as a serious person, but her solemn dedication to charity and her introspection can be deceptive. A fun-loving person, her resourceful and subtle sense of humor lurks not far beneath the surface. On a personal level, Mary Lou's sense of purpose imparts values and a meaning from which she derives satisfaction. She is serious about living life to the fullest, realizing a few goals that stretch the limits of feasibility, and about preserving a legacy for the future. She acquired this "serious" discipline and insight at an early age.

In 1953, Mary Lou was valedictorian of her high school graduating class, where she was known as "Brownie." In 1957 she graduated *magna cum laude* with a Bachelor of Arts degree in elementary education from Michigan State University. She was also elected secretary of her senior class and was named one of the Fifty Outstanding College Senior Women. In 1963 she received a master's degree from MSU in special education for the orthopedically challenged. In 1969 she was named one of the Outstanding Young Women of America.

The Tantons' family history corresponds with the Browns'.

John's paternal great-grandparents purchased their land from the government in 1880. The Tanton side of the family hailed from Devon, in the west of England. John's paternal great-great-great grandfather was a tenant farmer in 1850 near the town of Greater Tarrington. Workable land was in short supply, and there was a general surplus of labor. The family sold its possessions, packed the remnants, and set out on a seven-week voyage to New York. The elder Tanton was accompanied by his wife and eleven children. Subsequently the three youngest children returned to England with their parents.

John and Mary Lou have visited the family farm in Devon. They were able to locate distant relatives with the same surname. Headstones of deceased family members bearing the family name had by then been stacked against the churchyard wall. Ancient cemetery plots were being reused.

John's maternal great-great-great grandfather Koch was born in 1827. He served in one of the Germanic armies in the Saarland (now in southwest Germany). Upon discharge from military service he emigrated as quickly as possible. He was naturalized in Niagara Falls, New York, in 1854, and started farming in upstate New York. By 1880, the Koch family had proceeded toward the frontier, due in part to population pressures. The westward advance brought them to Sebewaing, Michigan. By then, railroads were already servicing some regions and Michigan's White Pine harvest was well underway.

Grandfather Koch built the family farmhouse in 1916 for the sum of five thousand dollars. Agricultural prices were high during World War I. This enabled him to pay for the home with the proceeds of one bean crop. The wine cellar in the basement was sixteen feet square. It had bunkers with troughs around two sides. Sixty-gallon drums of fruit wines and hard cider, made from the juice of home-grown grapes and apples and processed in the neighbor's press down the road, were stacked on the troughs.

His grandfather bought a carload of surplus dynamite at the end of the first World War to remove stumps. Dynamite also had other innovative uses. They called it a shivaree, that late night ritual celebration after a wedding ceremony that occurs after the newlyweds retire for the evening. Their first night together is expected to be an earth-moving experience. The marvel could be explained by either the detonation of dynamite (the shivaree) or some other equally earth-shaking event.

Families sustained themselves. Grandfather's fields were plowed with a team of horses. There was no need for the jug of homemade hard cider to carry a warning about operating heavy equipment. In the hot sun, the cider was metabolized without effect.

While working as a registered nurse at Harper Hospital in Detroit, John's mother, Hannah, met a chemical engineer from Canada. He had served with the Canadian Expeditionary Forces in World War I. Thereafter, he graduated from the University of Toronto. Though his family was involved in several business interests, his graduation coincided with the Depression, so he searched out opportunity (and eventually a wife) in Detroit. Hannah received a nursing degree in Detroit, the first in her family to receive an education beyond high school. John was born two years after their marriage.

They started raising a family on what was, at the time, the outskirts of Detroit, Michigan. The home was on Artesian Street, near the intersection of Grand River, Southfield, and Five-Mile Road.

John was born on February 23, 1934, in Detroit. His early life in the city was uneventful and largely unmemorable in comparison to the life awaiting him on the farm. By the time he was ten, in 1945, the war was nearing conclusion. The family became disenchanted with city life at the same time that many others were lured to the city for reasons that eluded John and his family. While much of the United States was escaping the rigors of agrarian life, the Tantons were fleeing the routines of city existence for a life on the farm.

Financial reversals had been visited upon the family farm in Sebewaing while it was in the hands of Hannah's brother, John's uncle. The farm came to the brink of a bank foreclosure just as John's folks were preparing to forego city life. By returning to Sebewaing, Hannah hoped to keep the farm in the family.

But there were still several obstacles to overcome. First, John's father, the chemical engineer raised in the city, possessed precious few skills transferable to a life on the farm. Second, farm implements were difficult for the family to acquire during World War II rationing. Against all odds, a tractor was procured. Third, the German community had a strong Lutheran orientation. Valuable information about farming was commonly shared at the local Lutheran Church, but the Tantons were not Lutherans, even though this was Hannah's childhood faith. There were sharp divisions along religious lines and stiff competition between the public and Lutheran parochial schools, which sometimes erupted in open animosity between the two groups. As Hannah had returned to Sebewaing as a member of the Evangelical United Brethren Church, a more fundamentalist denomination, they had to rely upon John's maternal grandparents to network with the Lutherans. This information stream, along with Grandfather's expertise, was essential to the farm's success.

As a child John was earnest in his religious beliefs, even though his parents were not particularly religious. Today, Mary Lou and John relate to a spiritual realm and to a Supreme Being, but they do not look to an intervening miracle worker. Some might seek divine intercession to free a parking spot on a busy day and deem themselves endowed from above when the parking space unfolds. Mary Lou's and John's spirituality has a more deep-seated dimension. Their spiritual side is more akin to the deism of Thomas Jefferson's day.

The intergenerational experiences of John's childhood are still cherished. He often reflects on the loss to our culture that results when children are unaware of not only one parent, but also of another generation. If civilization is an intergenerational relay race, then John perceives that a few generational gaps may cause us to fumble the baton. It will test the ingenuity of our successors to resume the race.

The escape from city life introduced the Tantons to subsistence farming. That wasn't exactly the objective; it just worked out that way. An urban world of childhood play yielded to a farm world of meaningful work. For John's father, an office of shuffled papers was exchanged for tangible results of a day's work: a bin full of grain, a mow full of hay, and a dinner table full of food raised by hand.

Today, we react to circumstances after the fact. Students under siege in a school shooting foster the anti-gun lobby. Highway carnage at the hands of a drunk driver prompts a temperance reaction. Similarly, we respond to environmental concerns only after the resource is devoured. But subsistence farming tolerates only a small margin of error. The land has no patience for inhabitants failing to anticipate the future.

An ounce of prevention is still worth a pound of cure. The cost of a cure was, however, often prohibitive on a subsistence farm. As a teenager, John became intimately involved in the family's administrative decisions involving crop rotations and planting cycles. Meticulous planning was imperative for fertilizers, nitrogen-fixing and nitrogen-releasing plants, and planting green manure crops. There was seldom a second chance.

Before John arrived on the farm, much of the land was used to pasture cattle. In an earlier interglacial period, the region was a lake bed, with fertile soil that provided fruitful bedding on one of Michigan's agricultural gems. Water retention, however, inhibited soil fertility and the Tanton farm had only an eight-foot slope over the half-mile distance from one end to the other. Thus, because it was ideally suited to tiles for improved drainage, much of John's childhood was devoted to laying tiles. The first tiles were four inches in diameter. They led to six-inch mains draining into eight-inch tiles. These were four rods (sixty-six feet) apart and extended across the farm. After school, John would typically be found loading the tiles into a wagon and laying them in carefully measured trenches. These efforts, of course, preceded the federal Wetland Reserve Program to restore wetlands drained by tiling. A delicate balance defines our relationship to our surroundings. Drain tiles on one farm in the '40s might not upset the overall balance. Yet the cumulative effect of drained farms and marginalized wetlands across the region reveal how people laying tiles can become the innocent multiplier in disrupting a delicate balance.

John milked the cows before school in the morning and worked the farm after school. Life on the farm left little time for studies. In John's words, the rural school was predictably not "big on homework." Unsurprisingly, his major writing project in high school involved field tiling technology. John claims the expertise he cultivated in the fields at home compensated for shortcomings in his writing skills at the time.

Since his earliest days on the farm, John recalls being captivated by his interest in life cycles and growth. He vividly remembers the soil's high fertility during the first few years after pasture lands and forests were converted to crop use. Certain crops, such as sugar beets, were hard on the soil, so they could be planted only once every four or five years. Navy beans were a known nitrogen-fixing crop. Corn returned green manure to the soil. Cows were pastured on some fields every three to four years. Fields were planted with oats then inter-sown with alfalfa. Perhaps they became alfalfa pastures for three to four years. After they were plowed, such fields became rich with organic matter. The rain was soaked up immediately, quite unlike the hard-packed soils following a sugar beet harvest.

John enjoyed gardening then and still does. In his words, he "just gets a kick out of seeing things grow." His contemporaries disliked working the fields and hoeing. He, on the other hand, enjoyed the outdoors and took pride in the view of a manicured, weed-free field with straight rows of crops.

There were four or five acres with trees near the back of the farm. To convert this to crop land they cut the trees, blasted the stumps with dynamite, hauled off the roots, picked rocks, and leveled the bumps.

His fascination with scientific agriculture led John to study new ways for growing legumes as interplantings and cover crops. Winter wheat was sown in the fall. It germinated, survived the winter, and started growing again in the spring. Alfalfa, or sweet clover, was then broadcast on the same fields. When the winter wheat crop grew, the alfalfa strained for sunlight in the shadows. When the wheat crop was harvested in August, the underlying legume was exposed to the full sun. It would vigorously grow for the remainder of that season. The nitrogen-bearing and nitrogen-fixing growth was then plowed under in spring to return organic matter to the soil. Keeping a finger on the pulse of the natural growth cycles was the necessary ounce of prevention that enabled the farm to succeed.

By the end of the '40s, agricultural prices were rising and the family was getting back on its feet. John continued working alongside his parents and grandparents, and Grandfather Koch taught him how to keep bees, a hobby John continues to pursue.

Genetics and the human genome project became a hot topic in the 1990s. For John, however, practical genetics were already a way of life in the 1940s and 1950s. The weed-free state of the family farm caught the attention of Michigan State University. Their farm was selected to grow Foundation wheat seed. The family received a small volume of a new variety and grew it to a larger volume. This then became seed for other farmers to produce commercial quantities of the innovation. The Tanton turkeys were Broad-Breasted Bronze, bred at the U.S. Department of Agriculture's Experiment Station at Beltsville, Maryland. The pigs were Yorkshires, longer and leaner, with less fat than others. The cows were purebred Holsteins, registered with the National Holstein Association at Brattleboro, Vermont. The foundation for John's medical school studies in genetics was established by his practical farming experience.

Putting up the hay ahead of a cloudburst always held a particular suspense. Wet hay combusts spontaneously; there was only a brief window of opportunity. Poor timing could render the barn vulnerable to a blazing fire. Gathering the hay, monitoring the cloud formations, and learning the growth cycles caused John to resonate with the pulsations of the land at an early age.

During these impressionable years, John cultivated an appreciation for the land. As the nation migrated to urban centers and learned the culture of the cities, his attention, of necessity, shifted to seasonal patterns, hidden pollinators, weather patterns, and the subtle complexities of crop rotations.

His was a world of balance and limits. Balancing his family's security against the available farm resources was a daily fact of life. His was not a world of surging stock markets with delusions of endless profits and growth. Rather, natural constraints governed every action. There were limits to how much hay could be gathered in the barn ahead of the cloudburst. There were limits to how many cows could be milked before pedaling to school in the morning. There were limits to sowing and harvesting cycles based on weather patterns. There were limits to the nitrogen-fixing capacity of alfalfa. Learning to live within limits was not optional. He inhabited a world of finitude.

When "Brownie" and John were in high school, the term "environmentalist" was not yet in use. The word "conservationist" was recognized, but its connotations did not always include the principles of conservation biology. In high school they would not have known either word, but by then they had already developed a sensitivity to our natural surroundings and a protective ethic for the land.

Even as an early teenager, John had formed the understanding that our role was not to multiply and subdue the earth. He believed we were to co-exist in an easy partnership with it and to study the natural world. Alexander Pope said that man was the proper study of mankind, but John found studies of the physical world more captivating. At this early stage he was already interested in assuring that we adopt a hands-off policy in at least some areas, to preserve both natural beauty and what we now call genetic biodiversity.

John's father had a disdain for politics. All too often, he found it self-serving and corrupt, yet he joined the school board when John was in late grade school and high school. John grew accustomed to the anticipated ribbing when a school board member's son drew enviable grades.

John's maternal grandfather was a "tinkerer." Nothing was discarded; everything was restored. John's brother Tom, four years younger, was less enthusiastic about farming and more interested in Grandfather's tinkering. Tom also played a bass violin in a band. He worked alongside his father and grandfather as he cultivated working skills with lathes, drills, and tools.

John's sister Elizabeth was six years younger. Because of their age difference they had little in common on the farm, but they have grown closer in their adult years.

The bicycle remained John's preferred mode of transportation on the four-mile trek to school during grade school and high school. The bus was used in winter.

In high school John played football, basketball, and baseball. He became the second highest scorer in basketball. He is quick to point out that there were only thirty-eight in his graduating class, but nevertheless, the team once took the district title. Participation in sports was almost obligatory if the school was to field a team.

After high school, John enrolled in the nearby land-grant college, Michigan State University. During his early years at MSU, he studied soil science in the School of Agriculture. He remained in the program for two years, but inspired by good grades, he transferred to pre-med in his junior year. In 1956 he received a degree in Chemistry with a grade point average just shy of 4.0.

During his undergraduate years, John was active in fraternity life but was not otherwise politically active. These were quiet years at Michigan State University. He assembled the fraternity's historical records and learned about organizational affairs, conducting meetings, making agendas, and keeping minutes. He produced the first alumni directory for the MSU chapter of the Delta Upsilon fraternity.

There was a strong medical tradition on his father's side of the family. A relative had been a Rhodes Scholar and became head of surgery at the university hospital in London, Ontario. This family history and his high grades prompted John to enter the Rhodes scholarship competition. The award requires strong writing skills, but there were virtually no writing requirements in John's farm life, soil science, chemistry, zoology, and calculus curriculum. Nevertheless, he emerged from the first round of Rhodes scholarship interviews in Detroit as one of two finalists and then attended the finals at the University Club in Chicago. Only six scholarships were awarded to the twelve hopefuls. He was eliminated in the final round after competing against students from Harvard and Yale.

In the fall of 1956, he enrolled in the University of Michigan medical school. Medical school became an all-consuming activity. John found time for Phi Chi, a medical fraternity, and Mary Lou Brown continued to play a prominent role in his life. They were married between his second and third years of medical school.

As a sophomore he worked as a researcher in the thyroid lab. During his senior year at the University of Michigan, John served as president of the Galens, a medical school honorary society. He also rewrote the organization's constitution and compiled the first directory of Galens' members.

John graduated seventh in a class of two hundred from U of M's medical school in June 1960. He and Mary Lou then moved to Denver for his internship at Denver General Hospital, where he was in "general rotation internship" between 1960 and 1961. The pay amounted to $105 per month, plus room and board. He circulated among twelve specialties in as many months. In the coming age of specialization such rotating internships would soon slip in popularity.

He then began a three-year residency at U of M in ophthalmology. His schedules relaxed slightly while in residency, which permitted him to accept an appointment as secretary to the Michigan Natural Areas Council.

John's brother Tom became ill in 1958 while a student at Michigan State University, a victim of a blood disease known as "aplastic anemia." He died within one month at the University Hospital in Ann Arbor, as John worked helplessly in the same medical ward. In John's words: "That experience reinforced my natural tendency to take life seriously, and impressed on me just how short and tenuous our time here is. It also encouraged me to make sure I didn't waste too much time. If you want to get something done, you'd better realize that the clock is running and get on with it."

Chapter 4

Foresight and Myopia

The vast, unexplored morality of life itself, what we call the immorality of nature, surrounds us in its eternal in comprehensibility, and in its midst goes on the little human morality play with its queer frame of morality and its mechanized movement; seriously, portentously, til some one of the protagonists chances to look out of the charmed circle, weary of the stage, to look into the wilderness raging round.
~ D. H. LAWRENCE

JR: If we hope to become good ancestors, how far ahead should we be thinking? The next generation? One hundred years? Like the Native American, seven generations?

JT: It depends on the topic. Some have short horizons (one eats a healthy diet one meal at a time), some intermediate (population changes equal several decades), some long (storing nuclear waste). The key I guess is to at least think about the future and pay it due consideration. Our current situation traces to plans our ancestors laid—at least in part. But much of life just can't be planned and must be lived on the fly in light of time-honored principles and moral/ethical codes.

MLT: We should span the history of several generations to help our children develop the values and perspectives required to guide them and their future.

MARY LOU'S AND JOHN'S DECISION TO MOVE TO PETOSKEY IN 1964 was influenced by their childhood homes on the farm. They wanted to keep bees, a skill John had developed under the guiding hand of his paternal grandfather. In northern Michigan, they could maintain a garden, chop their own wood, and still live close to the land while maintaining a modern medical practice. John was eager to join a group of physicians dedicated to providing comprehensive medical care. At the time, he was the twenty-fifth physician to join the Burns Clinic, one of the first large clinics established in the nation. It was patterned after the Mayo Clinic in the early 1930s by a visionary country physician, Dean Burns, M.D.

John was employed as an ophthalmologist at the Burns Clinic. He started in 1964 under a senior ophthalmologist whose interest in operations was waning. From John's earliest days at the clinic, he inherited an active surgical practice and also performed routine eye exams.

After their two daughters departed for college, Mary Lou began part-time work as a low vision specialist at the clinic. She matched low vision disorders with available products and offered suggestions to restore or maximize sight.

John's philosophy on the practice of medicine is captured in his essay entitled "Nothing More Can Be Done . . . A Fable for Our Times" in Appendix E. It bespeaks the personalized sensitivity and concern Mary Lou and John brought to their respected patients over the years.

When John began practicing in the early 1960s, cataract surgery required a week's hospitalization. It left the patient with heavy, thick glasses and distorted vision. Since then it has become an out-patient procedure that restores vision to pre-cataract levels.

John enjoyed a close relationship with many of his patients over the years. In retirement, he readily concedes this aspect of professional life is not easily replaced.

John always valued the input from patients, even if they might be of a different philosophical bent. He misses this exchange in retirement. His patients were generally interested in and supported his charitable causes. Even if they held differing opinions, their voice of opposition was not expressed by choosing an eye surgeon elsewhere, in part because the next practitioner was several hundred miles away. John's market position made it less venturesome to embrace controversial causes. Foresight collaborated with his liberation from the tyranny of the marketplace. He was uniquely well-positioned to raise divisive issues.

His patients reflected the broad spectrum of northern Michigan opinions. Even patients who disagreed with his views respectfully conceded he was striving, in good faith, to avert a problem before it arose. This was true for his vocation as their treating physician and for his avocation as a conservation activist. Where others could be found foraging for symptoms, John could be found rummaging for causes.

The demarcation between sight and foresight defined the zone where Mary Lou and John drew the battle lines for their charitable causes. It was the line between near-sightedness and far-sightedness. This line separates the priorities of a short-term profiteer from the long-term visionary. The line differentiates those aspiring to be a good consumer today from others hoping to become a good ancestor tomorrow. This is the severed continuity between near and far, short and long, consuming and conserving. These are the defining polarities for Mary Lou and John.

Their priorities are ordered to contemplate and accommodate the long-term and were established before the nation and its economic system became possessed by possessions and consumed by consumption.

In the relatively short time between their birth in the 1930s and their retirement in the 1990s, sweeping changes have affected the United States and the world. Mary Lou and John strive to maintain a sense of where we have been and where we are proceeding. The conservation ethic ingrained in their childhoods has survived the nation's transition to a consumer-based, resource-depleting, growth-oriented, waste-generating economy. To fit the self-sufficient, family-oriented talents of their childhoods into the dependent, here and now, self-absorbed psyche of today is to coerce a square peg into a well-rounded hole.

They recoil when resources are squandered and they bristle when the purveyors of consumption unfairly prey on our self-doubts and vulnerabilities. When financial consultants speak of the need to build economic growth, they hear an argument to pauperize the future quality of life at an ever-increasing pace.

They did not ask for controversy. That's just how it worked out if they were to remain true to their consciences. When action was required, they had essentially three choices: find someone else to do it (seldom a viable option), do it themselves, or conclude they couldn't be bothered. John often recounts the joke about the person who, when asked about ignorance and apathy in society, responded, "I don't know and I don't care."

Mary Lou and John readily concede their time and resources were often stretched too thin. Occasionally, something approximating the "I just can't be bothered" reaction was the only feasible response they could muster. But just how did they distinguish causes meriting their attention from others? How they drew these lines is no small part of the Tanton story. It illuminates their mastery of the art of the possible. Their causes were always on the outer reaches of the attainable. For example, the world had a daily net population gain of 230,000 people (births minus deaths) when they retired.[1] Did world population merit their attention? Of course. The global drama continues to unfold. But while the Tantons promoted international family planning efforts, they did not focus their time on this issue. The goalpost of their homespun causes was not quite this high.

In the April 5, 1976, edition of *Medical Economics*, John authored an article entitled "Get More Out of Giving to Your Favorite Causes." In this essay, John revealed how payments to charitable appeals were often followed by an even more compelling solicitation in the next day's mail. So Mary Lou and John established a budget and a special charitable account from which all charitable contributions would be paid. Realizing no one can contribute to all causes, John's article recommended focusing charitable gifts in areas of interest and striving for the best return on each donated dollar. It suggested contributions toward resolving fundamental causes rather than effects and not scattering the charitable shot. In the article, John stated, "Twenty-five dollars to help prevent unwanted pregnancies, for example, may return literally tens of thousands of dollars in benefits to the community in reduced expenditures for schools, social welfare, and so on."

The article also addressed the desirability of nondeductible donations: "The Sierra Club, for instance, one of our national conservation organizations, ran a full-page ad in the *New York Times* protesting the proposed construction of dams in the Grand Canyon. The next day, the organization was notified by the IRS that contributions to it would no longer be tax-deductible. Is it better to give ten dollars to a tax-exempt group that isn't going to get much done or to give the same amount to some non-deductible outfit like the Sierra Club that is really effective? Personally, I'll opt for the latter." John's proving ground on population advocacy traces back to his involvement with the Sierra Club. In the intervening years, the club has retreated from national population issues out of a concern that they could become divisive. A position relating population with urban sprawl would unavoidably lead the club to take a position on immigration reform (See Leon Kolankiewicz and Roy Beck, "Weighing Sprawl Factors in Large U.S. Cities," NumbersUSA.com, 19 March 2001). Interestingly, the Sierra Club would not shrink from addressing U.S. fertility rates, but it declines the immigration issue.

For Mary Lou and John, the decision to dedicate time to a cause followed a soul-searching effort. First, they determined whether there were attainable goals from the vantage of a husband and wife in northern Michigan. For example, could they have a meaningful impact on the population issue on a worldwide terrain or might their limited time be spent better elsewhere? Perhaps the problem of global population growth was beyond their humble means. With the benefit of at least partial hindsight, we can now consider whether their time was better spent elsewhere.

On June 30, 1998, and after four thousand surgical operations (according to a well-preserved list), John retired from active practice to expand upon his charitable pursuits. In the letter announcing his retirement to patients, John fondly reflected upon the one thousand patients assisted by Mary Lou's low-vision expertise. He expressed appreciation for the opportunity to blend vocational with avocational pursuits and mentioned such organizations as Planned Parenthood,

Little Traverse Conservancy, Sierra Club, Zero Population Growth, Federation for American Immigration Reform (FAIR), U.S. English, U.S. Foundation, Pro-English (previously known as English Language Advocates), and the *Social Contract Journal*. The letter indicated he would continue working on charitable causes while hoping to also make time for hiking, gardening, beekeeping, reading, and writing. John reflected on thirty-seven years of practice, concluding, "Like an aging ballplayer, one wants to leave before others start suggesting it—before the cheers change to jeers!"

CHAPTER 5
A Darwinian Casualty

Nature bats last.
~ Yogi Berra

JR: Describe your most recent walk in the woods.

JT: Unfortunately, I ended up at a paintball field, where a youth group from one church was trying to "kill" another church youth group . . . on a Sunday afternoon no less. Hmmm . . . the plastic balls with which they were littering the ground will be there until the Second Coming. Will that count as a plus?

MLT: I spent the late afternoon and evening by myself, on a familiar lakeshore, amongst tall fragrant pines. Fog was moving in; I was in completely silent surroundings. I have never before experienced such a satisfying sense of being—of solitude, peace, and silence.

OUR BIOLOGICAL CLOCKS RESONATE WITH THE WORLD around us. Sleep is regulated by solar cycles. Ovulation generally follows a lunar cycle. Our memories relate events to the seasons. We might not recall exactly when an event occurred, but we'll remember whether there was snow on the ground.

The pace of environmental change follows neither a solar, a lunar, nor a seasonal cycle. It does not resonate with our biological clocks. Environmental losses often are imperceptible to our senses.

To comprehend our dramatic impact on the world, it is necessary to telescope ten, twenty, fifty, or even one hundred years together. Only then can we begin to understand that ours might be the last generation to experience fresh water slipping through its hands.

An evolutionary psychologist might suggest that we have been hard-wired to react only to short-term changes requiring an immediate response. The predators confronting our distant ancestors one hundred thousand years ago presented short-term risks. Our ancestors either reacted swiftly or they were doomed. Impulsive responses became an essential lifesaving skill. If they did not neutralize short-term risks, their genetic fabric disappeared. Anyone seriously contemplating a two hundred-year volcanic cycle, rather than short-term risks, became lunch meat to the lurking predator. Genes that disposed one to the long view had little chance to survive into the next generation. The predisposition to contemplate long-term changes, if it even existed, would soon have been eliminated as a Darwinian casualty.

Today's predators, however, are of a different sort. Lions and tigers pose no threat to us. The "predators" of our time include ozone depletion, wetland losses, acid rain, groundwater contamination, greenhouse gas emissions, mass extinctions, population pressures, dwindling resources, and habitat losses. These contemporary predators are practically invisible to the near-term oriented human mind, yet they stalk us in a drama that unfolds in the blink of a historian's eye. Through the process of natural selection we have been finely tuned to react only to immediate threats. Yet these very skills, honed by eons of selection, are useless to equip us to react, as we now must, to the long-term predator. Reason, not instinct, will be our salvation in confronting the stealthy hazards now confronting us.

The ability to appreciate the significance of habitat losses spanning a period of, say, fifty years, is rare. It was rarer still in the early '70s. But for Mary Lou and John, it was an acquired skill. The cadence of their perception resonated with the accelerating pace of environmental loss. Their compelling affinity for the land and compassion for the wild was derived from the long-term management skills developed during their childhoods. These skills imbued them with unique sensitivity and insight but frequently elicited negative responses from those disposed to take a shorter-term view.

At an early age John became convinced that population pressures were at least part of the threat to the lands he loved. A clear cut virgin forest reflected a need for timber. One reason for extracting more timber was the need for more homes to house a growing population. This awareness implies a recognition that limits exist and that the forests of the earth do not extend infinitely beyond one person's horizon.

By the late 1950s, John encountered publications from the Population Reference Bureau (PRB).[2] This is the oldest demographic organization in the world and remains a leading source of population information. Influenced by the PRB information and by Mary Lou's interest in Planned Parenthood, he worked in the family planning clinic at Denver General Hospital as part of his internship. This was the first such publicly supported hospital clinic in the United States.

The Tantons know nature is not to be mocked and that we are not exempt from universal biological laws. They apprehended nature's revenge in the overpopulated, resource-depleted regions of the world. Those who believe we soar above nature's commands place blind faith in an exemption from universal biological principles. Every species on the face of the earth must learn to live within limits. We are not exempt from those limits. Garrett Hardin labels disbelievers as "exemptionists."[3]

To presume that we soar above the universal biological principles governing all other forms of life on the planet is to bet against nature. The Tantons see our successors becoming the unwary stakeholders in this losing wager. Whatever else may be said about exemptionists, they just don't make good ancestors. Mother Nature will determine our destiny. Although her jury is still out and time remains to correct the growing imbalance that threatens humankind, it is not clear that she will have the patience to await our awareness.

Some view history as a continual series of "improvements" in a chain of unremitting "progress." This superficial, materialistic view is defiantly indifferent to the consequences of overcrowding, biological extinctions, groundwater contamination, ozone depletion, global warming, and the loss of natural amenities. It dismisses incivility, road rage, and increasingly common forms of depravity as mere anomalies. The Tantons recognize these as symptoms of much deeper problems confronting us. Mary Lou and John understand that we are integrated in the natural world and that integration extends beyond the profit motive and involves an active relationship with natural processes. They are active participants in the natural drama.

By laying down roots, they became grounded. Theirs is a life of collaborative relationships with the natural world around them. Their search for meaning is rewarded by the discovery of patterns in nature, patterns that are all too often invisible.

CHAPTER 6

Prophecy and Charity

> *Those who cannot remember the past
> are condemned to repeat it.*
> ~ GEORGE SANTAYANA

JR: How do you manage your philanthropic budget?

JT and MLT: We save most requests for funds for a single year-end session where we try to match opportunities with the budget we've set for donations. We try to give to some non-tax deductible items as well—chiefly political ones. We look at philanthropy as buying into ideas—which, unlike material goods, have very low carrying costs. If you buy a good bottle of wine, what do you have to show for it in twenty-four hours? An idea, one can carry for a lifetime.

THE UNITED STATES IS THE MOST PHILANTHROPIC[4] NATION in the world. Charities thrive on the enthusiasm of well-intentioned, altruistic, selfless folk.

Mary Lou and John select their charities cautiously.

Ironically, charitable organizations often allocate their resources at cross purposes with the efforts of other charities. They respond to different perspectives on the same problem. The Tantons' charitable causes often are seemingly at odds with others but, on closer examination, the conflict is more apparent than real: The Tantons strive to address causes, rather than mere effects. Some charities work to alleviate hardship, while others address the poor planning that leads to hardship. The distinction is the difference between causes and effects. This difference may pit one charitable cause against another, thus dividing resources of the well-intentioned.

For example, water resource specialists in China might promote population control. By contemplating future needs, they strive to avert the distress that results from predictable water shortages. This effort clashes with charitably oriented organizations opposed to family planning while seeking to enhance food production with intensive farming practices. These practices, however, place further strains on water supplies. Both efforts are well intentioned, both address the problem of hardship, but only population control addresses the root cause of the problem. The Tantons anticipate the causes of future hardship. Thus, they would support efforts to avert future water shortages. Similarly, they would allocate charitable contributions and time toward family planning efforts.

Others, equally well intentioned but less prone to contemplate the future, might allocate their charitable contributions in ways specifically opposed to the Tantons' causes. Examples abound. Refugees experience a tragic plight in each of the forty-five violent uprisings that commonly rage around the globe in any calendar year. According to the United Nations High Commissioner for Refugees, there are more than twenty-one million refugees and displaced persons.[5] Some charitable organizations promote the permanent resettlement of a relatively few selected refugees in the United States by any available means. Others respond to their conscience by seeking fair treatment for all refugees.

The Tantons would propose a nonimmigration resolution, because immigration is not a solution. There are far more refugees in war-torn regions around the globe than there are available places for them to go. The masses will never have a meaningful chance to emigrate. The growing numbers of potential refugees require that hardship be alleviated at home. The refugees admitted to the United States—often the most talented and capable—lose the incentive and the ability to contribute to improving conditions in their nation of origin. By admitting (or luring) them to the United States, we may satisfy our conscience, but we may also be making matters worse for those left behind.

Many respond generously to televised pleas on behalf of the world's starving masses with unconditional food aid. Others would condition this aid on the acceptance of family-planning measures because unconditional aid will, generation by generation, add to the human suffering. Misery, alongside population, expands at an exponential rate. The starving masses in Somalia, for example, increase their number by 580 people each day according to year 2000 statistics maintained by the Population Reference Bureau.[6] Garrett Hardin claims that unconditional aid only adds to the starvation,[7] thus actually compounding the distress.

The Tantons' causes take us upstream in the chain of causation. Their charitable contributions of time and money must be an investment in the future, not merely palliatives that leave the underlying causes of distress unaltered. They invest in ideas, and their investments touch every one of our lives. Precisely because the purpose and effect of their contributions of time and money is to produce long-term changes that will improve the human condition, rather than the conditions of a chosen few, Mary Lou and John often find themselves in adversarial relationships with other charitably inclined folk. The difference is not of sympathy, but of sensitivity: sensitivity to the future and the need for change to ensure that there will be a future.

CHAPTER 7

Striking a Balance

*Just as there must be a balance in
what a community produces, so there must be a balance in
what the community consumes.*
~ JOHN KENNETH GALBRAITH, 1958

JR: What is the earliest memory of a conversation between the two of you when you thought land conservation might merit your attention?

MLT: From the early days of our relationship, we both hoped to see our family farms remain; we became aware that all progress involves change—and that all change is not progress. We often discussed conservation, which raised the question, "Saving the land from what?" This led to addressing population and family planning issues, and our involvement in both.

JT: I can't recall a time when I wasn't sensitive toward the land and its inhabitants. Mary Lou shared these feelings—this was one of the common traits that drew us together, and has had me thinking about running for the U.S. Senate.

IN 1958, DURING THE SUMMER AFTER THEIR MARRIAGE, Mary Lou and John backpacked the forty-five-mile length of Isle Royale, an island wilderness in Lake Superior. This is Michigan's northernmost land mass. During the trip, they met a group of hikers active with the Wilderness Society. After the trip, they visited Mary Lou's cousins from Knoxville, Tennessee, who were also enthused about the Wilderness Society. John and Mary Lou (M'Lou as she became known) were soon sold on the organization and joined.

Later in 1958, they were introduced to a natural area preservation group known as the Michigan Natural Areas Council. This organization identified and advocated the protection of significant botanical and natural features. John became secretary. Over the next few years, until the final enactment of the 1964 Wilderness Act, they became active in writing letters and offering testimony in Washington, to promote the passage of the act.

The Wilderness Act of 1964 was designed to provide the most permanent protection for wilderness areas. Wilderness protection designations had begun approximately forty years earlier, when Aldo Leopold, a member of the U.S. Forest Service, convinced the Forest Service to designate an area near Gila, New Mexico, for preservation. Over the next few years, the Forest Service identified other areas for protection but eventually, special interests attempted to expand access to these protected lands. On occasion, the Forest Service yielded to the pressure and protected lands were declassified.

Wilderness advocates sought a more secure form of legislation that would require an Act of Congress to lift the protections. To declassify land, applicants would be required to invoke the legislative process. This would afford notice and an opportunity for others to be heard. After negotiations spanning more than half a decade, President Johnson signed the act in November 1964.

This formative experience in advocacy led Mary Lou and John to the first of many land protection battles. It resulted from the friction created by efforts to protect seven thousand acres of still-virgin forest on the north shore of Michigan's Upper Peninsula. White pine and maple trees towered in the canopy of this well-preserved forest. At the time, Michigan's Senator Philip A. Hart proposed a shoreline drive through the area. The road would have invaded the still-virgin forests. In this battle the Tantons were introduced to the heated conflict between the defenders of long-term interests and the advocates for short-term profits. It led to a compromise that served to preserve the wilderness character of the land—a rugged gravel road allowing limited access without spawning the "Jellystone" parody of the wilderness experience. By preventing pavement they rendered the heart of formerly pristine wilderness inaccessible to large recreational vehicles.

Activism in public land conservation, and the often disappointing compromises that resulted, eventually led Mary Lou and John to become advocates for private conservation. During John's internship in Denver they learned about The Nature Conservancy (TNC) and then attended a TNC meeting in Wheeling, West Virginia. Familiarity with the operations of The Nature Conservancy sparked an idea to form the Little Traverse Conservancy (LTC), northern Michigan's first regional land trust. Eventually, LTC would protect thousands of acres and would emerge as a leading voice for the national conservation movement.

Conciliatory efforts to perpetuate the integrity of private land would be placed on the back burner for a while. There was still a little steam to vent—their concerns over the systematic dismantling of the biological integrity of the land they called home would lead them to invoke Michigan's newly adopted Environmental Protection Act, an experience that would also introduce them to frustrations with our legal system.

CHAPTER 8

"Unto the Breach"

Once more unto the breach, dear friends, once more . . .
~ WILLIAM SHAKESPEARE, HENRY V

JR: What principles should a judge keep in mind when evaluating the merits of a lawsuit brought by a group of concerned citizens to preserve the land?

JT: In Michigan, I would cite the Michigan Environmental Protection Act under which I was a plaintiff in three suits over land use. Also, the Tenth Amendment—I'm not impressed with judicial activism. And then there's the Preamble to the U.S. Constitution, with its closing regard for "ourselves and our Posterity." A judge should also have an eye toward the stakeholders not formally represented in the courtroom, as it's seldom possible to do merely one thing.

MLT: Precedent-setting cases acknowledge the validity of aesthetic considerations in the resulting decisions. Michigan's constitution requires that our legislators protect our natural resources; I believe this includes our state's scenic resources.

THE TANTONS' PERSONAL INTENSITY FOR PRESERVING THE land in the early '70s coincided with the adoption of the Michigan Environmental Protection Act (MEPA), one of the first such legislative enactments in the nation. MEPA is a plainly worded statute that, in theory at least, gives any Michigan citizen the means to protect any natural resource from impairment, pollution, or destruction. Plans to construct a dam on Monroe Creek in Charlevoix County were unveiled in the summer of 1971. This called for flooding four hundred acres of land to create a lake around which four hundred homes were to be interspersed.

Surprisingly, Michigan's Department of Natural Resources (DNR), the state's protectorate of natural resources, issued a permit to authorize the dam's construction. John attended the ill-fated public hearing in the state capitol. During the four-hour return trip to Petoskey, he resolved to explore the possibility of a legal challenge under MEPA.

Upon returning home, John called Peter Steketee, an attorney from Grand Rapids, and together they helped organize the Michigan Environmental Protection Fund. Their personal history traces back even further. Steketee was the great-great grandson of the Dutchman who accompanied Mary Lou's great-great-grandfather to the United States in the nineteenth century.

Peter estimated litigation costs might run between four and five thousand dollars. Since this was the first suit under MEPA, John knew this to be a crude estimate at best. Even if the litigation costs could not be raised, John delivered the personal guarantee to absorb the costs. Five thousand dollars might not sound significant today, but to place the sum in perspective, John earned sixteen thousand dollars during his first year at the Burns Clinic. Five thousand dollars represented a venturesome sum for the Petoskey surgeon at the time.

The suit was filed and, because it invoked landmark environmental protection legislation, became a newsworthy item across the state. Newspaper publicity caught the attention of Detroit-area attorney George Snyder, John's fraternity brother at Michigan State, who generously offered assistance.

Glen Sheppard (affectionately known as "Shep"), editor of the *Northwoods Call*, Michigan's voice for conservation, remembers John's unconditional commitment to Monroe Creek. In preparing the case, Shep and John accompanied a professor of biology, Gale Gleason, to the creek. Gleason had the misfortune of discarding a cigarette butt into the creek while in Shep's and John's presence. Big mistake! Bad timing! Before departing, there was little subtlety in John's demand that Gleason retrieve the cigarette butt from the creek . . . in his dress shoes. Gleason developed an appreciation for John's sense of resolve and commitment to the creek the hard way. After this initial test of their relationship, they soon developed a sense of mutual respect.

The case was tried in the spring and summer of 1972. Experts in the Monroe Creek case included Don Eschmann, a geologist from the University of Michigan and co-author of a treatise entitled *Michigan Geology*. Gale Gleason assisted by offering water quality testimony. Trout Unlimited (T.U.) became a co-plaintiff in the case. T.U. was represented by Attorney Joe Wilcox, an avid trout fisherman and a colorful addition to the courtroom drama.

The case was not decided by Circuit Judge Charles Brown until his last day in office, December 31, 1972. In light of the sensitivity we have since acquired for the value of fragile ecosystems it is difficult to conceive of a decision blithely affirming the right to flood four hundred acres for four hundred homes, but in 1972, judicial appreciation of emerging environmental concerns was still in the formative stage. While the court imposed minimal protective requirements, John was obliged to acknowledge that the case was lost in the circuit court.

Nevertheless, even the minimal court-imposed requirements delayed dam construction. This delay bought vital time. The owner, a pedophile, was often accompanied by young boys for a "weekend experience" at his privately owned North Fox Island. When this came to light, one of the young boys committed suicide. The owner abruptly absented himself from the area and never returned. The DNR permit eventually expired. A victory of sorts had been won, but at a high cost, and without vindicating the fundamental interests at stake.

A second suit was filed in the spring of 1973 against Birchwood Farms. This involved the construction of a sizable residential and golf project west of Harbor Springs. The Monroe Creek expert witnesses were again retained, as the case also involved ground water protection. This time Tanton and the co-plaintiffs prevailed. Strong court-imposed protective measures significantly affected how the project would proceed.

The third case arose at about the same time in an area east of Harbor Springs, Michigan. When the municipality built a sewage treatment plant, the owner of a tract of land fronting on Lake Michigan paid additional money for the sewer to run along her property. With the sewer servicing her property, her wetlands were compatible with construction and plans were announced for a hotel complex to be constructed on the property. Judge Ned Fenlon ruled against Tanton's MEPA challenge in the Emmet County Circuit Court. To avert an appeal, however, the owner voluntarily agreed to conditions that preserved the wetlands and substantially reduced the density of the development.

As it turned out, the Monroe Creek case fees were on the high side of five thousand dollars—they came to about thirty thousand dollars. Michigan's T.U. chapter shared in the costs, but most of the funding was raised by direct mail appeals to lake associations and summer visitor lists.

To fund the three suits, approximately $150,000 was raised in the early 1970s. Much of it came in the form of small contributions from concerned individuals. These contributions demonstrated an emerging sensitivity to human impacts and a growing grassroots commitment to conservation in northern Michigan. But they also revealed just how difficult it would be to save a few pieces of the biodiverse puzzle before we could even assess the loss—before the inventory was even taken.

Based on the *outcomes* (as distinct from the *rulings*) of these suits, it can be said that Tanton's group prevailed in all three cases. Their struggles seared an indelible imprint upon Michigan's legal environmental landscape. They were the first to litigate, and theirs was a baptism by fire. Victory came in spite of, not because of, judicial sensitivity to the needs of future generations.

In the Monroe Creek case, victory resulted from an unpredictable event: The authorities were catching up with a pedophile before the earth movers caught up with the land. The Birchwood case was resolved favorably only because someone took the initiative to file suit. And even after losing in circuit court, concessions were achieved in the third case. Success in litigation ultimately turned on the fortuity of Tanton's group being there to raise a voice in opposition.

This experience parallels that of other environmental causes. Success cannot be measured by prevailing in every endeavor. Sometimes it is just a matter of being there at the right time and deflecting the course of events enough to change the outcome. Environmental organizations were hapless ventures before the oil spill washed ashore in California several decades ago. "When the effluent met the affluent," activists conceded, "the environmental movement was born." John's litigation experience must have left him feeling something like that: He and his co-plaintiffs prevailed not because the courts demonstrated real sensitivity to the impact of human activity on our natural surroundings, but because they happened to show up at the right time to extract concessions from developers accustomed to having their way with the land. A bittersweet "victory" at best.

The litigation experience taught Mary Lou and John to appreciate northern Michigan's commitment to conservation, which found expression in generous contributions of ordinary concerned citizens. A few angels made substantial gifts, but the remainder of the funds came from direct mail solicitations to the northern Michigan community.

Beleaguered after three combative and costly court experiences, the Tantons returned to the more conciliatory efforts they had begun years before with the land conservation movement in the hope and prospect of producing more enduring results. But not without due circumspection.

CHAPTER 9

Confrontation or Cooperation?

> *An olive leaf he brings, pacific sign.*
> ~ JOHN MILTON, *PARADISE LOST*

JR: Why has the Little Traverse Conservancy been so successful in its mission and in its fund-raising efforts?

JT and MLT: It was the right idea at the right time and place. Lots of folks here have lived elsewhere, and have seen how bad it can get—and hence are willing to ante up the time and money to p<u>R</u>eserve and <u>R</u>estore what we have, and <u>R</u>eform the underlying systems (such as the zoning codes that lead to the degradation). Those are the three "R's" of the conservation movement.

FROM THE CLUTCH OF CONTENTIOUS LITIGATION THERE WAS a message about the heart of northern Michigan. Residents were committed to speaking up for the land, and they were willing to put up hard-earned cash for this voice.

But there was also a commitment to civility. Thoughtful sentiment for land conservation often originates in a conciliatory spirit. It is ideally neither bold nor confrontational.

The Tantons are life members in The Nature Conservancy. In 1972, Michigan's Governor William Milliken appointed John to the

51

Wilderness and Natural Areas Advisory Board within the Department of Natural Resources. Formulating the plan to organize the Little Traverse Conservancy (LTC) was part of a natural progression.

According to co-litigator and LTC co-founder Dave Irish: "The idea started with John. He was the catalyst. He was the force that made it happen. LTC would not have become a reality in the absence of John Tanton." The other co-founders of Little Traverse Conservancy also were involved in Tanton's lawsuits: Earl Larson, John Fischer, Edward Kosa, and Frank Pierce.

The co-founders had considered forming a chapter of The Nature Conservancy. Instead, they decided to form an independent regional conservancy. Conveniently, they were armed with a list of proven donors from the three lawsuits.

The Little Traverse Conservancy was founded upon a mission of conciliation and would avoid controversial causes. LTC has maintained a vigilant allegiance to this founding principle and remains an amiable forum for persons of diverse environmental persuasions.

This is true even on the contentious "property rights" issue. "Property rights" is one of the most heated environmental topics, yet all activists in the field find common ground at LTC. Invoking notions of "property rights," business interests often claim land owners have the right to destroy a natural habitat or wetland for private economic gain. If they are deprived of this "right," they claim a right to compensation at the taxpayers' expense. Others respond by asserting a community interest and claiming that "property rights" never included the ability to use one's land to a neighbor's detriment.

The conflicting interests are bitterly polarized on this issue. The battle rages on the constitutional terrain of the Fifth Amendment right to "just compensation" when private property is taken for public use. Nevertheless, both sides agree on one essential "property right": the right to preserve one's own land. Even divergent interests can unite under one roof in support of this property right.

LTC provides a common ground. Here the conservationist finds something in common with even the timber and mining industries. The naturalist meets the entrepreneur in a congenial venue. The conservation biologist here teams up with the venture capitalist. LTC's founders made these peace-keeping alliances possible by applying the lessons learned in the trenches of litigation.

When the Little Traverse Conservancy was incorporated in the summer of 1972, annual membership dues were one dollar. Life membership could be secured for a $100 donation.

The first brochure stated: "The Little Traverse Conservancy was established to help preserve natural lands for the general public benefit. It acquires land through gift or purchase, preserves and protects the land and makes it available for appropriate use by the public. The Conservancy operates in Charlevoix, Cheboygan, Emmet and Mackinac Counties. In addition to the primary role of identifying, obtaining and managing land, the Conservancy can assist other organizations or governmental bodies in attaining similar objectives."

LTC's history illustrates that effective organizational principles, a talented staff, and a committed board of directors can build successful programs. LTC's endowment at the turn of the millennium is more than $4 million in cash and deferred gifts. Its environmental education programs have become a favorite for northern Michigan's schools, and children participate by the thousands every year. More than eleven thousand acres have been protected permanently.

Today, LTC continues to develop innovative programs. It works cooperatively with Native American tribes to maintain culturally significant lands and recognizes donors in a conservation biography program. Its membership base is well over four thousand. This depth of penetration in the heart of a sparsely populated community is unprecedented in regional northern Michigan philanthropy. In the state of Michigan, LTC's protected acreage (nearly twenty square miles) ranks just behind The Nature Conservancy. These totals do not include partnership conservation "assists" achieved in cooperation with public agencies.

John served on the board of directors long enough to give LTC a healthy start and a formidable donor base. He then moved on to other philanthropic causes but never let LTC stray far from his heart. A conservation easement on the acreage around the Tanton home, including the foraging ground for their bees and a well-preserved woodland, is planned for LTC's protective custody.

Mary Lou and John not only provided a direction to the conservation movement in northern Michigan, but they also influenced the conservation movement on a national level. For example, it was while serving as the chair of the Sierra Club's National Population Committee (1971 to 1975) that John attended a population meeting at Lake Tahoe. While there, he walked the forest at Donner Pass and formulated the often quoted "3 R's" that have become the mantra of the conservation movement: Reserve, Restore, and Reform. *Reservation* is the effort to save a few pieces of the biological puzzle before they are lost. *Restoration* is the eventual transplantation of this preserved genetic material to biologically pauperized regions. And *Reform* involves environmental education efforts to assure reasoned and informed decisions on matters affecting our surroundings.

CHAPTER 10

Human Interest and Population Advocacy

What's past is prologue.
~ WILLIAM SHAKESPEARE, *THE TEMPEST*

JR: With respect to life-threatening toxins and contamination, it has been said that people are the multiplier. How does the "multiplier" affect your analysis?

MLT: We often [fore]see a problem only after it hits—"hindsight is better than foresight." Hopefully the solution prevents recurrence and results in more people with a common purpose taking a closer look and choosing a better course.

JT: The language of life is mathematics, according to Lord Kelvin. The fundamental human equation is the one we all learned with our multiplication tables: (multiplicand) x (multiplier) = (product). The things people do individually, whether positive (like donating time to community projects) or negative (like wasting resources), when multiplied by the number of people involved, yield the total effect. If we cut pollution per capita in half, but double the number of people, we're back where we started.

DURING HER CHILDHOOD, MARY LOU RECOGNIZED THAT children of smaller families generally received more personal attention and enjoyed a higher quality of life. When she and her mother visited local households to pick up knitting for the wartime effort, she noticed that large families were in persistent need of assistance. As a school teacher in 1957, Mary Lou again encountered children subject to abuse. The financial hardships of large families often seemed to correlate with the frequency of child abuse. Families with more children had a harder time getting ahead. The children were economically disadvantaged and often emotionally deprived. These observations prompted Mary Lou to provide needed information about family planning.

Mary Lou was initially drawn to Planned Parenthood by a personal interest in women and children. John was drawn to the movement by a concern over the imbalance between human numbers and available resources. In time, M'Lou's and John's interests would converge not only in effect, but also in purpose.

Mary Lou was named Outstanding Planner by the Northwest Michigan Council of Governments in 2000, after serving on the Emmet County Planning Commission and its committees for more than a quarter of a century. Here she acquired first-hand insights into the persistent human pressure on resources. This experience shifted the underpinnings of her population advocacy. While still maintaining a humanitarian interest in women and children, she eventually also came to appreciate the humanitarian need to maintain a responsible balance with biological systems.

The initial basis for John's involvement in population issues also has shifted over the years, evolving toward a new emphasis. Though he remains concerned about the impact of human activity on resources, his population and immigration advocacy have been informed by a growing awareness of culture, language, and civic affairs.

In Denver General Hospital where their first child, Laura, was born, Mary Lou noticed a table for dispensing birth control information to the women leaving the hospital with their newborn babies.

Upon returning to Ann Arbor, Mary Lou joined the local Planned Parenthood board in 1961. She and Nancy Bell Bates, granddaughter of Alexander Graham Bell, visited clinics and gathered contraceptive histories from women.

They soon found that many women were misinformed about contraceptives. Many women frequently confused feminine hygiene products with contraceptive products. Nancy and M'Lou asked drugstores to separate these products on the shelves. They also discovered that women often confused the word "germicidal" used on feminine products with the phonetically similar word "spermicidal." It became apparent that some women needed personalized assistance in identifying proper contraceptive products.

Between 1961 and 1964, John was consumed by academics while in ophthalmology residency at the University of Michigan in Ann Arbor. Their daughter, Laura, was born in June of 1961. Mary Lou was then pursuing a master's degree in special education while also tutoring children. Despite the family and educational demands on her time, Mary Lou continued to pursue her advocacy in family planning with Nancy.

When they moved to Petoskey, Michigan, in 1964, Mary Lou continued meeting individually with women in the maternity ward. She received a warm reception from obstetricians and gynecologists, and nurses alerted her when intervention was particularly needed. They often offered helpful comments such as: "Be sure to visit this girl. She is sixteen, just had a baby, and is just a child herself." Having given birth, often to an unplanned child, these new mothers generally welcomed contraceptive information. Intercepting these women before they left for home enabled Mary Lou to distribute necessary information efficiently and to achieve maximum effects. This maternity ward gave birth to the delivery of new concepts in northern Michigan. Here, in 1965, Mary Lou also gave birth to Jane, the second of the two Tanton children.

Some women were misinformed. Others were afraid even to ask for contraception information, fearing that their (usually male) physician might trivialize the question. Little information on family planning was available to women, so Mary Lou and her friend, Jean Beckley, converted an overnight case into a kit containing information on available contraceptives. The kit was easily transported.

Mary Lou's interest in Planned Parenthood originated in her concern for needy women and children who, throughout history, have borne the brunt of the hardship when resources are scarce. Her advocacy intersected with John's interests, although his commitment was grounded on related, but distinct, concerns. He was focused primarily on the competition of surging populations over dwindling resources.

Initially, the Tantons' conservation efforts were conciliatory. Upon arriving in Petoskey in 1964, for example, they took note of an underappreciated community resource: the Bear River. This river drained Walloon Lake and a network of spring-fed tributaries through much of the glacial architecture around their home town. The Bear emptied into Lake Michigan in downtown Petoskey. Old tires and trash were strewn along much of the river corridor. Mary Lou and John formed the Bear River Commission to remove refuse and to heighten appreciation for this resource. Soon thereafter they founded the Petoskey Regional Audubon Society (1967), the Hartwick Pines Natural History Association (1969), and the League of Conservation Voters for the 11th Congressional District (1970).

By 1967, Mary Lou and John became interested in establishing a Planned Parenthood affiliate and clinic in northern Michigan. This was one year before Paul Ehrlich wrote *The Population Bomb* and three years before the first Earth Day (1970). The Tantons observed that natural systems replenish themselves, much as soils on the farm are rejuvenated by proper crop rotation. Natural systems were, however, threatened. Wherever they looked they saw a new road, another clear cut, tires in an old riverbed, and a mounting waste stream. The problems of ever-increasing pollution and diminishing habitats had a common root cause: the sheer number of people. People are the multiplier. With an affinity for addressing causes, as distinguished from effects, the Tantons found a comfortable home in the population movement.

Two people inflict twice the damage of one. And six billion inflict at least two times the damage of three billion. For the Tantons to express respect for natural systems, it became necessary to speak out on population issues. Their voices first resounded in the councils of Planned Parenthood where they noted the alarming implications of the rising percentage of births to teenagers and single parent households. John wrote a letter to the president of Planned Parenthood World Population (PPWP) to urge that contraceptive information be made available to teenagers and single women. Today we would not expect Planned Parenthood to withhold information from the most needy and vulnerable. At the time, however, providing contraceptive information to teens and singles experiencing unplanned parenthood was still a revolutionary idea.

The hope for planned and wanted children in two-parent households was a worthy goal. Nevertheless, the president soundly rejected John's suggestion. The insight of those on the cutting edge can be obscured by the conventional wisdom of onlookers.

The organizational talents John developed as president of the Delta Upsilon fraternity at MSU were readily transferred to the formation of Northern Michigan Planned Parenthood (NMPP). John served as president from 1970 to 1975. During his tenure, in addition to expanding the informational services, NMPP instituted a direct health services program. It became a full service family planning organization with clinical services.

Concurrently with these efforts, during the late '60s and early '70s, M'Lou and John organized a local chapter of the Sierra Club and of the Audubon Society. Their co-founder of the Audubon Society chapter, Bill Sheldon, was a patient of John's. He had visited John for eye difficulty secondary to the tumor that eventually claimed his life. John had to inform his good friend of the tumor. The close relationship forged in their common endeavor made this physician's task a memorably distressing duty.

In 1968 Mary Lou became a founding member of the Michigan Women for Medical Control of Abortion (MWMCA) and also served on the board of the Michigan Council for the Study of Abortion. Mary Lou's views on abortion at the time are preserved in her op-ed found in the Appendix. MWMCA informed legislators and Michigan residents of the need for medical abortions to assure healthy and well-loved children. The organization promoted the ideal that motherhood is a vested right of every woman. The right was to be exercised at the individual discretion of the mother and her physician, within the confines of responsibility to the child, the family, and to society.

MWMCA spearheaded an initiative petition drive to reform Michigan abortion laws. The initiative would have allowed abortions for the mother's physical and mental health. Mary Lou sought and received support from the American Association of University Women as well as from Methodist and Presbyterian women's groups. After working on this initiative for four years, market opinion research polls revealed Michigan voters favored reform by a margin of two-thirds to one-third. But then, on the eve of the election, the opponents hired advertising men who blanketed the state with red-filtered photographs of fetuses. Many were even displayed on church doors. By the time of the election, voter support waned. Michigan voters rejected the initiative by a margin of two-thirds to one-third. Soon thereafter, the U.S. Supreme Court superseded this vote with the landmark decision in *Roe v Wade*.

The late '60s and early '70s also afforded Mary Lou and John a series of opportunities to acquaint their friends with the natural amenities on state lands. They organized campouts at Wilderness State Park, where an old Civilian Conservation Corps building housed about eighty of their friends from across the state. These outings became fund-raisers for the Sierra Club. They hired a cook, bought the food, and made all the necessary arrangements. The outings, usually in the last weekend of February, introduced many to cross-country skiing in the northern Michigan area. For one of the outings, lessons were offered by a former Olympic cross-country skier from Czechoslovakia. The last weekend in February remains a favored date for their cross-country gatherings, now commonly held in Canada.

In the late 1960s, Mary Lou and John joined the newly formed organization known as Zero Population Growth (ZPG) as soon as they learned of its existence. This led to active involvement in planning the first Earth Day, an unforgettable event in the environmental movement. It was celebrated in April 1970. While preparing for Earth

Day, they met Roger Conner. He would eventually become the first executive director of the Federation for American Immigration Reform (FAIR).

John and Mary Lou were on the road during Earth Day week in 1970. They traveled the state and gave thirty speeches on population growth. As chair of Michigan Women for Medical Control of Abortion, Mary Lou spoke on and debated the need for medical control of abortion. When discussing these concerns, John was careful not merely to complain but to offer helpful advice. Thus, his talks examined the components of the population growth equation: unplanned children in unwelcome settings, teen pregnancies, single parent households, families financially strained with five or six children. He also noted that immigration accounted for ten to fifteen percent of total population growth.

While there was a receptive audience for the message about voluntary fertility reduction in the United States, he also detected an aversion to the topic of immigration. While the United States was willing to voluntarily reduce its population by bringing down its fertility, it was reluctant to discuss population growth due to immigration.

John began to ask questions about this disregarded component. He found no one knowledgeable. Many believed it was not a proper subject for discussion. Undeterred by the prevailing reticence, he began opening files and accumulating materials, hoping someday to deliver the information to a qualified writer on the subject. None was to be found. At the time, it was already clear that the topic would become a rising national concern. John trusted that eventually someone would follow his or her conscience to advance meaningful discussions on the topic.

Advocacy on population issues soon led John to a select group of activists. In retrospect, this activism may have produced one of the most effective charitable media campaigns ever. Its message left an enduring mark on the nation's demography. In June of 1970, John attended a conference in Chicago, the "Congress on Optimum Population and the Environment" (COPE), joining writers Paul Ehrlich, Garrett Hardin, Willard Wirtz (secretary of labor under

Presidents Johnson and Kennedy), Stuart Udall, and others. Hubert Humphrey addressed the general meeting (having the misfortune to show up in alligator shoes).

In the early 1970s, Richard Salarius asked John to organize a population committee for the Michigan Sierra Club. Salarius was an instructor at the University of Michigan and eventually became a member of the national Sierra Club board of directors. In the wake of Paul Ehrlich's classic *The Population Bomb* and Earth Day 1970, population studies soon became a familiar, even fashionable, topic.

John's formation of the Population Committee for the Michigan Chapter of the Sierra Club led to a meeting of Midwestern Sierra Club activists at the Morton Arboretum in Chicago in the fall of 1972. George Treichel, a geographer from San Francisco State University, attended the meeting. Treichel was on the national ZPG board. Impressed with John's work with the Sierra Club, Treichel recommended John for ZPG board membership. John was elected in April of 1973.

John was appointed chair of the national Sierra Club Population Committee in 1971. There he learned that Garrett Hardin was a member. Having read several of Hardin's works, John wrote to him enthusiastically. Hardin's jarring response left a lasting memory: He announced his immediate resignation! Hardin was singularly a writer, not a committee-type person. Until he received John's letter, he had not even been aware of his appointment to the committee several years earlier. Despite his resignation, a bond formed between the two. His letter of resignation was the first in a series of hundreds of letters exchanged between Hardin and John over the ensuing years.

In early 1974, John chanced upon an ad in *Science* magazine for an essay contest held in conjunction with the upcoming Limits to Growth Conference, underwritten by Texas oilman George Mitchell. The conference followed the acclaimed Club of Rome book entitled *Limits to Growth*.[8] John submitted a synopsis of his thoughts on immigration and was selected to write a final paper on the subject.

The paper on immigration placed third in the contest. A fellow contestant, Englishman Teddy Goldsmith, was editor of *The Ecologist*, a British periodical. Goldsmith did not place, but he liked John's paper well enough to run it as a cover story in *The Ecologist* in 1976.[9] John was now armed with a handout with which to promote his concerns over the unmentionable topic. This essay on immigration is reproduced in Appendix A.

As soon as John became a ZPG board member in 1973, he undertook efforts to steer the organization toward immigration reform. This led to his appointment as chair of an immigration study committee. The committee produced two papers over the next two years. The first analyzed the immigration situation and the second made recommendations for change in basic immigration laws. Both papers were adopted by the national board and the executive committee, but John's ZPG efforts foundered at that point. Eventually the Sierra Club also refused to advocate for immigration reform. The subject was simply too sensitive.

During his two-year term as president of ZPG, John unceasingly suggested that the organization recognize the importance of opening a national dialogue on immigration. Although most board members were unable to conceptually switch from domestic fertility to immigration, this was not true for everyone at ZPG. Gerda Bikales, also an early ZPG member and Holocaust survivor, was employed as a medical social worker in Newark, New Jersey. Here Gerda directly confronted the effects of legal and illegal immigration. Even during the early days with ZPG, Gerda offered John enthusiastic support for his still-controversial writings on immigration reform.

At the end of his presidential term in 1977, the issue was still a taboo subject for the ZPG board. John remained on the board through December 1978, but it became increasingly apparent that the ZPG board was beyond reach on the issue. In late 1977 and early 1978, John entertained the idea of establishing a new organization devoted to immigration issues. Thus it was that during his last year with ZPG, John was organizing the Federation for American Immigration Reform. FAIR opened its doors on January 2, 1979, and Mary Lou eventually became the president of the U.S. Immigration Reform Political Action Committee (IRPAC). The Tantons had enlisted in yet another cause.

CHAPTER 11

"Of Grass and Grassroots"

*There are a thousand hacking at the branches of evil
to one who is striking at the root.*
~ HENRY DAVID THOREAU

JR: How do we honorably discharge our responsibility to the less fortunate in foreign lands with exploding populations?

MLT: Any humanitarian relief program should be evaluated regularly. Does it maintain low overhead costs? Does it reach the target population? Does it "teach one how to fish"? It should address the root ailment, not just treat the symptoms.

JT: As to their brightest and best, the ones with the best education and a vision of a better future—help assure they stay at home and develop their own country, rather than bail out for the MDCs (more developed countries). We then need to provide them with all of the information and at least some of the tools they need to realize their dreams and aspirations (ad astra per aspera!).

IN 1999, MARY ELIZABETH BROWN, AN ASSISTANT PROFESSOR in the Social Science Division of Marymount Manhattan College, published *Shapers of the Great Debate on Immigration, A Biographical Dictionary*.[10] This book traces the history of U.S. immigration policies through its leaders, starting with Thomas Jefferson and including such other notables as Booker T. Washington, Henry Cabot Lodge, Theodore Roosevelt, Henry Ford, Edward M. Kennedy, and Alan K. Simpson. Of the twenty persons whose histories are memorialized in this book, only four are still living. Of the four, John Tanton is the youngest and is the subject of the last chapter entitled *Of Grass and Grassroots* (from which the title of this chapter is respectfully borrowed). Explaining her rationale for entitling John's chapter *Of Grass and Grassroots*, Mary Elizabeth Brown states:

> *The play on words in the title is deliberate. John Tanton first became interested in immigration questions through a lifelong interest in the natural environment. When he determined that immigration was a significant danger to American natural resources, he also found that there were no mechanisms in the political system for getting his views across and for affecting legislation. Hence, he turned to a grassroots effort combining mass appeal, leadership by a few dedicated individuals, and attempts to influence officials at the highest levels of the federal government.*

If you were to ask for John's nomination of the most influential person in recent history, whom might he select? John Locke? George Washington? Thomas Jefferson? Abraham Lincoln? Martin Luther King Jr.? Albert Einstein?

Wrong. His nomination is Emma Lazarus.

When the history of the twenty-first century is written one hundred years from now, the effect of demography will be impossible to ignore. Estimates are that well over one hundred million additional U.S. residents during the first fifty years of the twenty-first century will alter indelibly the nation's environmental conditions, culture, language, air quality, and water purity. This population expansion will intensify the competition for resources and drastically effect countless other aspects of life. This population surge, demonstrably driven by immigration rather than a fertility increase, is only the first installment of the demographic portrait expected from the U.S. Census Bureau.

The unprecedented high wave of immigration results largely from a revisionist interpretation of the Statue of Liberty. The poem authored by Emma Lazarus in 1883 beckons the "huddled masses yearning to breathe free." Despite the dramatic changes in the earth's demographics since the days of Emma Lazarus, the open-bordered imagery of the poem prevails in public discourse on the immigration debate. Images trump reason. Accordingly, it elevates the author to the most influential person of our times, according to John's calculation.

Emma Lazarus (1849-1887) wrote "The New Colossus" as part of an effort to raise funds for the pedestal of the Statue of Liberty. When French sculptor Bartholdi assembled the 152-foot statue as a gift from the French nation, he intended to commemorate the successful American experiment in republicanism, our cherished freedoms, liberties, self-governance, and the rule of law. Thus, the statue became known as "Lady Liberty." The Lazarus poem, only one of many manuscripts on the statue, shifted the symbolism from "Liberty Enlightening the World" to a beacon for immigration. The poem's title refers to the Colossus of Rhodes, a bronze statue of the sun god, Helios, that overlooked the Greek city's harbor. It became one of the seven wonders of the world. The Lazarus poem reads:

> Not like the brazen giant of Greek fame,
> With conquering limbs astride from land to land;
> Here at our sea-washed, sunset gates shall stand
> A mighty woman with a torch, whose flame
> Is the imprisoned lightning, and her name
> Mother of Exiles. From her beacon-hand
> Glows world-wide welcome; her mild eyes command
> The air-bridged harbor that twin cities frame.
>
> "Keep, ancient lands, your storied pomp!" cries she
> With silent lips. "Give me your tired, your poor,
> Your huddled masses yearning to breathe free,
> The wretched refuse of your teeming shore.
> Send these, the homeless, tempest-tossed to me.
> I lift my lamp beside the golden door."

The immigration debate provides a unique insight into how an idea in our democracy can build on the strength of a singular image, a phenomenon of Emma Lazarus's poem. In the face of this tendency, the Tantons' immigration reform efforts illustrate how, even today, the power of such an image can be affected by the energy the Tantons have devoted to their tireless conservation ethic. The Federation for American Immigration Reform became Mary Lou's and John's vehicle for delivering this conservation ethic to the public, and with it they have moved a national debate.

In 1977, John arranged for Roger Conner to be invited to join the ZPG national board. Two years later, John recruited Conner to become FAIR's first executive director. Roger had served in the trenches of Michigan's early environmental movement. His experience included an appointment to the Michigan Air Pollution Control Commission by Governor Milliken, and he became the second executive director of the West Michigan Environmental Action Council.

Roger characterizes an early visit to the Tantons as his "trip to the mountaintop." He met M'Lou and John at their home in Petoskey overlooking the valleys, the bay, the hills, and the Tantons' beloved beehives. They discussed the need for a new organization. Roger had dedicated five years to the West Michigan Environmental Action Council but was not planning to become a lifer. He was ready to expand his professional horizons. This was a new endeavor on the national scene, and that is where FAIR's story begins. Roger and John agreed to commit five years to determining whether it was possible to achieve any definable goals.

Roger's verbal skills as a national champion debater at Oberlin complemented John's disciplined organizational skills. As an example of this discipline, John carried a notebook everywhere to record ideas as they dawned on him. He also acquired a small tape recorder for his night stand. When thoughts emerged in the middle of the night, the handy tape recorder was in close reach to record them.

Maybe too close.

Before long, John was given the choice of sleeping with his tape recorder or with M'Lou. Since then, the tape recorder has been spending lonesome nights in distant corners of the Tanton home.

Roger and John would compare their respective checklists and monitor the progress of the organization on Mondays. The issues involved not only immigration reform advocacy but also the customary problems of operating a charitable organization: identifying the strengths and weaknesses of the staff, filling new positions, and maintaining a cooperative spirit in the workplace. There was a sense of mutual respect for the other's resolve and unique talents.

Staffing the new organization was a challenge. If its concerns had been strictly conservation and environmental issues, any number of other organizations in the same field would have offered a vast pool of mobile employees to fill new positions. Immigration reform was a new and disquieting subject, however, and no prospective employees experienced in the field were readily available.

Staff was recruited from college graduates with a certain vision of the world, its future, and a commitment to ideological aspirations. Well-educated people dedicated to the cause had more to offer than uncommitted writers merely capable of grinding out press releases on any subject. Because no one was schooled on the immigration issue, college recruitment involved discussions on the applicant's world view and ideology.

They located basement space on New Hampshire Avenue, N.W., in Washington, D.C. To find ground zero in the immigration reform movement at an organizational level, this basement crevice was a good place to start. After hiring secretarial help, they found a writer in Gary Imhoff. Barnaby Zall, then attending law school at night, was engaged as a lobbyist. Gerda Bikales was enlisted as a writer and policy analyst "on loan" from the National Parks and Conservation Association.

It was thought, or at least hoped, that by opening an office in Washington, D.C., the environmental and population interests would come to FAIR's aid. This did not prove to be the case.

The U.S. fertility rate had dropped precipitously in the wake of Paul Ehrlich's *Population Bomb*, Earth Day 1970, and the efforts of organizations such as ZPG in the early '70s. Population control groups had shifted their focus to the surging fertility rates overseas, but a number of conservation groups had not yet made the transition to working on these root causes rather than effects: They were still vigilantly trying to save selected patches of wilderness rather than seeking ways to relieve the population pressure and resource hunger that jeopardizes all wilderness.

John knew Sherry Barnes through the ZPG executive committee and her work for Planned Parenthood. Unlike other colleagues at ZPG, Sherry was able to discuss topics such as immigration meaningfully. Bill Paddock, another ZPG board member and a writer on population issues, was also sympathetic to the cause. Otis L. Graham Jr., a historian from the University of California, Santa Barbara, shared a sensitivity to the need for immigration reform. Sydney Swensrud, former chairman of Gulf Oil and acquainted with Sherry Barnes through International Planned Parenthood, also joined the board. This was FAIR's original board: Barnes, Paddock, Graham, Swensrud, and Tanton. Their first meetings were held in the basement space on New Hampshire Avenue.

John established an organizational structure with an active, cohesive board having a manageable number of members. Each board member was selected for at least two of the three W's: Wisdom, Wealth, and Work. With Otis Graham, they also found value in a fourth "W": Wit.

If FAIR enjoyed any measure of success in the early days, it was because of its ambition and persistence. On all fronts, it was outgunned and outmanned by groups advocating open or relaxed borders. "John," according to co-founder Otis Graham, "did it all with a partner [Mary Lou] of crucial importance—the vision, find the people, find the language, find the money, build the organization, run the organization, start another one, keep playing on all these strings. We need a word larger than *philanthropist* or activist to describe him."

The board established a disciplined organizational routine. They met quarterly and rigidly followed a defined agenda. They insisted on staff reports assessing accomplishments to date and projecting specific anticipated achievements for the upcoming quarter.

Individual board members brought diverse talents to the organization in its formative years. Mr. Swensrud was a prior chair of Gulf Oil Corporation. As a successful investor, he readily drew upon an assortment of maxims that distilled his decades of business success to their essence. In 1980, Swensrud's business sense impelled him to recommend an "emergency fund" for FAIR. Five percent of all contributions plus interest earned was placed in an emergency fund that often was used to tide FAIR during precarious times. The funds were replenished when support improved.

Bill Paddock combined vast experience on the population issue with an enthusiastic spirit. Sherry Barnes had strong organizational skills, was fluent in population issues, and had the intellectual courage to deal with challenging issues crucial to the nation's future.

The immigration issue is not conveniently characterized as either liberal or conservative. High immigration levels undercut employment opportunities for disadvantaged labor (a liberal concern) while straining the bonds of national unity (offending a conservative agenda). Immigration reform draws on support—and excites opposition—from both the left and the right. Of the five board members, Graham and Barnes gravitated toward the left, Swensrud leaned to the right, and Paddock and Tanton were centrists.

Now, how to raise money for the movement? As 1980 was a presidential year, direct mail solicitations would draw little attention, so it was necessary to rely upon individuals. Donations of more than $174,000 were needed during the first year to keep the organization afloat. One of the primary sources of early support was Jay Harris, John's predecessor as ZPG president. Harris was a descendant of Henry M. Flagler, a lawyer and associate of John D. Rockefeller. He established the railroads down the east coast of Florida and built up Palm Beach. Sympathetic to John's interest in the "unspeakable" immigration issue at ZPG, Harris pledged $100,000 over five years to launch the Federation for American Immigration Reform.

Early funding was also provided through the Environmental Fund. Bill Paddock and Garrett Hardin were on the board to which John was admitted in 1980. Eventually, the Environmental Fund became known as Population-Environmental Balance (PEB).

The early days taught a fund-raising lesson: The areas most responsive to FAIR's appeals, California, Texas, and Florida, were those that felt the consequences of immigration most acutely. To their surprise, FAIR soon learned that the political system in these jurisdictions was unresponsive. Politicians in the areas most dislocated by rapid immigration found it difficult to withstand the pressure for expanded immigration. Thus, paradoxically, FAIR's most outspoken political allies in the immigration reform movement were from states least threatened by immigration, including Senator Walter D. Huddleston and Congressman Romano Mazzoli from Kentucky and Senator Alan Simpson from Wyoming.

Opposition to reform came from those subject to political pressures from the immigrants themselves and their advocates in California and Florida. Nevertheless, Roper Polls have consistently revealed that seventy percent of U.S. residents believe U.S. immigration should be under three hundred thousand per year. The same polls have revealed that approximately fifty-five percent of U.S. residents, including minorities and recent immigrants, believe overpopulation is a major national problem needing immediate attention.[11] Perhaps the minorities and underprivileged understand that their jobs are the first threatened by the next wave of immigration. Increasingly, employment prospects of college graduates are also being eroded as U.S. immigration policies lure the best and brightest from underprivileged nations.

Formulating a conceptual framework for the immigration topic resembled the taxonomic efforts of early botanists. FAIR needed an organized system of classification, so its initial efforts focused on creating categories and terminology for describing and analyzing legal immigration, illegal immigration, immigration volume, optimum population, employment policies, and others. It soon became apparent that immigration issues could be distilled into three fundamental questions:

- ✦ How many people should be admitted?
- ✦ Who should be admitted?
- ✦ How should the rules be enforced?

FAIR's introductory monograph, "Rethinking Immigration Policy," was derived from John's 1975 Mitchell Prize paper, which became the cover story in *The Ecologist*.[12] Gary Imhoff reworked the article for FAIR.

Legal and illegal immigration numbers were increasing. As a matter of priority, the first, and theoretically easier, question pertained to illegal immigration. According to John, "It didn't make much sense to change the rules if nobody was following them anyway." Thus, FAIR supported the Simpson-Rodino Bill of 1986, which principally addressed a component of the third issue: enforcing the laws on illegal immigration.

In early 1987, Roger Conner left the position of executive director and became president of FAIR. This enabled him to focus on fundraising. Dan Stein filled the executive director's shoes as FAIR made the transition from advocating for passage of the Simpson-Rodino Bill of 1986 to advocating for its enforcement. Over the years, Stein has distinguished himself as a leading voice in the national media on immigration reform. His wife, Sharon, has served a similar course of advocacy as director of Negative Population Growth (NPG).

It was impossible to predict which themes would appeal to the public and which allies would step forward. It was also unclear from what quarter opposition would materialize. The early strategy had to be resilient enough to accommodate emerging issues and opposition.

At the start of the 1980s, FAIR was only able to react. Refugee issues demanded a humanitarian response, yet even in that context issues were already brewing. The arrival of Cuban prisoners in the Mariel Boat Lift drew national attention and caused considerable consternation even in proimmigration circles. The new organization's finite resources were strained in the struggle to deal with all aspects of the immigration policy. This was a new challenge for the board and its executive director, all of whom emerged from the well-funded population movement. Although immigration reform was the logical next step for population advocates, it required a new discipline, a new emphasis, and a new constituency. The transition was not free of challenges.

Population issues are essentially biological. In any biological system, the demand for resources is balanced against the available supply. Immigration, on the other hand, involves a complex cluster of interrelated, and often politically volatile, issues. These issues included economics, social welfare, English education, bilingual ballots, political fragmentation, job security, burgeoning ghettos, resource conservation, the brain drain in foreign lands, a host of cultural issues, and many more.

If FAIR expected an informed and sophisticated Congressional perspective on the issue of immigration, it sadly misjudged the nation's representatives. Years earlier, Sam Ervin, head of the Senate Judiciary Committee when the 1965 immigration bill passed, indicated this was the single most sensitive topic ever to have reached Congress. More than one hundred organizations testified in connection with that legislation. John complimented Sam Ervin for his judgment in insisting upon a ceiling on immigration from the Western hemisphere. Ervin denied possessing foresight. He said it intuitively felt like the right thing to do. Congress established a ceiling of one hundred twenty thousand from the Americas because it "sounded good."

Elected officials seemingly had little appreciation for immigration's eventual role in population growth or its impact on a national population policy. For example, on, July 12, 1971, Michigan's Senator Philip A. Hart responded to a letter from John as follows:

> Your letter of June 17 has not been an easy one for me to answer . . . My own judgment is that since immigration into this country is not a major factor in the population problem we would do well not to separate it out for special treatment.

Thus, FAIR could not wait for instant adherents to come forward and help the organization. Of necessity, FAIR's early efforts in Congress were focused on building coalitions by helping others engaged in immigration issues. Senator Alan Simpson and Congressman Romano Mazzoli, who served on the Select Commission on Immigration near the end of the Carter years, were educated on immigration issues. Senator Simpson became chair of the Judiciary Immigration Subcommittee. Simpson and Mazzoli were dedicated to addressing the immigration issue, and FAIR was eager to provide support for its staff.

In the early days, FAIR was running against prevailing American pro-immigration sentiment and going it alone. "One of our goals," according to Roger, "was to make the discussion of immigration a legitimate topic for thinking people." FAIR's founders envisioned three stages in the immigration debate. The first stage was the "Statue of Liberty" phase. Whenever someone brought the topic up, the Emma Lazarus poem was quoted in response. It was a sufficient answer to any possible argument.

Phase two was designated the "Caveat" phase. Here people would say: "Now, I want to make sure you understand I am not a nativist, racist, or mean-spirited, but I've been thinking about immigration, and maybe there are some important points here. For example, what about the effect of the brain drain on the nation of origin?"

The third, "Mature Discussion," phase will emerge when immigration is accepted as a legitimate topic for discussion, *sans* pejorative epithets, and without having one's parentage questioned.

The frequency of news reports on immigration and its effect on politics, language, and the environment suggest that the twenty-first century will deliver us to the third phase.

Chapter 12

Practice on Loan

> *In no country in the world has the principle of association been more successfully used or applied to a greater multitude of objects than in America. Besides the permanent associations which are established by law under the names of townships, cities and countries, a vast number of others are formed and maintained by the agency of private individuals.*
> ~ Alexis de Tocqueville, *Democracy in America*

JR: How did you strike a responsible balance between employment and charitable pursuits?

JT: My ophthalmology practice was very concrete: One could see results in the short term. But being good at it was built on endless reputation. My public-interest life was the opposite: long-term and abstract, and thus hard to measure, but very stimulating and constantly changing. This made for a nice contrast and balance, which I adjusted as circumstance and feelings dictated. Since few are so favored, I felt a responsibility to spend extra time on the public interest side.

MLT: My teaching career spanned part of John's medical school, internship, and residence years. Motherhood was then balanced with babysitting, private tutoring, graduate school, and volunteer counseling and board membership for Planned Parenthood.

THE TANTONS ARE THE DESCENDANTS OF IMMIGRANTS, SOME of whom fled to the United States to escape political oppression in the early nineteenth century. They sought a place of refuge and they found it here, on our sea-washed, sunset shores, in the land of the free and the home of the brave; in the land of opportunity, where every child can legitimately dream of becoming president; where amber waves of grain and purple mountains' majesty nurture the image of seemingly endless frontiers. This place became their sanctuary. They came to a place where their descendants could satisfy their yearning to breathe free, acquire advanced degrees, build a life of comfort, and perhaps even lift their lamp beside the golden door.

Is it an act of irony, or a natural progression, for the heirs of these immigrants to advocate a greater respect for the nation's borders? Are Mary Lou and John fulfilling their ancestors' legacy? Did the descendants and intellectual heirs of nineteenth-century immigrants change the circumstances? Or did the circumstances change them?

The paper trail suggests that the circumstances have changed—that the world has become a different place. John organized his thoughts in an essay addressing the shifting paradigm in this new world. This essay is set forth in Appendix B. It might eventually be seen as his opus. The essay's title poses a salient question: "End of the Migration Epoch?" Here John draws on years of experience as a seasoned advocate. He squarely confronts conclusions drawn from the cliché that "We have always been a nation of immigrants."

When Mary Lou's and John's immigrant ancestors were arriving in the United States during the early nineteenth century, the world's population was approximately one billion. At the time it took more than one hundred years for the population to double. Since then, the world's population has swelled to more than six billion, and it doubles in less than fifty years. In a world of one or two billion, the dissatisfied could pack their bags, find a new place with deep rich soils, fresh waters, and abundant resources. Here they could settle into a new home. But in a world of six billion, where are these verdant unoccupied lands? Realistically, they are not to be found. These changes led John to frame the poignant question others were afraid to address: "Have we reached the end of the migration epoch?" Long before he framed the question in his essay, John and Mary Lou understood that an organized effort would be required to move the issue forward on the national agenda.

De Tocqueville observed U.S. democracy in action when visiting from France in 1831. His treatise, *Democracy in America*, remains a respected account of America's early experiment in self-governance, one that is consulted even today by those seeking insight into the nature of our democracy. One of de Tocqueville's most perceptive insights was his recognition of the importance of organizations in the American democratic process. De Tocqueville suggested that organizational skills in building associations were a prerequisite to achieving goals in our system. This observation about the character of our democracy remains as true today—indeed, perhaps truer—than it was in de Tocqueville's day.

As a result of the Tantons' experiences in s and sorority life and in numerous charitable nonprofit organizations, they understood organizational structures. Bylaws, agendas, the ritualistic recording of minutes, and the peremptory motion to adjourn were familiar tools for organizing a group effort and directing it toward achieving a selected goal. In the early days, FAIR needed the Tantons' organizational skills. But M'Lou and John were still tucked away in northern Michigan, removed from Washington by a distance of some six hundred miles.

In 1980, the three ophthalmologists of the Burns Clinic decided to add a fourth. That year's class of residents was expected to finish training in July 1981. The candidate would be found in this crop of graduates. Timothy Van Every, M.D., was selected and accepted the position.

John had experienced the challenges of starting a practice and he knew it takes a while to get established. In John's words, "A little light went on." He could take a year's leave of absence while "lending" his ophthalmology practice to the newcomer. After building his practice for sixteen years, it was, at the time, the largest in northern Michigan. The opportunity to take it over for a year would be an irresistible lure with which to attract the best possible candidate.

John was forty-seven. Daughter Laura was in college. Daughter

Jane would be entering her junior year in high school. Though it might not have been a prudent decision financially, it was nevertheless the right time for a midlife hiatus from his practice. It would free him to turn his hand, full-time, to the issue that had become all-consuming for him.

Jane willingly left her high school class as a junior, knowing she would return for her senior high school year to graduate with hometown friends. M'Lou harbored the same apprehensions as others in the family but on balance knew this was the right move. So, on September 1, 1981, M'Lou, John, and Jane loaded a share of worldly possessions into a rented truck and headed for Washington, D.C. The glacial topography on the outskirts of Petoskey requires travelers to scale a series of hills. But they were "in the truck that couldn't." Red indicator lights on the dashboard signaled engine failure only minutes after they were under way. The threesome wondered whether this was a foreboding omen of the year that lay ahead. But the truck was quickly exchanged for another and their journey unfolded uneventfully.

It proved a productive year for the family. The Tantons resided in Arlington, where Jane enjoyed her high school junior year experience. Two-thirds of John's salary was paid by FAIR and one-third by the Environmental Fund. Monthly revenues of $2,500 covered the essentials, but not much more. While Mary Lou served as a lobbyist for FAIR on the House side of the Hill at a nominal wage, John's assignment included substantial travel and fundraising. He also continued to develop FAIR's organizational infrastructure.

The trip to Washington, D.C., was timely not only because the nation was entering an era of lower fertility rates but also because the Simpson-Mazzoli Bill was being debated in Congress. This bill emerged as the United States was experiencing large-scale immigration resulting from the 1965 immigration bill. Debates on the Simpson-Mazzoli Bill began in 1981 and continued to 1984. The Tantons' one-year sabbatical in Washington, D.C., and the founding of FAIR coincided with the entry level of the Congressional debate on the Simpson-Mazzoli Bill.[13]

This early experience in the trenches of the legislative process introduced M'Lou and John to the arguments for increased immigration, the adversaries in the debate, the vested interests, the immigration bar, and religious groups (curiously both for and against increased immigration).

John found that the chief roadblocks to immigration reform were tradition and inertia, with the scales weighing heavily in favor of the status quo. To pass a bill, lobbying efforts had to succeed in the subcommittee and the full committee in both houses before the bill could move to each chamber. That meant six opportunities to fail, even assuming the bills passed each house in anything like their original version. If different versions were passed along the way, then the bill went to a conference committee, where the conferees for each house voted separately. Then the conference report went back to the floor on both sides and there were more votes. That meant ten opportunities to fail. Then it proceeded to the president, for an approving signature.

Thus, eleven "yes" votes in a row are required to pass a bill, while to defeat a measure the opposition need only prevail in one of eleven stations. It is much easier to defeat a measure than to pass it. In John's words, "The legislative system is stacked against getting anything done."

The most frequent reaction to immigration reform proposals is the "nation of immigrants" argument. Although opponents of immigration reform commonly invoke this argument, John points out that it does not withstand scrutiny. All nations, with the possible exception of an area near central Ethiopia, are peopled by immigrants, yet only a handful of nations, such as the United States, still accept immigrants in any substantial numbers.

The Population Reference Bureau, one of the leading demographic organizations in the world, publishes an annual *World Population Data Sheet*. This data sheet includes no immigration data because, on a worldwide scale, the volume of migration is literally insignificant. Indeed, restrictive immigration policies in all but a few countries already have been established.

In the United States, approximately one in eleven persons is foreign born. This means that ten in eleven are native born. Thus, notwithstanding its high levels of immigration, the United States remains a nation of the native born.

When the Simpson-Mazzoli Bill for immigration reform was introduced, opposition had not yet reached a fever pitch. Groups joining the opposition later in the 1980s were not as polarized as they later became. Nevertheless, the advocacy required to achieve passage of the Simpson-Mazzoli Bill consumed millions of dollars.

During the early days, amnesty for illegal aliens was also a difficult issue for FAIR to confront. People around the world were standing in line, following the rules, waiting for a chance to migrate. Amnesty confers special status upon those who cut the line and enter out of turn. FAIR was concerned about the precedent established by granting amnesty. It also had to accept the political reality that all illegal immigrants were not going to be deported.

FAIR found Senator Simpson generally receptive to immigration reform legislation, but he also maintained a firm commitment to amnesty. The staff and board at FAIR wavered on the issue. Amnesty was difficult to square with the fundamental notion that a nation unable to control its borders cannot control its destiny. Ambivalence led to delay, and by the time FAIR resolved the issue within its ranks, it was too late to influence the debate.

John found it challenging to establish firm policies on several knotty issues that arose in FAIR's formative days. There was an occasional lack of unanimity among the staff and board, which split on whether the organization should be reactive or proactive. There was also a need to build a membership base and well-reasoned positions to influence the debate. As the organizer and chair, it was difficult to strike a healthy balance between maintaining a united front and avoiding micromanagement of the staff, particularly before FAIR had formulated policy decisions on major issues.

Raising money and building membership for an organization devoted to this issue was difficult. Immigration was still not on the national radar screen; its effects on culture and language and the strain it exerted on natural resources were apparent only in a few isolated regions. In many circles, immigration was not a comfortable topic for discussion. Nevertheless, a few benefactors came forward.

Fund-raising efforts can bloom unexpectedly. John recalls one benefactor offering $42,000 to run a full page ad in the nationwide edition of the *Wall Street Journal*. Though it struck the FAIR board as a waste of money, the gift was graciously accepted. The ad drew only about one hundred responses, but a Texan, K. C. McAlpin, was one of the respondents. K. C. soon became a staff member of FAIR. His loyalty to the organization and to the Pro-English movement spans the decades. His contributions have been immeasurable. So the $42,000 ad became a profitable investment, notwithstanding the paltry response.

FAIR used direct mail to build its membership base, but because there were no lists of donors committed to the cause of immigration reform, FAIR's mailings to "cold lists" seldom broke even. Nevertheless, subsidizing direct mail programs to find members was not a matter of choice. It was essential. The organization needed members to build credibility, even if the cost of identifying them exceeded their contributions. When money was in short supply, the direct mail program suffered. Understandably, this impaired FAIR's long-term prospects of building membership, but even in the tight-budget conditions of the organization's early stages, scarce resources were allocated to achieving this crucial goal.

By 1985, FAIR had a membership base of approximately fifteen thousand. FAIR has never been willing to write the kind of appeal that would attract the far end of the political spectrum, so its membership traditionally has been composed of moderates on both the right and the left.

FAIR's moderate position allowed new immigration organizations to employ a more emotional appeal. For example, Palmer Stacey, a staffer for Senator East, a conservative southerner interested in immigration, founded the American Immigration Control Foundation (AICF) by using appeals far more strident than FAIR's. Though AICF raised money, its reaching and emotional appeals could have undermined its effectiveness in the legislative process.

As FAIR's chair, John worked to procure an effective commitment from the staff by giving them "ownership" of the issues. The only way he moved an issue forward was for the staff person to move with it.

Thus, the staff person responsible for the issue was expected to write the paper on that subject. It then became a part of the author.

John planned one of these commitment-building experiences for Roger Conner in the summer of 1980. They spent a week on a sailboat in the North Channel of Lake Huron. This is an unblemished scenic area in the Great Lakes. Granite outcroppings, tranquility, and protective coves make this an environment for serious thought. It is a favorite destination for mariners and inspiration-seekers. During the week, Roger formulated a case statement for FAIR.

The idea of forming coalitions with other public interest groups is seductive to new organizations, but it proved difficult. FAIR had its agenda, and other organizations had theirs. Signing on to the policy statement of another was seldom productive because it diluted the focus on FAIR's issues. John learned that the best way to form coalitions with other organizations was not to become formal allies, but rather to share mailing lists. By contacting them directly, John would find which of their members agreed with FAIR's views and sign them up as members.

John developed a policy of promoting from within the organization and of working with people well known to him. At this early phase in the immigration reform movement it was still difficult to find people committed to the cause.

The politically and socially active often belong to a variety of organizations. Perhaps this explains why special interest groups become highly focused on a single issue. When too many causes combine under a single umbrella, some members will lose interest and drop out. The FAIR board, for example, coalesced around the population issue. Had they included gun control, zoning policy, international trade, or protectionism, some would have fallen by the wayside. According to John: "That's not bad; it's just human nature. So we continually try to form coalitions. These coalitions are not among organizations, but rather among individuals who happen to agree on one issue. The individuals may disagree substantially or even profoundly on another issue."

The anticipated longevity of the organization became an important consideration in its early stages. Some thought that FAIR might have a life of five to ten years, complete its mission, and then fold its tent. This happened with the U.S. immigration reform movement after 1924, when Congress adopted measures to stem the tide of immigration. The prior heavy wave of immigration had produced ghettos across the United States in the early 1900s. The successful advocates disbanded into the night after the bill passed.

History shows, however, that the opposition will persistently peck away, day after day, week after month, month after year. If no one is present to defend the gains, in time the beachhead will be eroded and a distorted history of the efforts will have been composed by the opposition. Several facts suggested that FAIR should plan to be engaged for the long-term:

1. Rampant population growth around the planet,
2. Dire circumstances in countries of origin, and
3. Declining fertility rates in a nation obsessed with economic growth.

Finally, John recognized another principle: "Don't take the credit; take the blame." He recalls the words of Lao-Tse, the Chinese philosopher: "He leads best who, when the job is done, finds his people saying: we did this ourselves." From John's perspective, to make the organization successful it was necessary for the leaders to be quick to take the blame and slow to take the credit. He knew the truth of the saying that "Success has a thousand fathers; failure is an orphan." He conferred credit for FAIR's successes to those who, by claiming "parentage," also became allied with FAIR and its goals.

These early efforts, born of his methodical leadership and his hiatus from medical practice, secured John's position as the eventual "dean"[14] of the immigration reform movement. The flat-earthers in the environmental movement had just met their Columbus.

Chapter 13

Nation of a Billion

The stewardship of environment is a domain on the near side of metaphysics where all reflective persons can surely find common ground. For what, in the final analysis, is morality but the command of conscience seasoned by a rational examination of consequences?
~ Edward O. Wilson, The Diversity of Life

JR: What will it take to prevent the United States from becoming, like India and China, a nation of over one billion people?

JT: The "core" population, i.e., those here in 1970, now has sub-replacement fertility, which dictates reaching a peak population in several decades, and then a slow retrenchment back to present-day levels. It is immigration that is making us grow, and that must be cut to levels where immigration equals emigration if we're to avoid continuous population growth—even to one billion.

MLT: Conservationists and others concerned with balancing numbers of people with resources and quality of life issues must weigh in all components of population growth: births, deaths, and fluctuations due to migration. A population policy for the United States can then be revisited.

JOHN MET ROY BECK THROUGH THE IMMIGRATION REFORM movement. Beck was a journalist in the Washington, D.C. area, with an interest in environmental issues. He had a broad writing background in religious issues as well.

John hired Beck as the Washington correspondent for *The Social Contract*, a quarterly journal on environmental and migration issues. John was the initial editor. Beck's familiarity with the immigration issue led him to author a well-recognized article entitled "The Ordeal of Immigration in Wausau" in the July 1994 *Atlantic Monthly*. The article chronicled the experiences of a small town in the Midwest.

In Wausau, Wisconsin, well-intentioned Lutheran church members arranged for several Hmong refugees from Southeast Asia to be accommodated in the city. This was a goodwill gesture from the outset. There were plans for the few refugees to swiftly become assimilated into the city. But the 1965 Immigration Act had another outcome in mind for the small town.

The Act allows for family members to be reunited in the United States under so-called "chain migrations." These provisions are peculiar in that they permit the longest migration chains from the very nations having the highest fertility rates. The voluntarily low fertility rates of U.S. residents are offset by the fecundity of "chain immigrants" from high fertility nations.

In Wausau, the nature, educational opportunities, and culture of the town were rapidly and markedly transformed. Southeast Asian gangs became a recognized threat. Teenage pregnancies, culturally permissible and encouraged in Southeast Asia, were noticeably affecting welfare rolls. Language barriers in the schools affected education for all students. Over time, out of concern for their own children's education and safety, many bedrock families found it necessary to pull up stakes and leave town.

The story in the *Atlantic Monthly* prompted a CBS *60 Minutes* documentary on the effect of immigration on Wausau. This national exposure, in turn, provided Beck the opportunity to author a book published by W.W. Norton entitled *The Case Against Immigration*.

Through Beck's affiliation with John, the www.NumbersUSA.com

Web site was developed under U.S. Foundation. The site has become an interactive resource for persons interested in stabilizing U.S. population. It is also a springboard for direct communications with the body having the singular constitutional responsibility to regulate our nation's borders: the U.S. Congress.

Pursuant to a grant from the Cowell Foundation, Roy Beck also authored *Re-Charting America's Future* for the Social Contract Press. Published in 1994 to correspond with the national high school debate topic dealing with immigration, each chapter of the book states a general claim against stabilizing the population of the United States. Each argument was derived from the common arguments of special interest groups advocating population growth or increased immigration. Beck's book, which systematically dissects each argument, was a helpful handbook for high school debaters and others interested in becoming familiar with the issue.

Beck's graphic depiction of demographic information from the U.S. Census Bureau, shown on page 82, was central to the book. The chart has been updated with the year 2000 projections from the U.S. Census Bureau. It illustrated John's reflections when first addressing the issue as he toured Michigan on Earth Day 1970.

The chart begins in 1970, when the United States had just over 200 million residents. This coincided with the first Earth Day. Population was then high on the nation's conscience, following the publication of Paul Ehrlich's *Population Bomb* in 1968. The United States became a "replacement level fertility" nation shortly after 1970.[15] Notwithstanding this dramatic reduction in the native born birth rate, the U.S. Census Bureau projects that the U.S. population will expand to 404 million by the year 2050!

Beck's chart includes two components. The lower chart depicts the growth in the U.S. resident population from 1970 to 2050. In other words, it includes those here in 1970 and their living descendants. The upper graph depicts the U.S. population growth resulting from immigrants arriving between 1970 and 2050 and their offspring.

The upper portion of Beck's chart indicates the U.S. Census Bureau's midrange U.S. population projection of 404 million by the

This is a future that does not have to happen!

But the United States Census Bureau says that the projections on this chart are inevitable UNLESS Congress cuts immigration.

Growth from post-1970 IMMIGRANTS and descendants

Growth from AMERICANS already here in 1970

We Are Here

Total U.S. Population in Millions

Growth of U.S. Population in Millions

Year	Total	Americans already here in 1970
1970	203	—
1980	—	227 / 218
1990	249	232
2000	275	243
2010	300	250
2020	325	255
2030	351	253
2040	377	245
2050	404	236

SOURCES: Census Bureau and Leon Bouvier

year 2050. Thus, the post-1970 growth is principally attributable to immigration. Demographers will often find the U.S. Census Bureau projections to be on the low side.

This chart illustrates a favorite Tanton saying: "Only Congress can now determine whether we become a nation of one-half billion, or like China, a billion people."

A word on population momentum was commonly included in John's speeches and writings. Even though the United States became a "replacement level fertility" nation shortly after 1970, the Beck chart reveals an increase in 1970 U.S. residents, and their descendants, until approximately 2035. This is because of "population momentum."

If the United States were to maintain "replacement level fertility" (2.1 children per woman), then one might expect no further growth in the resident population. But there is a momentum to population numbers. A growing population will continue to grow for several decades even after the nation moves to replacement level fertility. The population will not stabilize until the young children move through their child-bearing years. For example, even if the fertility rate in Mexico plummeted from 3.1 in 1998 to 2.1 by 2020, its population still would surge from 91 million in 1998 to 154 million in 2050, when it would still be escalating.[16]

Thus, Beck's chart contrasts the voluntary, noncoercive decision by the United States citizenry to reduce its fertility with the effect of a Congressional policy to relax the nation's borders. Were it not for immigration, the 1970 resident U.S. population would have stabilized at approximately 240 million by the year 2035. But while our fertility rates are down, John would still be quick to mention concerns over our rate of consumption. With only five percent of the world's population, the U.S. is generating seventy-two percent of the world's toxic waste.[17]

In the United States, political influence is often rationed among ethnic groups. John points out that the federal government claims to disfavor discrimination based on ethnicity, yet it actively continues to promote ethnic political separation. Tax-exempt status and grants are conferred upon nonprofit organizations for advocating the rights of particular ethnic groups. This is a tax benefit subsidized by other taxpayers. The political influence of one group can grow only at the expense of the influence held by another because politics is still a zero-sum game. Thus, the political influence of Native Americans and African Americans is diluted when the influence of another organization expands.

Studies from the Population Reference Bureau reveal how immigration will influence future political power in the United States. Approximately one in ten U.S. residents is Hispanic at the millennium. By 2050, the proportionate Hispanic population is projected to become one in four residents. In just fifty years this surge in resident population and demographic transition will continue to affect resources, language, culture, and politics. The influence of the existing ethnic groups will correspondingly yield to this demographic shift.

If the nation's drinking water is endangered by contaminated groundwater with 275 million Americans, what will it be like with 400 million? If our national parks are loved to death with 275 million Americans, what will it be like with many more clamoring for admission? If forty percent of Americans are breathing air unfit for human consumption with 275 million Americans, what will the air be like with a fifty percent population increase in fifty years?

Immigration reform's position on the national agenda falls somewhere between international terrorism and White House lawn maintenance. Many environmental organizations have embraced the cause of immigration reform, but others still shrink from the issue. Even among those who vigorously advocate a reduction in the nation's fertility to reduce environmental threats are those who still refuse to address immigration. Why? Roy Beck joined Leon Kolankiewicz in analyzing just this issue in their paper entitled "The Environmental Movement's Retreat from Advocating U.S. Population Stabilization (1970-1998): A First Draft of History."[18] The study looks to a variety of social, religious, political, and cultural factors in explaining the environmentalists' retreat from population issues.

When the sink is overflowing, some will fetch the mop while others reach for the faucet. The Tantons do both.

For example, Mary Lou and John identify this major concern:

There is no sunset provision to require periodic reevaluation of our immigration policy. Agricultural programs, for example, are debated in Congress, agreed upon, and then given a certain life that expires in the absence of further legislative action. The program might be authorized for a period of years. It then requires periodic reauthorizations. This enables Congress to monitor how the plan is working.

Immigration laws, on the other hand, have a theoretically perpetual shelf life. They have no date for reevaluation. No sunset. As a practical matter, an immigration policy continues until circumstances become so severe that Congress is forced to react. As the numbers build, constituencies become more divisive, differences are accentuated, problems proliferate, and, according to Mary Lou and John, they become harder to resolve. The compromises required to enact new legislation yield partial solutions. At best they address conditions as they existed years before the debate started. Legislation is often rendered obsolete by the time it is adopted because by then new conditions have developed. One of FAIR's goals over the years has been to provide a periodic review of immigration legislation. Periodic review would encourage Congress to address current and future conditions.

The effects of massive legal immigration are compounded by illegal immigration. As to illegal immigration, FAIR advocated three measures. First, within the United States, legislation could impose employer sanctions and tightened immigration controls. Ultimately, employer sanctions could be effective only if Congress prescribed a system of identification on which the employer could rely to assure compliance. If employers were unable to determine who is entitled to a job, employer sanctions would fail. FAIR also advocated that Congress adopt a statement on the purpose of immigration policy. U.S. immigration law is largely ad hoc; it has no particular purpose at present. It is fundamentally unlike the Full Employment Act of 1946, which states the objective of full employment. It is unlike the Wilderness Act of 1964, which defines wilderness and provides a mechanism for protecting some of it. FAIR proposed that the purpose of immigration policy should be debated and discussed. The national interest of the United States, and possibly even that of the nations of origin of potential immigrants, should be considered when formulating a policy.

The second measure was to strengthen the borders and points of entry.

The third was to assist in resolving conditions in the nations of origin. This would enable the citizenry to be satisfied where they reside. When there is sufficient education, employment opportunity, and freedom, there is little impetus to flee.

Of the planet's daily net population gain of approximately 230,000 people (births minus deaths), the vast majority (more than ninety percent) are being born into impoverished circumstances. All could advance a legitimate claim on the collective conscience of the United States. More than one billion people go to bed hungry every night and several hundred thousand slip beyond the brink of malnutrition annually.[19] How may the interests of the needy billions in distant lands be advanced meaningfully and respectfully?

During the 1990s, the United States admitted more than one million immigrants every year. Compelling sympathies extend to the newcomers, but those left behind are far more numerous and have nowhere to flee. Those deciding to "cut and run" are typically better educated than the law abiders left behind. Those who aspire to the freedom we offer might flee their nation of origin, but they would also be the most likely citizens to agitate for change at home. Every dollar spent on assisting recent immigrants and in meeting responsibilities for bilingual education will be unavailable to help the far more abundant and needy foreigners lacking the means to flee.

Immigration reformers question whether the United States has a responsibility to open its borders to the world's underprivileged. Can the United States meaningfully address the hardship in foreign nations by admitting a select few? Is this problem solvable with open, or relaxed, borders?

The issue for Mary Lou and John is not whether the United States should act with compassion. Clearly we must. The issue is what form our compassion should take. How should it be expressed? Soaring world population figures confirm that the problem defies resolution through open borders.

Immigration is one of the most divisive issues confronting the nation. It strikes to the heart of a nation's culture, language, identity, and demographics. It is neither liberal nor conservative, democrat nor republican. It engages environmental activists and anti-environmental forces alike. Some right-wing religious organizations favor immigration reform. Other religious sects try to pry the nation's borders open. Forces aligned on this issue for different reasons can make for strange bedfellows.

As U.S. immigration policy promotes a brain drain overseas, it is also courting a "brain restrain" in the United States. Every high tech job awarded to a highly trained recent immigrant is a job not available for a U.S. graduate. Over time this translates into a disincentive for U.S. students to pursue an education in high tech fields. It also discourages employers from providing training and educational incentives to local employees.

Just how should the issue be framed to embrace the differing views? From John's perspective the issue does not even necessarily involve a debate between "anti-immigration" and "pro-immigration" factions. The immigration reform movement is not anti-immigrant; it acknowledges the patent truth that immigrants have enriched America. The movement recognizes that this enrichment will, and should, continue. Rather, the reform movement is opposed to a policy that opens our borders to unprecedented levels of immigration at a time when the bonds of national unity in the United States are fraying and population pressures are noticeably straining the natural resource base. Moreover, this surge in migration paradoxically coincides with a voluntary fertility reduction by the native population. A realistic prospect of achieving a more favorable balance with our biological surroundings and natural resources exists, only to be undermined by our immigration laws.

John believes reasonable people should be able to agree on reasonable limits. Even "pro-immigration" advocates do not favor the immigration of criminals or supporters of apartheid. The issue cannot be framed as either "pro" or "con." Rather the issues are how much, by whom, and how to enforce the rules. John draws on a dietary analogy: "Dieters are not just for food or against food. Rather, the issue is how much food, what kinds of food, and how to achieve specific goals."

Some might favor immigration policies that would cause the United States to become a nation of 500 million and eventually one billion. The Federation for American Immigration Reform favors policies that would achieve a balance. Approximately 225,000 people emigrate from the United States every year. Immigration levels of approximately 200,000 would cause the U.S. population to stabilize within a few decades. FAIR continues to advocate stronger border controls to achieve this goal. Present policies, by contrast, offer no prospect for eventual stabilization.

Perhaps it will just take a while for the nation to awaken to the Tantons' message, which cannot be reduced to a punchy cliché or slogan. It was Goebbels who said that the art of politics consists in reducing all beliefs to a slogan. In current political circles this represents the triumph of the sound bite over reasoned thought. The Tantons have no slogan. Their message defies abatement to the dimension of a bumper sticker. Goebbels was wrong. Communicating complex and far-sighted concepts is where the true art is to be found.

Would Mary Lou and John like to envision a borderless world? Perhaps, but they are constrained by global realities. In John's first article on immigration in 1976,[20] which garnered the Mitchell Prize and presaged the activism that would claim his future, he lamented the lack of equilibrium that makes borders essential:

> *Happily, it is possible to envision a world in which international migration could become free and unfettered. Appropriately, it is the world of a stationary state, in which people in different regions are in equilibrium with resources, and in which there is a reasonable chance in each region for self-fulfillment, matched with social equity. Under these conditions, international migration could be unfettered, because there would be little incentive to move. Contentment with conditions at home, coupled with man's strong attachment to things familiar, would serve to keep most people in place. While the*

freedom to migrate at will is incompatible with the physical realities of today's world, it is one of the many things that can be restored as man achieves balance with his environment.

Eventually, as we overburden the nation's physical limits, immigration is destined to emerge as a leading issue. Until then, the voices of concerned citizens will continue to draw some attention and prompt an anticipatory thought process. As the following section demonstrates, even the U.S. Census Bureau sometimes needs a wake-up call on the issue.

CHAPTER 14

The Great American Paradox

For about two decades, the federal government has sabotaged the American people's dreams for environmental quality, economic security, and social stability and equity.
~ ROY BECK, RE-CHARTING AMERICA'S FUTURE, 1994

JR: While the U.S. voluntarily reduced fertility, why is immigration increasing at unprecedented levels?

JT and MLT: Fertility has fallen all over the developed, modernized world to replacement levels or below—not due to government policy, but traceable to economic, social, cultural, and other factors. Immigration is much more in the purview of government policy, but we have no government population policy to guide it. Hence tradition, myth, and short-term considerations dominate.

A CURIOUS THING HAPPENED AT THE U.S. CENSUS BUREAU between 1989 and 1992. Its significance is apparent only in the context of this demographic data.

In 1989, the Bureau projected U.S. population would peak at 302 million people by 2040. Then it was projected to begin a slow but steady decline toward lower numbers.

Then, in 1992, a little known revision to this projection was buried in the mountain of paperwork churned out by the U.S. government. By then the Bureau had determined that it had miscalculated by a wide margin. The U.S. population would peak not at 302 million, but rather it would rise to 383 million (later increased to 404 million) by 2050. Prospects for a plateau or reduction were no longer in sight.

Population projections regularly undergo marginal revisions from year to year, but there was nothing marginal about this revision. What went wrong?

By April 1975, when John was elected president of ZPG, the U.S. birth rate was dropping precipitously. In 1957 the United States experienced the peak of the U.S. baby boom. The nation's Total Fertility Rate (TFR)[21] was then 3.767 children per woman. A total of 4,308,000 domestic births were recorded in 1957. U.S. births ran over four million annually from 1954 to 1964 (the end of the baby boom). By 1977 total annual U.S. births had dropped to 3,326,632, down almost one million from 1957. The nation's 1977 TFR stood at the record low of 1.7. By contrast, the TFR between 1960 and 1964 was 3.5!

Interestingly, the Census Bureau's 1997 Population Profile reports that the U.S. population grew by 52 million between 1950 and 1970, when the population was 203 million. Then growth slowed between 1970 and 1990 when 46 million individuals were added. Census Bureau projections reveal our population growth between 1990 and 2010 will likely exceed even the baby boom era. Moreover, "Beginning in 2012," reports the U.S. Census Bureau, "the number of births each year will exceed the highest number of births ever achieved in the United States."[22] This increase in sheer numbers will occur even though the fertility rate of native-born U.S. residents is expected to remain at subreplacement levels.

Why? Because immigration emerged as an increasingly important population factor in the nation over the last half of the twentieth century. In 1950, immigration accounted for only one percent of the population growth in the United States. It steadily increased year by year. By 1996, immigrant families and their children were responsible for sixty-one percent of the nation's population growth![23]

The sharp decline in domestic fertility in the 1970s understandably caused the U.S. Census Bureau to project that our population would plateau at 302 million in 2040, and then decline. This 1989 determination was not entirely unfounded, so long as immigration continued to be of marginal importance. But the U.S. Census Bureau failed to take the Tantons' concerns into account and overlooked the unprecedented high rate of immigration. Then, in 1992, they began to recognize the effect of immigration on U.S. population.

This oversight illuminates one of the great paradoxes of our time: Just as U.S. citizens were reducing fertility, Congress began increasing the population. It actively undermined the efforts of U.S. citizens to address population growth. As the United States was beginning to curtail its population growth for a more favorable balance with available resources, Congress began tilting the scales with increased immigration. Under 1965 and 1990 legislation, our nation's borders have been opened wider than ever before to waves of migration.

Although the U.S. Census Bureau remained oblivious to the Petoskey ophthalmologist's message for several years, eventually it was obliged to take note. The Bureau concluded that the nation's 275 million residents at the millennium would swell to more than 400 million in just fifty years because of immigration. And it will not peak there. The continuing increase has no end in sight.

Over the centuries, immigration surely has been beneficial for America. It has enriched our lives and immigrants merit recognition in our noble history. But today, the issue is not whether immigration is beneficial for America. Rather, the issue is one of proportion and limits. The Tantons' concerns are becoming more clearly reflected in our strained landscapes, overburdened water resources, air impurities, and quality of life. In a March 19, 2000, study on urban sprawl called "Weighing Sprawl Factors in Large U.S. Cities," Leon Kolankiewicz and Roy Beck found that approximately one-half has been found to result from land-consumptive decisions. The other one-half results from population (See NumbersUSA.com).

Success remains elusive. Since the time they embraced the issue, the impact of immigration has, year after year, increasingly added to the nation's census by number.

Between 1925 and 1965 the U.S. averaged 178,000 legal immigrants every year. Between 1989 and 1997 annual admissions more than quintupled, averaging 1,063,000 annually.[24] This high volume of immigration is unprecedented in our nation's history. Congress is leading the nation toward less environmental security and more congestion. The Tantons' tireless efforts have been met with increased migration. We can nevertheless conclude that the pressures on U.S. borders would have led to more migration had their voices never been raised.

Chapter 15

A Good Thing

> ... *this much I think I do know—that a society so riven that the spirit of moderation is gone, no court can save; that a society where the spirit flourishes, no court need save.*
> ~ Learned Hand,
> The Contribution of an Independent Judiciary to Civilization (1942)

JR: How has immigration benefited the United States?

JT and MLT: It obviously had its pluses and minuses. Do you want the American Indian viewpoint? The black viewpoint? The viewpoint of the countries that lost their Nobel laureates? The viewpoint of Bill Gates? The engineers he fired to hire cheaper Asian Indian substitutes?

The right question is what factors should be given what weight in setting immigration policy—how can we reach an agreement and implement the results?

In politically correct times, concern for the culture of a nation tends to draw fire. For expressing an interest in preserving the nation's culture and language, John has endured his share of name-calling. Few words are as compelling as "racist." Perhaps the word "heretic" in the Middle Ages had a similar effect. The label has a mind-numbing influence, even when it is unjustly applied.

Those first in line for discrimination under relaxed immigration policies are the under-employed minorities in the United States. Where we stand on the immigration issue often depends on where we sit. Interests finding it advantageous to maintain access to cheap foreign labor erode the employment gains of minorities within the United States. Ironically, these special interests often freely label anyone concerned about immigration as racist.

There is a hard truth about America: Social change will fail to occur when only the underprivileged and politically powerless are adversely affected. Massive immigration levels undercut employment opportunities for those hardest hit and least able to protect themselves. Stiff foreign competition for low-wage jobs with no benefits ravages the household income of America's minorities. A globalized work force erodes hard fought gains for the American worker. Mary Lou's and John's advocacy upholds the dignity of labor for the United States workforce, yet their efforts to control our borders invite perverse charges.

A "politically correct" movement purports to be based on tolerance, but there has been surprisingly little tolerance for the Tantons' concern for U.S. jobs and the well-being of its minorities.

Mary Lou and John see diversity as a good thing, but so is preserving the common bonds of a nation. While diversity maintains an engaging atmosphere in which new ideas can be tested, too much diversity strains the foundational roots of a nation. Achieving both objectives requires a sense of proportion. John observes that as we undergo the present national transformation, we may find ourselves creating precisely the circumstances from which our immigrants fled.

The cultural shift will test the limits of toleration and compromise. For example, religious freedom in the United States is upheld only by vigilantly maintaining the separation of church and state, but other, less tolerant, cultures are based on their fusion. John questions how a nation that respects the separation of church and state will accommodate the views of newcomers favoring such a fusion. How might these antithetical notions be reconciled in a single nation? Other cultures practice female genital mutilation (FGM). Should the United

States allow this time-honored practice in the name of tolerance, political correctness, and multiculturalism?

The transformation by immigration will also alter the marketplace of ideas in the United States. Perhaps we could promote the use of the world's six thousand languages in a small town in the name of diversity. But as John points out, communications would become hopelessly tangled. The exchange of ideas would be compromised by this level of diversity. The issue is one of balance. John asks just how much of a good thing really is a good thing.

CHAPTER 16

Mondays with John

The world is too much with us; late and soon,
Getting and sending, we lay waste our powers:
Little we see in Nature that is ours;
We have given our hearts away, a sordid boon!
~ WILLIAM WORDSWORTH, "THE WORLD IS TOO MUCH WITH US"

JR: How did you select Mondays as your day off?

JT: Partly because few other doctors took time off on Mondays, so it helped spread the workload at Burns Clinic, and partly because it gave us a long weekend.

HIS PARTNERS AT THE CLINIC KNEW NOT TO EXPECT HIM. After all, it was Monday. Other considerations competed for his time. Tuesdays through Sundays were vocational days, but on Mondays, it took an emergency for John to show up at the ophthalmology practice. If anyone asked how he spent his day off work, they would soon find themselves engulfed in a long and captivating conversation.

Since the time he began practicing at the clinic in 1964, Mondays have been reserved for avocational pursuits. For John, his profession was never a means of amassing vast personal wealth. He provided the essentials for the family, with enough to spare for rewarding family excursions. We can now reflect upon his medical career and his practice of setting aside avocational time with the benefit of hindsight.

Over the course of a career, one day each week has a cumulative effect, but it comes at a price. Does John have any regrets? Perhaps. Working to become a better ancestor correspondingly reduced his time as a parent. Extended family trips only partially compensated for this lost family time. Moreover, the national controversies exacted an emotional toll. This limited the residual energy available for patients and profession.

On Mondays, at his personal expense, John hired Donna Pikur, secretarial co-worker at the clinic, to perform typing, filing, and mailing related to his charitable pursuits. Until FAIR was formed in 1979, this one-day arrangement worked fairly well. The dramatic increase in the workload in the spring of 1980 demanded a full-time assistant. John recruited Kathryn Bricker, who had served as the first executive director of the Little Traverse Conservancy.

With a full-time assistant for charitable projects, it became necessary to organize a separate office. John rented space from the Burns Clinic. He purchased the necessary typewriters, filing cabinets, and phones.

It soon came time to incorporate. With a portentous and seemingly uneventful stroke of the pen at the time, John signed the articles of incorporation for the Conservation Workshop on July 6, 1981. The Conservation Workshop changed its name to U.S. Foundation in 1982 to reflect its broad purpose of serving as an incubator for a variety of new projects. Over the years, Mary Lou and John had been involved in forming a number of charitable nonprofit organizations. The red tape in starting each entity became an impediment for new projects. Under the umbrella of the U.S. Foundation, Mary Lou and John hoped to establish a nursery for new projects without incurring hefty start-up costs. Funding was derived from a variety of farsighted sources. In 1983, for example, a donor agreed to contribute $90,000 per year, for a period of three years, to John's charitable efforts. All projects were related to conservation objectives. Once a satisfactory cash flow and donor base were established, a fledgling project was expected to take wing and explore its heights independently.

Over the years, U.S. Foundation has become the extension of Mary Lou's and John's personalities and commitment to conservation. It has undertaken projects to conserve natural resources, balance national unity with diversity, encourage foreign language studies, promote English in official government speech, support discussion groups, assist the vision impaired, and facilitate charitable ventures. Employees of U.S. Foundation range from one to twenty-five per project. All are on a central payroll, which allows for heath, disability, and retirement plans. Each constituent project has its own board of directors but operates under the broad supervision of the U.S. Foundation board.

A review of some of the U.S. Foundation projects—some ongoing, others concluded—lends insight into the Tantons' broad vision and commitment. Following is a brief summary of these projects.

- ✦ Raptor Research provided support for the field work of ornithologist Sergej Postupalsky on the great birds of prey, such as eagles, hawks, owls, and ospreys, in the upper Great Lakes region.
- ✦ Regrants Program raises funds for studies on population, resources, environment, immigration, language, and assimilation. Typical grants underwrite the preparation and publication of papers and continuing education courses.
- ✦ PROWILD promotes the ranching of native animals in East Africa and the dry land parts of the United States as an alternative to cattle ranching.
- ✦ U.S. English, starting as a project of U.S. Foundation in 1983, attained independence on June 30, 1988. This national organization was the catalyst for constitutional amendments making English the official language of state government in Colorado, Arizona, and Florida. John's ties to U.S. English have now been severed.
- ✦ Recycle North started the local citizens' recycling program in northern Michigan. It is now a function of county government.
- ✦ U.S. Foundation sponsors the study of literature gathered by the Great Books Foundation and from the Foreign Policy Association's Great Decisions Series. It holds annual workshops

for writers, academics, politicians, and philanthropists to discuss population, resource conservation, environment, immigration, language, and assimilation policy questions. U.S. Foundation also sponsors town meetings, periodic discussion groups on current issues, and foreign language meetings.

+ American Alliance for Rights and Responsibilities is a national organization exploring the interrelationship between rights and correlative responsibilities. It is predicated on the recognition that every right is supported by a reciprocal responsibility. AARR became independent after three years in the U.S. Foundation "nursery." It eventually became known as the Center for Community Interest.

+ Bringing out the Best in Ourselves is a series of small grants to local public and parochial schools to emphasize and encourage academic excellence.

+ Alcohol and Drug Awareness Hour was a series of public lectures and other programs designed to address and prevent alcohol and drug abuse.

+ Growth & Development Forum was a public forum for the study and debate of growth and development issues confronting local communities.

+ The Social Contract Press publishes a quarterly journal, *The Social Contract*, on immigration, language, population growth, and individual rights and responsibilities. The Press also publishes and promotes books relating to environment, immigration, national bonds, and conservation.

+ The Emergency Committee on Puerto Rican Statehood is a citizen-based organization addressing the implications of Puerto Rican statehood for national language, unity, and cohesiveness.

+ Pro-English and its precursors, English Language Advocates and E Pluribus Unum, has been a national membership organization working for English to become the official language of government. It opposes bilingualism at the ballot box but promotes bilingualism in the schools for educational and transitional purposes. Its early acronym, ELA, might someday correspond with the abbreviation for the English Language Amendment to the U.S. Constitution.

+ Conservation News Service was formed to restore an interest in conservation. CNS arranges for and circulates articles on conservation in the media and it sponsors the Conservation Summit, an annual conference of leading environmental and conservation organizations.

U.S. Foundation projects span diverse topics. They are designed to avert hardship before, rather than after, it becomes unmanageable. All are united by principles of conservation and foresight.

It is possible to overstate the role of a founder and it is also easy to underestimate the contributions of others. While Mary Lou and John have been the catalysts for U.S. Foundation projects, the organization relies upon a talented staff, including Rev. Robert Kyser, Niki Calloway, Dorothy Koury, Faith Peruzzi, Marion Kuebler, Wayne Lutton, Ph.D., Linda Purdue, and Roy Beck.

Over the years, John's medical practice provided much needed "immediate gratification" when, for example, he surgically restored a patient's eyesight. Few of us will ever experience the elation John has felt when a patient reports, "Doctor, I can see again." This sense of accomplishment was a needed antidote to John's long-term, contemplative, and often frustrating charitable endeavors.

U.S. Foundation projects remain controversial. For example, even today, some still are not convinced that we are in the most severe extinction spasm since the age of the dinosaurs. They remain in a perpetual state of indecision, seemingly unaffected by the alarming findings of biodiversity studies.[25] Indecision carries consequences. At U.S. Foundation, however, there is little risk of sleeping through an era with indifference.

CHAPTER 17

Frames of Reference

Thou shalt not exceed the carrying capacity.
~ GARRETT HARDIN, HARDIN'S ELEVENTH COMMANDMENT

JR: How do you define an optimum population?

JT: Conceptually one can envision four levels of population:

1. **Maximum**: The maximum that can be stuffed in; for the short-term.

2. **Carrying Capacity**: A smaller number, one that can be accommodated long-term without spoiling support systems. It can weather adverse turns of events, such as a drought, due to reserve capacity. One exact number can't be fixed, since it's technology-influenced, and this changes over time.

3. **Optimum**: Doubtless smaller yet, but also inexact, as values modify technology: How much peace and quiet, wilderness, wildlife, do we want? Requires an even larger reserve capacity.

4. **Sub-Optimum**: Much smaller yet, but too small to sustain culture and economics, enable division of labor, etc. Theoretical.

MLT: Let's take a community as an example. Isn't it optimum size when crime is low, when you know the people in your school, your neighborhood, and when you are held accountable for your actions? Apply these same concepts in communities nationwide.

MARY LOU AND JOHN HAVE NO PRESENT WITHOUT THE PAST. By invoking principles of biology, humanity, history, and literature, they strive to discern coherent patterns.

Different people will look at the same facts and arrive at different conclusions. Mary Lou and John explain the different perspectives by positing two contrasting views of the world. These world views tend to overlap within both the individual and the issues. The two views were discussed in *A Conflict of Visions* by Thomas Sowell.[26] The line separating these views distinguishes many of the Tantons' views from others. In John's words:

> *One view is the constrained view of mankind, which basically sees man as being born a savage who needs to be civilized and brought into society. This view does not expect the ideal and sees, as did the framers of the Constitution, that governments were instituted because men were not ideal, and there was a need for restraint in human affairs.*
>
> *The other side Sowell characterizes as the "unconstrained" view, which would be the Rousseauian view that man was born free and is everywhere in chains. This view holds that man is innately noble, that it is human institutions that are basically at fault and need to be changed. It holds that we should strive for the ideal. If there are social costs like the killing of millions of people in Cambodia in order for the ideal government to be brought into place, that is unfortunate, but a cost that can be easily borne in pursuit of the ideal. That side does not believe in trade-offs, but rather looks for absolutes and perfection. Sowell acknowledges there are gradations of these attitudes along issue lines and within each of us as individuals. I have found it a helpful framework.*

John sees the immigration battle as a "skirmish in a wider war."[27] The wider war embraces fundamental ideas regarding limits to population, economic growth, national bonds, and language diversity.

In the fall of 1988, John wrote down some of the differences between these conflicting views of the world.[28]

The first difference arises out of a basic biological principle that all species live within limits and boundaries. The limits are not easily defined. The opposing view, held by the Julian Simon and Ben Wattenberg school of thought, would claim that people are the ultimate resource and there are no limits to resources on the planet. Under this world view, universal biological principles do not apply to the human species. We would be considered exempt to these universal biological laws because our intellect can perpetually push back the limits.

The second difference arises out of John's belief that "the nation" is still a valid concept. While there is a need for local and state governments, and also a need for global authority to address transnational issues such as global warming, chlorofluorocarbons, and acid rain, a need also exists for structure at the national level. Even those theoretically opposed to national governments and nationalism would not be prepared to cede their sovereignty to a global authority. Mary Lou and John see validity in the concept of a nation. And here lies another point of difference between the two sides in the immigration debate: Orthodox, politically correct notions suggest that all mankind should fit somehow within a single mold. Even if that is a valid ideal for some, John's understanding of history, biology, evolution, and instinctive territorialism suggests that it just is not a workable idea.

The third difference arises out of the "melting pot" metaphor. Mary Lou and John see the United States now striving to accentuate the differences among people, while minimizing the similarities. John points out that the Civil Rights Act of 1964 was based on Martin Luther King's admonition that we judge others by "the content of their character rather than the color of their skin." We were then prohibited from inquiring into race, religion, creed, or national origin in hiring practices. Since then, the nation has seemingly turned its back on Martin Luther King's message. We are now compelled to base employment decisions explicitly upon race, religion, creed, or national origin. The goal of integration has been replaced with the ideal of separatism. National unity is being sacrificed on the altar of diversity.

A fourth difference relates to the need for commonality in the official language of government. The U.S. Census Bureau reports there are 322 different languages spoken in the United States.[29] In a democracy, unlike other forms of governance, the exchange of information among the populace is essential. It would be difficult for an effective democracy to maintain a lively and informative debate without the bond of a common language. John observes that individualism might be benefited if each of us had our own private language, but the experiment in individualism would undermine our ability to function as a democratic community.

A fifth difference relates to the question of culture. Mary Lou and John believe that an American culture exists, even though it may be difficult to define. For example, the United States is the most philanthropic society on the face of the earth. All of the Tantons' charitable projects are supported by a spirit of philanthropy. Undermining American culture erodes American philanthropy.

After having been subjected to personal attacks for advocating his charitable causes, John identifies a final difference, one unlike the other differences mentioned above. It reveals his personal rules of engagement in a controversy. According to John: "Attacking an opponent personally, impugning the person's motives, or making the individual appear in a poor light, are no substitutes for debate. Rather, we should deal with the issues." He will challenge views and perspectives, but he is not known to lodge a personal charge.

While changes from one day to the next might be unnoticeable to many, the same changes impose a stressful disquietude upon John. He often awakens at 4:00 a.m. pondering the nation's future. He visualizes the pendulum on an historic course. By John's internal clock, these changes are advancing rapidly, and not for the better. The biodiversity losses, increasing congestion, rising tensions, diminished civility, and erosion of family life in the United States introduce personal strains. John is also apprehensive about the adoption of hate speech legislation. This legislation has been used to threaten population activists concerned about immigration. It could intimidate concerned citizens from addressing openly the root cause of disunity in the United States.[30]

CHAPTER 18

Litter on a Stick

> *The concept of public welfare is broad and inclusive . . . The values it represents are spiritual as well as physical, aesthetic as well as monetary. It is within the power of the Legislature to determine that the community should be beautiful as well as healthy, spacious as well as clean.*
> ~ U.S. SUPREME COURT JUSTICE WILLIAM O. DOUGLAS
> IN BERMAN V PARKER.

JR: Define the attribute of billboards that you personally find the most troubling.

MLT: Years ago, Burma Shave forty-four-inch square signs amused us as we traveled. Today, billboards defile a drive through the countryside. *Merriam Webster's Collegiate Dictionary, Tenth Edition*, defines "defile"—"to make unclean or impure: as to corrupt the purity or perfection of (the countryside defiled by billboards.)" I find billboard alleys and highway "yellow pages" both excessive and offensive.

JT: My personal objection is to their furtherance of the dominance of the commercial over other aspects of life. One just can't escape their message to "Buy! Buy! Buy!" as one can with radio, TV, or print . . . which one can turn off.

Beauty is in the eye of the beholder—and they (billboards) are not in my eye (or Mary Lou's either!).

WHY WOULD MARY LOU BECOME AN OUTSPOKEN CRITIC OF billboards? Why would she organize Scenic Michigan, a nonprofit entity? Why would she become a defender of the night sky?

Situated next to their greenhouse, their garden, and the fields that provide nectar and pollinating opportunities for their bees, Mary Lou and John still enjoy a relatively undiminished view of the night sky. But signs of "progress" abound. Urban sprawl devours the farmland and the agricultural heritage around their home. The sense of place and serenity is incrementally compromised.

We were a nation built upon principle, but now the dominant principle seems to be shifting toward consumption. Descarte's axiom has degenerated into "I shop, therefore I am." Shopping has become a form of recreation. Even our July Fourth parades have become a stream of advertising messages promoting more consumption. Commercial messages lurk at every corner; we are besieged by three thousand commercial messages every day.[31] Even though we do not respond to each of the advertisements, the central theme is reinforced: Buy it now! Happiness is expected to be derived from immediate self-indulgence. And even our valued viewscapes have yielded to the principle of consumption.

John Miller, founder of the Washington, D.C.-based Scenic America, condemns the proliferation of billboards in his 1997 book entitled *Egotopia*:

> In years past, the marketplace was clearly defined and physically limited. The physical space and influence of the family, the neighborhood, the school and the church stood distinctly uncompromised by the attractions and the seductions of the market. In the New American Landscape, designed to enhance self-indulgence, the entire society must become literally a perpetual, omnipresent, round-the-clock market . . . What we are dealing with is not so much the evidence of a Madison Avenue conspiracy haranguing us to buy snake oil as our collective cultural need to be the constant recipients of instructions in the liturgy of consumption.[32]

There is no more intrusive form of advertisement than billboards. They intrude upon our public space and have an oppressive presence.

Picture this. On returning to the historic section of a well-preserved hometown or university in the heart of America, you find billboards have been installed. They cling to the rooftops. They clutter the roadsides. And even a few old growth trees have yielded green space to the commercial message.

The experience defies description. Its sheer ugliness evokes U.S. Supreme Court Justice Potter Stewart's oft-quoted dictum, "I know it when I see it."[33]

We are outraged when cherished historic settings are surrendered to billboards. Yet, we remain silent when billboards claim ever more space along roadsides, in community centers, and on pastoral open space. Mary Lou believes that apathy has betrayed aesthetics. Can treasured architecture and respected places still find a safe refuge in the face of such indifference?

The issue is one of balance. Just how should we balance the serenity of space and communal values against a billboard owner's right to profit from a captive highway audience? Freedom of choice hangs in the balance. Billboards have no "off" switch, like a radio. The right to avert our eyes from an unwanted message vanishes in the presence of billboards.

If good citizenship and cherished traditions are nurtured by a place worthy of our respect, where history is revered and where individual choice remains a priority, then our priorities are being dishonored by the purveyors of billboards.

The Web site of a major billboard merchant carries its philosophy: "Pure and potent and *impossible to avoid*." Billboard profits come at the expense of a defenseless captive audience. Our personal freedom in our road-bound cars becomes the stock in trade for billboard purveyors, but not all communities are willing to surrender these unavoidable spaces to the highest commercial bidder. By striving to preserve a unique identity, M'Lou squarely confronts the well-funded billboard lobby.

Mary Lou co-founded Scenic Michigan, an affiliate of Scenic

America. Both organizations promote respect for our revered scenic places. By necessity, this places them in the billboard industry's line of fire.

The influence of the outdoor advertising industry trumps aesthetics when billboards encroach on the public realm. The legal balance and the scales of justice are under steady pressure from the billboard industry. Unsurprisingly, this is one of the most formidable lobbying forces in the nation, because it derives its lifeblood from the alcohol, fast food, automotive, and other industries that dominate our consumption-oriented epoch. It is resisted by the charitable efforts of Scenic America which seeks to preserve a sense of community and respect for a community's scenic past.

M'Lou's sense of presence and identity and her rich sentiment for the land are not isolated traits. These values derive from her life's experiences. They originate from the same sense of awe she experienced under vast starlit skies on her childhood farm. They were nourished by her appreciation, as a child, of the unblemished vistas on her family farm. And they nurtured a resolve to act as her sense of personal identity, defined by the place she calls home, was threatened by ugliness "impossible to avoid." She recoiled at the proliferation of billboards on the countryside and cringed when historic places yielded to oppressive in-your-face commercialism.

It is difficult to improve upon Mary Lou's description of her sentiment for the land:

> *The villainous assault and intrusion on one's spirit—mine anyway—are the insidious effects billboards embody as I travel the highways. I resent their demeaning presence in pristine farm settings, on the historic Sauk Trail that threads through the community of my childhood and youth, and their invasion into the skyline; scarring a city's or village's unique character and identity. Without billboards blighting the roadsides, I concentrate on my surroundings; feeling an almost eerie peace and sense of humility and belonging as I become part of the land around me. Curious and appreciative of the changing geography, flora and fauna, and glimpses of history that enrich my*

journey, I hope for at least a few more miles before the next onslaught of commercial images is displayed on the behemoth lollipops in the sky.[34]

An appreciation of the magnificence of the land, an affinity for the landscape, and a compelling sense of place enable us to become a more caring people and a more civil society. Indeed, it is a peculiar fact that those who respect our sense of place have a strangely endearing quality. Even when railing against billboards, they radiate a love of the land.

Mary Lou's efforts to preserve the scenic amenities of our cities and roads are not without mixed success. Billboards continue to proliferate, yet Mary Lou's organization has claimed judicial victories in the United States and Michigan Supreme Courts. Favorable legislation has also been adopted. Perhaps her success should be evaluated by asking, "How many more billboards would clutter our streets had she not risen to this challenge?"

Billboard purveyors beware. Someday you may find yourself tormented and oppressed. Perhaps you will find a measure of comfort in understanding your oppressor. The bane of your existence is really only a warm-hearted, soft spoken, kind-spirited, sincere, altruistic, charitably-oriented, and doggedly persistent grandmother with a disarming smile in Petoskey, Michigan.

CHAPTER 19

The Road to Ruin

The most precious lesson The Crick taught me was the joy of cooperating with nature instead of forever beating my head against the wall of biological logic.
~ GENE LOGSDON, YOU CAN GO HOME AGAIN

JR: Can we build ourselves out of a state of congestion with more roads?

JT: Not if the number of vehicles and our auto dependency continue to grow—and they are growing even *faster* than the population. (In California, from 1980-1990, population increased by twenty-five percent and vehicles increased by thirty-three percent.)

With stable car numbers and usage, a good system of roads is a target we could probably hit.

MLT: Building more and bigger roads to ease congestion can be not only invasive upon a community, but likened to fighting obesity by loosening one's belt. We can plan fewer auto trips per day, walk or bike when possible, and create walkable communities.

GROWTH-ORIENTED, CONSUMPTION-BASED ECONOMIES provide distractions from our appreciation of the unsullied natural world. We dwell on trivialities with the measure of our self-worth often determined more by what we consume than by who we are.

Amid the distractions, life in the fast lane has not obscured the view for everyone. The Tantons' perspective of a planned bypass around their small northern Michigan hometown exemplifies their sense of place. It also demonstrates how their activism comfortably moves from issues of national significance to matters of local concern.

They were among the first opponents of the proposed Petoskey bypass in 1987. This was long before the town folk thought they might have the wherewithal to influence a governmental undertaking of this magnitude. They prompted the concerned citizenry to believe in themselves. Even decades later, many in the community are still waging the battle, but the Tantons are remembered as among the first to sound the alarm on this controversy.

Ten thousand years ago, rich and deep soils were deposited by receding glaciers on the hills surrounding Petoskey. The most productive agricultural land in the region is situated on these hills, and a dynamic agricultural heritage has become a natural legacy here for several generations.

In 1987, U.S. Representative Bob Davis represented the Tantons' northern Michigan district. As a result of Davis' nonpublic meetings with several members of the Petoskey business community, a $28 million "highway demonstration project" was arranged for Petoskey in 1987. There was no public input for this pork-barrel legislation.

As soon as plans for the bypass around Petoskey were announced, Mary Lou and John began organizing efforts to oppose the project and to respect the land. They were the catalysts for the Growth & Development Forum, a project of U.S. Foundation. In a letter to the editor of the local newspaper, John invited townsfolk to attend a town meeting on the need for a bypass and possible alternatives. The auditorium at the high school was filled, a mailing list from this meeting was developed, and the cornerstone for transportation planning with concerned citizen input was set in place. With a modest nudge and a healthy dose of foresight from Mary Lou and John, the movement soon developed a momentum of its own.

Admittedly, Petoskey was experiencing traffic congestion. As a resort destination on the shores of Lake Michigan, Petoskey's traffic patterns are seasonal. Congestion affects local roads during July,

August, and a few skiing weekends in winter. Michigan Department of Transportation origin-destination studies reveal that approximately eighty to ninety percent of the traffic was *Petoskey-bound*. So the bypass would only serve the traffic passing through, namely, ten to twenty percent of the total. A nine-mile bypass removed from the downtown by several miles would not accommodate traffic destined for Petoskey, so eighty to ninety percent of the congestion would likely remain. And some of the ten to twenty percent just passing by might opt for the more traditional and scenic waterfront route, even if it took a little longer.

Just how much longer would it take? According to the Michigan Department of Transportation, motorists might save one and a half to two minutes on the longer, but faster, bypass!

This savings would come at the expense of bisected farms, degraded wetlands, an indelible scar on the land, and more than 60 million in tax dollars. "These scars," noted John, "only ratchet their way in. They do not ratchet their way out."

As natural amenities gradually slip from our reach, a respect for the past and the future seems to elude us. The bypass would cut not only through valued lands, but also it would sever the continuity of a rich heritage. These scars might be imperceptible to some, but they would sear the Tantons' consciences. For others rooted in the place they call home, for those who derive a sense of place for the inhabited grounds that would be paved, and for Mary Lou and John, the bypass would cleave their hearts just as surely as it would slice through lands and homes.

The Growth & Development Forum began by conducting town meetings. It arranged for Henry Richmond, founder of the 1,000 Friends of Oregon, to appear for a town meeting. Mr. Richmond's organization had led the charge in passing Oregon's urban growth boundary legislation. The Growth & Development Forum also arranged for other public meetings to study transportation issues. The speakers pointed out that bypasses only became a planning tool after World War II. They observed that this post-World War II remedy was only a Band-Aid and that we now needed a cure for twenty-first-century wounds.

During the town meetings a common theme emerged: The cultural, civic, historic, and commercial town centers of communities across the nation have yielded to bypasses. The report card on these notions of "progress" is now in, and the marks are not encouraging. The result is homogenized urban sprawl that, in Michigan, daily devours 240 acres of agricultural land. This translates into two and a half average-size counties per decade.[35] Bypasses in the United States first attract strip malls. Then low density, auto dependent, land consumptive residential projects become the "last cash crop" of the obliterated agricultural heritage. Roads form the skeletal frame upon which urban sprawl hangs. Mary Lou began busily circulating James Howard Kunstler's *Geography of Nowhere*. In Kunstler's words:

The road is now like television, violent and tawdry. The landscape it runs through is littered with cartoon buildings and commercial messages. We whiz by them at fifty-five miles an hour and forget them, because one convenience store looks like the next. They do not celebrate anything beyond their mechanistic ability to sell merchandise. We don't want to remember them. We did not savor the approach and we were not rewarded upon reaching the destination, and it will be the same next time, and every time. There is little sense of having arrived anywhere, because every place looks like no place in particular.[36]

The federally funded bypass threatened to carve a gouge in the land as it bisected the surrounding agricultural communities. In April 1999, the Taxpayers for Common Sense published the "Road to Ruin."[38] This report documented the "50 Worst Tax Wasting Road Projects in America." These are the projects harming our communities and damaging our surroundings. The Petoskey bypass drew national attention as one of the fifty worst. At the beginning of the millennium, efforts to resist the bypass have remained successful.

Eventually, the most beleaguered side is likely to lose the bypass battle. To date, Mary Lou and John maintain their resolve and keep the fires of opposition glowing, exhibiting no signs of fatigue.

Interestingly, ten years after Congress arranged for the 28 million in bypass funds, the Petoskey Chamber of Commerce hired out-of-town consultants to study regional economic strengths. Upon completion, the consultants conducted a public forum on how the small town might improve its business climate. At this meeting, the consultants' opening remarks admonished chamber members to oppose the bypass! Not surprisingly, because the chamber had led the pro-bypass charge for years, more than a few jaws visibly dropped. Others in the audience exchanged consoling nods while silently acknowledging the wisdom of the Tantons' early opposition.

CHAPTER 20

Ability or Agility

> *... the mind unaided by factual knowledge from science sees the world only in little pieces. It throws a spotlight on those portions of the world it must know in order to live to the next day, and surrenders the rest to darkness.*
> ~ EDWARD O. WILSON, CONSILIENCE, THE UNITY OF KNOWLEDGE

JR: How would you improve upon the schools?

MLT: More emphasis on music and the arts is a positive trend. Learning at all educational levels would be enhanced by smaller classes and individual attention. "High tech" should be balanced with "high touch," and responsibility for one's academic and personal performance should be emphasized.

JT: There is certainly no one-paragraph answer. But I'd prefer not just smaller classes, but smaller *schools*. (My graduating class numbered 39.) I don't want uniform schools, certainly not at the federal level, or even the state. Also, we need students to come from stable two-parent homes where there is a respect for learning. That's a big assignment, but there are some things that can be done, such as cutting teen pregnancy.

EDWARD O. WILSON OBSERVES THAT "WE ARE DROWNING IN information, while starving for wisdom."[38] In the information age we have the means to amass a wealth of information in finite fields of specialization and subspecialization. Biologists unveil new secrets of life every day. Social scientists expose a never-ending stream of information affecting the human drama. Yet in our persistent quest for knowledge, we become more specialized in narrow endeavors.

The ability to expand the store of knowledge in a finite field is empowering but also confining. We are constrained by the straitjacket of our disciplined field of specialization. The more we know about one discipline, the less we understand about another. Abilities in one field detract from the agility to flow into another. Ability and agility can become inversely related properties.

The Tantons' most distinctive trait is their unique combination of cross-disciplinary agility and ability. For example, when economic reports assume growth is good and more growth is better, the Tantons adroitly move within the framework of mathematical and biological information to counter that assumption. The Tantons' world knowledge is not limited by the perspective of economists and financial consultants striving to gain a competitive short-term business edge. Growth-based rhetoric does not satisfy their demand for information. They apply biological, social, and historical information. An affinity for the land nurtured in their childhood years imparts a view of growth-based dogma from a different perspective.

The Tantons distinguish themselves by the way they frame issues and process information. In the words of Edward Abbey, "Growth for the sake of growth is the ideology of a cancer cell."[39] No economic system on a finite planet can accommodate perpetual growth. Mary Lou and John are quick to invoke biological principles in pointing out that we must attain sustainable levels of economic activity. Their insight derives from their agility in navigating among fields of specialization.

When community planners propose a bypass around a historic small town, the Tantons' minds leap to the consequences for a valued agricultural legacy, the sprawl-inducing effect of automobile-dependent lifestyles, the fragmentation of a community, the loss of biological habitat, the increased tax burden imposed by the cost of infrastructure and services, the loss of open space, and the inevitably dispiriting influence of architecturally uninteresting strip malls along the corridor. These are insights born of ability and agility.

CHAPTER 21

Addition and Division

Language and religion are the ultimate dividers of mankind.
~ IMMANUEL KANT

JR: Explain the role of language in a culture or in a civilization.

JT: A huge question: Language is the carrier of culture. Forms of address, for instance, reflect and influence class structure. In German, the formal "Sie" versus the informal "du" influences personal relationships. Becoming fluent in Chinese script is said to take ten years of intense study, and still yields only forty-five thousand characters, as opposed to three hundred and fifty thousand words in English. The Arabic decimal system of mathematical language was a huge advance.

MLT: I enjoy the study of language. As a teacher, I took pleasure in the growth of my students' language skills and abilities. I enjoy reading selections challenging in content and vocabulary. A good command of our written and spoken language binds our culture and enhances social interaction.

IN 1982, JOHN VISITED STANLEY DIAMOND, WHO RAN Senator S. I. Hayakawa's San Francisco office, to discuss population and immigration. Although the senator was not prepared to embrace immigration reform, his concern about the divisions resulting from language prompted him to introduce a constitutional amendment to make English the official language of the United States.

Mary Lou and John were and remain interested in upholding bilingualism at an individual level. Thus, U.S. Foundation has offered discussion groups in Spanish, German, and French. But at the level of official government business, they see bi- or polylingualism as a divisive movement. This is evidenced by the experience of our neighbor to the north. The separatist movement in Canada is based principally on language. Both sides share a common background in Western civilization, self-governance, democracy, and liberty, yet they are divided, chiefly by language.

Population growth and the divisive effects of bilingualism are not related issues for everyone. While immigration issues may remain abstract, there is nothing abstract about the inability to communicate with neighbors. The link between the two is plain; the unprecedented wave of immigration strains the national bond of language.

For an economic system to function, there must be common units of exchange. Thus, we use the U.S. dollar. For schedules to be maintained, common measurements of time are required. For manufacturing, exchanging merchandise, and transacting goods, common units of weight and measure are needed. And for an experiment in self-governance to provide a meaningful "marketplace of ideas" (the foundational purpose of our First Amendment), the Tantons respectfully submit that a common language is essential. By combining disciplines, the interrelationship between language and immigration comes into view.

Their language advocacy, while promoting familiarity with foreign tongues, encourages one common language *for government purposes*. Thus, because statehood for Puerto Rico could lead to dual languages in Congress, the issue drew their attention. They oppose the use of multiple languages in all government activities, from administering driver's exams to printing election ballots.

For a nation grappling with its identity in a politically correct environment, English language advocacy is viewed as a form of heresy in many circles.

In the fall of 1982, John brought the issue of bilingualism to the attention of the FAIR board where it met with a cool reception. Once again, the Tantons were confronted with the option of either concluding they couldn't be bothered or, alternatively, starting a new movement. They had a proven track record of starting organizations. They understood direct mail, knew organizational structures, understood the process, and knew they had an important issue on their hands.

John arranged another meeting with Senator Hayakawa, who was about to leave the Senate. He was willing to pursue the matter further after leaving office and provided a list of campaign donors. John returned to some of the original FAIR donors for seed money and also received some support from FAIR itself, even though it was unwilling to dilute its main message with the language issue.

A staff person at FAIR was also particularly interested in the subject. Gerda Bikales had worked on population and migration issues with the Tantons for many years. An immigrant to the United States, she had learned English upon arriving as a teenager. She authored a 180-page paper in which she concluded that multiple official languages would become a divisive drain on resources and tax our national bonds.

John recruited Senator Hayakawa, along with two of his friends, Stanley Diamond and Leo Sorenson, as board members. Along with Gerda Bikales and John, the first board consisted of five members. Walter Cronkite and Alistair Cooke became members of the board of advisors. The organization was known as U.S. English. Eventually it attracted more than four hundred thousand members and was responsible for initiatives making English the official language of state government in Colorado, Florida, and Arizona. In Colorado, the initiative passed sixty to forty percent; in Florida eighty-four to sixteen percent; and in Arizona fifty-one to forty-nine percent.

The fledgling organization received a favorable response in ten percent of its first direct mail solicitations. This is eight to ten times higher than the norm. It was apparent that U.S. English struck a chord with America. The rapid success of U.S. English was atypical for a Tanton project. In most cases it took much longer for their championed cause to catch on.

Even so, those on the front lines will be the first to trip land mines. As often as the Tantons were on the forefront of emerging issues of national importance, it remains a tribute to their sensitivity to the conventional wisdom that more land mines were not tripped along the way. One such land mine lay in waiting in 1988, when the opposition chose to focus its attack on the individual, rather than the issue.

The history of this controversy requires insight into John's basic observations. His view of natural history suggests that individuals have never fared as well as a group. Our biological past reveals that evolution selects for the survival of the fittest group, rather than the fittest individual. Birds of a feather flock together. "It's not surprising that a flock of geese would fly overhead," according to John, "but it's interesting that there are no sparrows in the pack." In his study of the natural world, John found survival in numbers and an affinity for group identity. "Life," claims John, "remains a group sport." During a trip to the Galapagos Islands he was particularly impressed with the harshness of life's condition. If a species was not eating, it was being eaten. As Alfred Lord Tennyson observed, "Nature, red in tooth and claw."[40]

While John and Mary Lou remain individualists in forging new ground, at heart they nurture a spirit of altruism and community values. For some, the concern for community extends to family, to civic organizations, to their town, and to their state. For Mary Lou and John, the sense of community also extends to the nation's impoverished minorities, who are the first to experience an erosion of household income as a result of progrowth immigration policies. These policies tend to cement the underprivileged and minorities in their socioeconomic level. At the same time, as the ranks of the poor swell through immigration, a new political force emerges, reflecting the transplanted ideals of the failed systems from which recent immigrants have fled.

John addressed these issues in a memo dated October 10, 1986, for use in a discussion group. To prompt the thinking process, John openly shares ideas on an issue. He is trusting and open, perhaps to a fault. With his characteristic candor, John posed questions on the demographic destiny of the nation. Opponents of the U.S. English message in Colorado, Florida, and Arizona decided to move beyond the message to launch an attack on the messenger. They labeled the author a racist. By maligning the integrity and motives of John Tanton and, thus, U.S. English, they hoped to thwart the initiatives.

John's memo drew fire for this quip: "Perhaps this is the first instance in which those with their pants up are going to get caught by those with their pants down." As a population activist and a land conservationist, John would readily address threats to the natural environment. The threat was metaphorically coming from those with their pants down. Yet, his adversaries were quick to twist the metaphor by ascribing improper motives to the statement.

Interestingly, the issues appearing in John's memo have since been addressed openly in a variety of newspapers, including the Sunday, November 1, 1998, edition of *The Washington Post*. This time there were no charges of racism. *The Post* reported that "Competing ethnic groups too often waste their energy—and squander their country's resources—trying to dominate and sometimes exterminate their rivals." Similarly, in the July 12, 1999, *Newsweek*: "The Latin wave will change how the country looks—and how it looks at itself." Comment on the same issues now commonly passes as unobjectionable observation on matters of fact. Yet when John first raised them from a land conservationist's perspective, the opposition seized upon them as an opportunity to mount a personal attack.

In a move that John would later regret, he resigned from the board of U.S. English in order to refocus the debate on language, rather than on him. The strategy was successful. Arizona, at fifty-one to forty-nine percent, had the closest margin, a mere eleven thousand votes out of one million cast. "I console myself in the unpalatable step of resigning," conceded John, "with the conviction that my action likely made the difference in the Arizona victory."

After John resigned from U.S. English, the organization's temperament seemingly changed. It became less assertive, more interested in public relations, and more accommodating to the status quo. Tax documents from 1998 revealed that the president of U.S. English, Mauro Mujica, received a salary of more than $427,301![41] By contrast, John served without compensation.

John's polite resignation did not signal his abandonment of the cause. To maintain the public interest perspective within the movement, John Tanton, Gerda Bikales, and Leo Sorenson have formed Pro-English, previously known as English Languages Advocates (ELA), under the auspices of the U.S. Foundation. John's work to protect the common bond of a single national language in government continues.

Chapter 22

A Barrel of Ink

We can never do merely one thing.
~ Garrett Hardin, Hardin's Law

JR: How do you contrast "responsibilities" with "rights"?

MLT: Scales should at least balance our individual and communal rights and responsibilities. Then we should individually and collectively accept the challenge to apply more weight to the responsibility side of the scales.

JT: We need to distinguish between legal "rights," which often impose responsibilities on someone else, and "rights" to physical goods, such as food, health care, clothing, and education, which require physical resources and labor/intelligence. There can be no requirement that others have to work without quid pro quo to supply us with the physical goods of life. The world does not owe us a living.

Mark Twain reminds us never to pick a fight with someone who buys ink by the barrel.

In the fall of 1990, John Tanton launched a program to begin buying his ink by the barrel. As a project of U.S. Foundation, the inaugural quarterly issue of *The Social Contract* was published. In the first edition, editor and publisher John Tanton answered the foundational question "Why another journal?" in the editor's note. The note summarized much of his twenty-plus years of experience with population and immigration controversies. As early as 1970, John had observed that a number of issues bear on human population growth, such as its absolute size, distribution, and rate of change. This had resulted in the formation of the Federation for American Immigration Reform (FAIR). It had also led John to consider the question of balance.

"There is a balance," he said, "between rights and responsibilities. The right to swing one's fist stops at the end of the other's nose. And the other fellow's nose is going to be a good deal closer in the future than it has [been] in the past." While many raise the banner of rights, John reminds us that for every right there is a corresponding responsibility. If someone has the right to proceed on a green light, someone else has the responsibility to stop on red. This led to his formation of the American Alliance for Rights and Responsibilities (AARR).

As with the development of any social idea, literary efforts were needed. Mary Lou's and John's organizations had produced a long series of newsletters and a few books[42] but few magazine-length articles.

Responding to the need for a coherent body of literature on these issues of emerging importance, *The Social Contract* was born. The journal provided an opening for new authors as well as an opportunity to solicit articles from thought-provoking writers known to John. The title of the new journal was resurrected from Rousseau's day to correspond with John's theme of balancing rights and responsibilities.

The first article in the inaugural *Social Contract* was Garrett Hardin's essay "The Tragedy of the Commons," reprinted from the December 13, 1968, issue of *Science*. This article is still commonly cited today. It led to Hardin's recognition as one of the great thinkers of our times. In this essay, Dr. Hardin invokes biological laws in developing ethical principles based upon the concept of "carrying capacity."

Themes for *The Social Contract* reveal John's evolving thought during his eight-year span as editor. They also reflect his ability to anticipate issues meriting our attention. Always a step ahead of his time, the issues penetratingly addressed in this journal were reliably on the cutting edge of environmental and migration topics.

The Social Contract's quarterly themes (a brief summary is set forth in Appendix D)[43] often commemorated historic events or writings, such as Booker T. Washington's September 18, 1895, speech encouraging the employment of underprivileged blacks called "Cast Down Your Bucket Where You Are." Another edition recognized the twentieth anniversary of the 1972 report of the Commission on Population Growth and the American Future by John D. Rockefeller III as submitted to President Nixon. In so-called "Occasional Papers," The Social Contract reprinted significant historic writings, such as Frederick Jackson Turner's 1893 speech entitled "The Significance of the Frontier in American History."

In a particularly thought-provoking edition, John focused on the fortieth anniversary of C. P. Snow's renowned "Two Cultures" lecture as the theme for the summer 1999 issue. On May 7, 1959, Snow, a British scientist and writer, delivered his justly famous lecture at Cambridge University entitled "The Two Cultures and the Scientific Revolution." According to Snow, scientific and literary endeavors were worlds apart.

John drew an analogy to the polarity among the participants in the immigration debate. The hard scientists, biologists, ecologists, and those working with numbers take a longer, more objective view. Their studies are readily projected into the future. Meanwhile, individual consumptive interests tend to focus on the here and now. Community considerations clash with individual interests, reflecting the same divisions Snow explored in 1959.

The Social Contract remains a rich source of information on issues of emerging import. All editions can be found at www.thesocialcontract.com. The Web site has become an effective research tool.

Chapter 23

Bell of Freedom

> *I got a hammer. And I got a bell.*
> *I got a song to sing all over this land.*
> *It's the hammer of justice. It's the bell of freedom.*
> *It's a song about love between my brothers and my sisters.*
> *All over this land.*
> ~ Peter, Paul, & Mary

JR: Which freedoms would you be willing to compromise in order to promote the cause of equality?

MLT: I am willing to have my freedom of movement curtailed in order to conserve fuel and help others enjoy a healthier environment.

JT: We need a balance between the antithetical properties of freedom and equality. I'm willing to sacrifice some free speech so we can have sworn oaths in court or copyright and patent laws; I'm willing to pay some taxes to support common facilities; and I'd be willing to have some search and seizure to cut down on drinking and driving deaths.

In population and migration studies, regional disparities of opportunity are palpable. It is impossible to ignore the plight of impoverished masses. Attributing the oppressive disparity to corrupt political systems and failed cultures provides no relief for their victims. Inequality abounds.

Five percent of the world's population resides in the United States, yet the United States accounts for twenty-five percent of the world's annual fossil fuel consumption, we use thirty-three percent of the world's paper, and we generate seventy-two percent of the world's hazardous waste.[44] Our pets eat a diet higher in protein than many of the world's poor. When there is no place left to go in Manila, the impoverished resort to a landfill known as Smoky Mountain. Here the housing is fashioned from scraps of discarded tin and cardboard. Fertility rates are high and the human drama unfolds literally on the rubbish heap of an inequitable social system. The student of demography unavoidably becomes an expert on the inequality of life.

John's persistent quest for fundamental causes led him to seek an explanation for this global inequity. In that search, we in the United States are not exempt from blame. In our pursuit of the ideal we may have deceptively sought unity in opposing forces inherent in our system.

Liberty and freedom are fundamental to our system of self-governance. These foundational principles are associated with conservation, according to Tanton's view. By protecting natural resources John sees himself as defending fundamental principles inherent in the freedoms we cherish. In an article published in the *Graphic* (a northern Michigan publication) on September 4, 1980, reporter Tom Dammann quotes John's statement correlating freedom to resources: "Freedom as we know it in this country is tied up with the ratio of population to resources." It follows, if John's observation is correct, that freedoms will vary inversely with population.

John's interest in this issue reveals his affinity for root causes of problems, causes that are often harbored in our daily assumptions. Over time, we no longer question the unexamined convictions in our conventional wisdom. The Tanton mind, however, would have us revisit the relationship between liberty and equality. We commonly believe these two properties are mutually reinforcing. If we extend freedom to all, we expect greater equality to follow. John believes that, in fact, Peter, Paul, & Mary's "Hammer of Justice" and "Bell of Freedom" strike disharmonious chords.

We might prefer that history accommodate the prevailing notions that liberty and equality are complementary and mutually reinforcing attributes. In fact, history teaches that liberty and equality are inherently conflicting concepts locked in a timeless struggle. John reminds us that liberty and equality toss about in our legal system much like two rabbits in a gunny sack.

Liberty and equality are related to each other much like investment income is related to security. Security comes only at the expense of income, and vice versa. Liberty succumbs to the gravity of equality. And equality shoulders the weight of liberty. A homely example illustrates the point. We could decide to defend the liberty to ingest any substance of choice during pregnancy, but this liberty comes at the expense of equality. We can't expect the offspring of this pregnancy to begin life at the same starting line as a child nurtured in a toxic-free uterus. Conversely, by curtailing a pregnant mother's freedom to consume controlled substances, the offspring will have more equal footing in life's unremitting race. But the mother's liberty is curtailed in the quest for equality.

The harsh reality of the world's inequity can be easily ignored. We prefer to drink from the cup of freedom undiluted. We strive to nurture the assumption that the forces of equality will triumph if freedom is just given enough of a chance. In fact, we might do ourselves a great service by recognizing the polarity between liberty and equality. To ignore this polarity is to create unattainable expectations for ourselves and for our system of justice.

On November 20, 1992, John wrote a letter to the editor of the *Atlantic Monthly*. It quietly slipped onto the editor's cutting room floor. Since then, the subject has not resurfaced in John's writings, although it remains one of the principal pillars of his intellectual framework. In this letter John critiqued an article in the November 1992 *Atlantic Monthly* that asserted, without analysis, that the Declaration of Independence makes "enduring affirmations of liberty and equality." John pointed out that "these are antithetical properties." The unpublished letter stated:

> We are all unequal as to nature: Some of us are short, others tall; some are fat; some are thin; some are strong, others weak.

As to our individual genomes, about which we're hearing a great deal these days, we are likewise unequal, with the possible exception of identical twins. Surely the child with an inborn error of metabolism, a hereditary eye degeneration, or Down's Syndrome is not equal to one not so afflicted. Among those with more conventional genetic endowments, some of us are bathed while still in utero in alcohol, nicotine, cocaine, or the AIDS virus. These, and many other influences, make for decidedly unequal footing at the starting line of extrauterine life.

We are all unequal as to nurture. Some of us start life as orphans, others with one parent or two. Some are loved and nurtured; others are beaten and rejected. Some of us have good food so that our brains can develop properly and then good education so we can take advantage of that development. William Julius Wilson, the University of Chicago sociologist, characterizes life as an "intergenerational relay race." Some individuals have a lot more relayed to them than others.

Finally, we are all unequal as to luck. It can make a big difference whom we happen to (or happen not to) make friends with, run into, or are assigned as a roommate. Diseases and accidents, in some measure parceled out in a random and statistical fashion, strike some of us and not others. If they could respond, the marines assigned by chance to that barracks in Beirut might have comments on this point.

The net result of all these factors is that we end up with vastly different abilities, training, ambition, and circumstances. If each of us were completely free to express these differences at will, we would end up with wildly unequal results. The only way this outcome can be avoided is through strictures on this freedom, whether through social conventions, customs, or statutes that restrain one individual and favor another.

We need some degree of such restrictions on liberty, if society is not to self-destruct from the disparity that would otherwise

> result. Caveat emptor is on the way out; caveat venditor is on the way in. On the other hand, we need a certain degree of freedom, if all initiative and productivity are not to be stifled. The classic political conundrum is exactly how to balance these opposites of freedom and equality.
>
> Doubtless, none of this would have been lost on Mr. Jefferson. What he probably meant by the phrase was more fully expressed by George Mason's antecedent Virginia Declaration of Rights: "All men are born equally free." It would be interesting to know if the phrase as it made it into the Declaration was among those edited by the Continental Congress.
>
> Freedom and equality—at least of results—are in eternal conflict, just as are high return and security in an investment. We could enrich our debate on public policies if we quit pretending that they both can be maximized at the same time and instead discussed the proper balance between two opposites.
>
> Cordially,
John H. Tanton, M.D.

The oft-quoted preface to the Declaration of Independence might suggest that our founders were unconcerned by the conflict between liberty and equality.

> We hold these truths to be self-evident, that all men are created equal, that they are endowed by their Creator with certain inalienable Rights, that among these are Life, Liberty and the pursuit of Happiness.

This interpretation is reflected in a bestseller on the life of Thomas Jefferson,[45] which suggests that the author of the Declaration of Independence perceived no tension between liberty and equality:

> It was the vision of a young man projecting his personal cravings for a world in which all behavior was voluntary and therefore all coercion unnecessary, where independence and equality never collided, where the sources of all authority were

invisible because they had already been internalized. Efforts on the part of scholars to determine whether Jefferson's prescriptive society was fundamentally individualistic or communal can never reach closure, because within the Jeffersonian utopia such choices do not need to be made. They reconcile themselves naturally.

From their assertion of self-evident truths about equality and the inalienable right of liberty, it might, at first blush, appear that Mr. Jefferson and the Declaration of Independence brook no compromise or accommodation between the two. If the opening lines of the Declaration of Independence were the only words by which to divine his views, one could conclude that he never acknowledged the eternal struggle between liberty and equality. But the early exposition in the Declaration of Independence was not Jefferson's last word on the subject; the tension between liberty and equality did not elude Mr. Jefferson.

The conflict between liberty and equality is not, however, a new idea. It has perhaps just been forgotten. Even the founders of our system considered it in framing the complex systems of checks and balances. Jefferson knew that the limits to "rightful liberty" were circumscribed by the "equal rights of others." In 1819, admittedly long after penning the Declaration of Independence, he wrote:

> *Of liberty I would say that, in the whole plenitude of its extent, it is unobstructed action according to our will. But rightful liberty is unobstructed action according to our will within limits drawn around us by the equal rights of others (emphasis mine). I do not add "within the limits of the law," because law is often but the tyrant's will, and always so when it violates the right of an individual.* Thomas Jefferson to Isaac H. Tiffany, 1819.[46]

Jefferson's sensitivity to the issue was also evident in other letters written after 1776. For example:

> *Being myself a warm zealot for the attainment and enjoyment by all mankind of* as much liberty as each may exercise

without injury to the equal liberty of his fellow citizens (emphasis mine), I have lamented that . . . the endeavors to obtain this should have been attended with the effusion of so much blood. Thomas Jefferson to Jean Nicholas Demeunier, 1795.

John would point out that the polarity between liberty and equality is evident when viewed from the perspective of human history. In 1968, after completing their monumental work on human history, an exhaustive eleven-volume collection entitled *The Story of Civilization*, Will and Ariel Durant summarized their overall conclusions in a concise 117-page book. This resource is frequently quoted by Mary Lou and John. It is entitled *The Lessons of History*. In Chapter Three, entitled "Biology and History," the Durants connect human history with natural history: "History is a fragment of biology: the life of man is a portion of the vicissitudes of organisms on land and sea." In this chapter the Durants correlate the study of humankind with basic biological principles. "Nature," they observe, "loves difference as the necessary material of selection and evolution; identical twins differ in a hundred ways, and no two peas are alike." The Durants found similar operational principles governing civic affairs. Within our civilization, the Durants observed:

> *Nature smiles at the union of freedom and equality in our Utopias. For freedom and equality are sworn and everlasting enemies, and when one prevails the other dies. Leave men free, and their natural inequalities will multiply almost geometrically, as in England and America in the nineteenth century under laissez faire. To check the growth of inequality, liberty must be sacrificed, as in Russia after 1917. Even when repressed, inequality grows; only the man who is below average in economic ability desires equality; those who are conscious of superior ability desire freedom; and in the end, superior ability has its way.*[47]

The issue did not escape the attention of our forebears and it does not elude the Tantons. The immense inequality introduced to the student of demography bespeaks the polarity between freedom and equality. Today, the Tantons call upon us to cautiously reexamine the reliability of assumptions underlying our decision-making processes.

CHAPTER 24

A Crash Course on Population

Voluntary population control selects for its own failure.
~ GARRETT HARDIN

JR: Which ideas are most endangered by the increasing global population?

MLT: Perhaps we take our quality of life blessings too much for granted; good health, freedom to move about in relative safety, and to express ourselves. More people means more rules, tighter zoning regulations, stricter rules, and more infringements on the rights of others.

JT: One of the major prices to be paid for increasing population is in individual liberty: Bigger crowds require more crowd control. And, of course, the idea of perpetual growth will run up against experiential reality.

AFTER HAVING SERVED AS ADVOCATES FOR POPULATION reduction during the better part of their adult lives, Mary Lou and John now find themselves poised on a new threshold. In the early days, Mary Lou regularly joined in the chant that "2.2 is the number for you" and sported the button "Only's are OK." But now that the effects of population advocacy have been settling in for several decades, the "one size fits all" remedy needs to be reexamined.

Italy, headquarters of the Roman Catholic Church, has one of the lowest fertility rates in the world. Since the middle of the twentieth century, Italy's fertility rate has been steadily declining. Italy's total fertility rate (TFR) has reached almost one child per woman[48] and still seems to be in decline. The TFR in many European nations is slightly higher than Italy's, but it is still substantially below replacement level. The population activists of the 1970s could have concluded that fertility rates might stabilize at or about replacement level. But for many nations, they continued to drop below replacement level. In John's words, "We need to start talking about this."

With a total fertility rate of almost one child per woman, Italy's population soon will attain a negative momentum. This will cause the next generation of Italian parents to drop by one-half in every generation: Where there were once four Italians, the next generation will have two, and the third generation will have one. Gains on the goal of sustainability through cultural practices will prove illusory if population reduction is eroded by massive increases in immigration from high fertility areas.

Not long ago demographers were concerned about exponential population growth. Mary Lou and John are becoming equally concerned about the fate of nations such as Italy, which eventually will encounter an exponential population decline. The population movement sought to achieve a more responsible balance between people and resources, not the extinction of a civilization.

Fertility reduction in a number of nations, such as Italy, results from a variety of social influences. In part, it results from environmental concerns. It also follows urbanization. On farms, children are generally an economic benefit. In a congested urban setting, on the other hand, more children impose more costs. Fertility reduction also follows from gender equity and improved educational prospects for women. Children exact an economic opportunity cost from women with meaningful job prospects. Where two incomes are needed to maintain a household and where the costs of child care are high, there will be fewer children. Thoughtful, caring parents are concerned about how they will provide for the next generation. They limit the number of their offspring out of recognition that the children of smaller families will enjoy a greater concentration of resources and parental attention.

John and Mary Lou effortlessly move from the social to the biological realm. In any biological system, certain attributes will have survival features and others will not. When a population drops by fifty percent in each generation, a vacuum will result. Consider a crude mathematical example involving two groups of differing fertility. In the first group, the population doubles every generation; in the second, the population declines by fifty percent in each generation. If the two populations initially had twelve members, then by the first generation, the higher fertility group would have twenty-four members and the other would have six. By the second generation, the ratio would be forty-eight to three. Thus, in two brief generations, populations of equal fertility would be separated by a sixteen-fold difference!

Mary Lou and John suggest that at some point it will become necessary to begin dispensing different advice to different populations. What works in one place will no longer work in another. Nations with a dwindling population will become extinct at some point if their population continues to decline by fifty percent in each generation. To suggest that all populations should reduce their fertility, no matter what their total fertility rate (TFR) might be, will cause some populations to suffer a Darwinian extinction, while others will continue to surge. In an extreme example, the early Shakers successfully advocated sexual abstinence. The laws of biology relegated their experiment in voluntary fertility reduction to an historical footnote, hence Hardin's dictum at the beginning of this chapter.

The biologist would tell us that a dwindling population in a borderless area eventually will disappear. The human attributes leading to substantial fertility reduction will disappear with its proponents. These attributes include female empowerment, educational opportunities for women, and environmental awareness. These worthy developments and aspirations, when placed in borderless competition with a highly fertile population, eventually will vanish.

Surely nations experiencing exploding population growth still require intense family-planning efforts. On the other hand, in nations with aging populations and thus fewer workers for every pensioner, at some point a slight increase in fertility to replacement levels will be necessary.

As John observes, there are three ways to slow a car: You can apply the brakes gradually, you can slam on the brakes, or by colliding, you can bring the car to an abrupt halt. Fertility collision has occurred in many of the advanced nations and even in others, such as China.

A declining fertility rate in the 1970s eventually creates an aging U.S. domestic population. Evermore elderly dependents will rely upon fewer and fewer workers. According to a report published by the United Nations, the U.S. dependency ratio of worker per retired person will decline from 5.21 to 2.82 between 1995 and 2050.[49] According to this United Nations report, the dependency ratio could be preserved only if our retirement age were postponed to approximately seventy-five.[50] The U.N. study also reveals that by admitting 10 million immigrants every year until 2050, the retirement age could stay at sixty-five and the elderly dependency ratio of 5.21 to 1 could be preserved. This will present an interesting dilemma for the twenty-first century. Will the fertility-reducing generation cash in the environmental chips to preserve its ability to retire at sixty-five?

The aging workforce in Western subreplacement fertility nations contrasts with burgeoning numbers of unemployed workers in other lands. This has prompted John to question the future prospects of Western civilization. The nations with reduced fertility generally recognize gender equity. Unsurprisingly, the high fertility nations provide fewer educational and employment opportunities for women. What are the prospects for gender equity if emissaries of high fertility (and thus low gender equity) nations continue to stream into low fertility nations?

John is likely to devote more of his time addressing this upcoming dilemma for subreplacement-level-fertility nations.

Over the long course of history, it will be necessary to carefully thread the eye of the population needle to maintain a balance. If it were possible to identify an optimum population, we would strive to stabilize at that level, perhaps with a TFR of 2.1 children per woman. At the millennium, U.S. fertility stands at 2.03 children per woman.

Once an optimum population is reached, replacement level will make it necessary for one family to have three children for every family having one. And for each childless couple, another family will be needed to offset with four.

Fertility reduction in a nation maintaining a firm resolve to regulate its borders would leave a more sustainable future for subsequent generations. If, however, fertility reduction merely becomes a safety valve for exploding foreign populations to transfer surplus numbers across borders, then the system will select against thoughtful and voluntary fertility reduction. Conscience selects against itself. Mary Lou and John remain avid population advocates, but the advice they dispense in the future will be based on a fact-intensive analysis of the demographic factors peculiar to each nation.

CHAPTER 25

Do You Know the Type?

How shall we live?
~ MORTIMER ADLER

JR: Pick one of your idiosyncrasies and try to explain it to the satisfaction of a detached reader.

JT: I don't mind getting stung by my bees—it seems like just retribution for pilfering their hard-won honey! One of my greatest pleasures is to spend a hot summer afternoon in the bee yard, observing and wondering at the bees' comings and goings and complexities.

MLT: I enjoy observing "washday." I enjoy hanging out the laundry, seeing it blow in the wind, savoring the aroma of fresh air in clean clothes and bedding.

WE NEVER NOTICED. JARS OF HONEY WERE STILL STOCKED on store shelves, but the Tantons' bee colonies, like many others, were devastated by an infestation of mites in 1997. A few hives miraculously survived and the colony was restored in 1998. During the mite infestation, Mary Lou's and John's domain grew quieter by the flutter of a bee's wing and paler by the hue of a yellow jacket.

Here is an anecdotal glimpse into the lives of Mary Lou and John. Do you know the type?

Their days of charitable causes have become a life of shared gratitude. This gratitude asserts itself in their well-maintained garden, in their greenhouse, in tending the bees, and in life's simple pleasures. They read poetry to each other while traveling.

They define themselves by reference to our natural amenities. They bristle when historic viewscapes, the night sky, and open space succumb to well-lit malls and commercial messages on billboards. They live to be a part of, not apart from, nature. For them, the loss of wildness marks a loss of depth and complexity. They wince in pain when a habitat is threatened.

To them, even the seemingly monotonous landscape holds endless fascination. A walk in the woods becomes a botany exercise. Celestial formations mark the seasonal migration of species. Weather patterns and growing cycles bring life to the land and a sense of wonder to their surroundings. Biological events inform their sense of place. They will plan to protect a biologically developed region before the species it harbors are threatened.

Conservation is not just a concept or even an ideal. It's a passion. It's as though they were hard-wired to maintain and restore a balance. They'll deliver their latest botanical findings to you in a coffee shop.

While others might forget an extinct species or, worse yet, never even notice it missing, they will not forget. The loss exacts a spiritual toll from them long before others become aware of the loss.

Vanishing habitats along migratory corridors cause birds in their yard to slip beyond the brink of extinction. The music in their life slips into disharmony one note at a time. When conventional wisdom suggests that we have a land of vast, untapped frontiers, they respond with an explanation of this complex reality: The frontier has become a mirage. The next frontier is not "out there," but "in here," in our hearts, in our communities, our nation, our citizenship, our personal values, our mutual relations, and our natural surroundings.

When limited natural resources are thought to be boundless, their future becomes dim. History's problems have been solved by moving elsewhere. That "solution" is no longer an option; the future they envision begs for a new paradigm.

Mary Lou and John have been influenced by photographs of our fragile spaceship Earth from outer space. They see a defenseless orb with a resilient, but finite, ecosystem. The image defines the outer limits of our growth. It constrains our horizons and commands an ever-present sense of symmetry and balance. The image from which the works of man cannot be detected might also, for others, inspire a claim for the vastness of opportunity.

The flowers in their garden are carefully planned to maintain an uninterrupted, colorful, and ever-changing display throughout the season. The aligned rows in their vegetable garden are an expression of earlier days on family farms. Having mastered the art of using compost to conceal carrots from foraging deer, they'll serve up fresh garden treats in mid-winter. In their garden and on a grander scale through their advocacy, they defend a biodiverse past and a dignified future. When our consumptive imperative asserts itself by blazing yet another new trail into the nation's natural resources, the loss is registered on their conscience.

When telling you about a weekend trip to their cottage, they'll describe the silence. And they'll explain it with clarity. The silence becomes palpable.

The Tantons call upon us to recognize the physical constraints of biological systems. Though the Tantons need the security of natural systems, the natural systems may actually need them more. The choice is not between nature and humanity, because they choose both. When discussions of congestion, incivility, road rage, and resource depletion are imbued with unexamined assumptions, they fearlessly examine the root causes of our consumptive tendencies.

They contemplate seizing a compassionate future from the all-consuming jaws of the materialistic present. For them, the future must be met with resilience, not resistance. They don't just study the future domain; they dwell in it. When they observe the beginning of a trend, they ask, "How will this work out?"

Their charitable efforts are intended to protect the magnificent complexity of our fragile planet. And like features of our planet, their efforts are layered. Above the surface, on a superficial view, they can be as invisible as the atmosphere to all but the most inquiring minds. The next layer, like the earth's flora and fauna, comprises a rich diversity and an allegiance to basic biological principles. Beneath their surface, like the earth's solid core, they are firmly grounded. They are bonded by patriotism, a love of nature, a shared conservation ethic, and, not least important, shared values, love, and mutual respect. To know them is to encounter them at all levels, at once.

They place a premium on both valued friendships and solitude. And there is no contradiction. Both are essential to complete them.

History is the handmaiden to their conservation ethic. They draw upon history in three ways: first, in their chosen mentors, such as Aldo Leopold, Rachel Carson, and Sigurd Olson; second, in learning from yesterday's heretics; and third, in drawing strength from historical figures who withstood withering opposition. This empowers them to absorb criticism without damage to their souls.

When their biographer turned fifty, they gave him a plaque bearing an inscription reflecting their ethic:

> *Press on. Nothing in the world can take the place of persistence. Talent will not; nothing is more common than unsuccessful men with talent. Genius will not; unrewarded genius is almost a proverb. Education will not; the world is full of educated derelicts. Persistence and determination alone are omnipotent.*

The trimmed saplings on their Chandler Hills tree farm will produce valued timber decades beyond their lifetimes. In caring for the trees, their lives incline now, as they have always, to the future.

They cringe when political candidates exchange the common good for campaign financing.

When the media reports that public officials in California hopelessly shrug their collective shoulders at the prospect of becoming a state of 50 million within a few decades,[51] the Tantons sigh in disbelief.

They wonder how to connect the dots for a nation with daily news headlines on impending water shortages, streams unsafe for human or aquatic life, polluted beaches, urban sprawl, loss of open space, degraded ground waters, loss of wildlife, and increasing divisiveness among groups.

When we discuss how to become better parents, they remind us to think also about how to become better ancestors. They tirelessly review the past to obtain a coherent glimpse of the future and identify patterns and discerning where they lead. They find themselves by discovering the future.

They address the implications of exploding population projections before finite resources are squandered. When the conversation turns to mistakes of the past, they ask which of our own cherished beliefs and self-evident truths will be disproved when we become the distant ancestors.

They lament the loss of natural amenities to fleeting notions of "progress." When the prospects for economic expansion stir the soul of a nation, they ponder whether a finite planet can accommodate perpetual growth. They appreciate the relationship between ecological health and sustainable economic prosperity. When the discussion moves to economic gains from extracted natural resources, they talk about the consequences of intruding upon the biological cycles in which our lives are intertwined. When we hoist the banner of economic growth for the sake of growth, they see us lowering the boom on the future.

John and Mary Lou prepared a list of a deceased parent's top two hundred expressions to preserve his humor, wisdom, and world view for descendants who will never know him. The list includes classics such as: "Age before beauty," "Big enough to drive a Mack truck through," "Different kettle of fish," "Gone to his reward," "Got his wires crossed," "It's all over but the shouting," "Learn to play a poor hand well," "My first wife (when referring to his only wife)," and "Virtue has its own reward." The list is organized by topic, such as answers to "How are you?": "On my last legs." "Not in bad shape for the shape I'm in." "Fair to middling." "In the pink." And then, for good measure, they organize the sayings in alphabetical order. More profound than the sayings themselves is their understanding that these fragments of a parent should be preserved. Their effort assures that distant descendants will have some sense of who he was and how he saw the world.

They understand the value of getting away and making time for extended vacations. But the getaway often becomes a busman's holiday. While visiting Australia, they researched the immigration challenges Australia has experienced and made lasting contacts with interested citizens. While visiting friends in Paris, they toured the ancient, yet still functional, infrastructure. Exploring the Parisian sewer system became a highlight of the trip. And for summer fun each year, they become residents at the University of Michigan Biological Center ("bug camp" on Douglas Lake) for a week and sample the joys of entomology.

After dinner, one of them might sit down to a piano and effortlessly stroke out a few familiar songs, only to apologetically confess that his other fingers always have been too short to span the octaves. The complaint generally elicits little sympathy.

In conversations they move comfortably from abstract projections to concrete particulars. They channel even trivial discussions into substantive issues. They form discussion groups to address timely topics. They tend to shy away from aimless chatter, yet it is impossible to think of them without recalling their subtle and insightful humor. When you ask for their opinion, they may respond with a quotation from Alexander Pope or Mortimer Adler.

Fear of controversy does not cause them to shrink from the demands of their conscience. With reasoned discourse and by holding to their beliefs, they enable others to build friendships and a stronger community.

To save paper, they'll scratch you a note on the back side of junk mail. The doctor, however, will realistically entertain no more than a faint hope that his penmanship will be legible to any but his closest intimates.

When the conversation turns to rights, they turn the dialogue to reciprocal responsibilities.

When someone close to them was afflicted with an alcohol problem, they reached out to resolve it. They then limited themselves to nonalcoholic beverages to provide an encouraging example and helped organize an Alcohol and Drug Awareness Hour (ADAH) to assist others confronted with similar challenges. When asked whether the ADAH sessions were measurably successful, they responded with other questions that strove to find a constructive response: "How do we prove what has been prevented?" and "Is there heightened community concern?"

Their collection of tapes and CDs includes memorable speeches on philosophy, economics, history, and politics. An assortment of classical music is also in the mix.

Their sense of self-worth is not dependent upon the opinions of others. They draw upon the strengths that lie within them.

They instinctively exercise a conservation ethic and know that we are precariously embedded in a fragile biological system. Their acquired vision is no accident. It draws on the venerable authority of biological and human history as well as their childhoods while working hand in hand with parents and grandparents on historic homesteaded farms.

They believe that if we are to have companions in our dotage, then friends must be cultivated among the young, while there is still time.

Before it became readily available, they offered family-planning counseling to avert the hardships of unintended pregnancies. Before others had the courage or the insight to discuss our demographic destiny, they opened the debate on establishing an appropriate level of immigration. They achieved what others charitably inclined could not by confronting issues lying at the core of our national existence.

They are willing to confront the possibility that the United States could become a mere address for disparate groups arguing over values in different languages, honoring different cultures, and divided by countless differences. They boldly question whether this is the future we should choose. When politicians profess that diversity is our strength, they agree in principle but ponder how to balance the blessings of diversity with the need for unity and public commitment in a nation drifting from its foundational bonds.

When we analyze the justice of our actions, they consider the survival value of our decisions. When we elevate the value of individuality, they remind us that the human condition has, for the most part, been collective.

While others monitor stock market exchanges with dizzying accuracy, they transact exchanges in the marketplace of thoughts, trafficking in ideas.

They contemplate where constitutional boundaries should be drawn. They also note when the boundaries have been disrespected, misunderstood, and ignored. By probing our national conscience, they force us to test our fundamental beliefs and belief systems.

They are respected by some, scorned by others, and misunderstood by many. Armed with the tireless habit of reason, they are humbly successful, inquisitively confident, solemnly humorous, and overtly subtle. When others disagree with their opinion, they will reevaluate their position methodically and, in the process, cause those who disagree to reexamine their own foundational assumptions.

As modern-day successors to yesterday's pamphleteers, they distribute news clippings to friends and acquaintances.

They are stubbornly undeterred by the statistically accurate assumption that one person in a world of six billion souls cannot make a difference. Explicitly or implicitly, directly or indirectly, their quiet advocacy has touched each of our lives.

They are not likely to ask an empty question such as "How's the weather?" They would rather take the time to engage in a meaningful exchange and perhaps form a new friendship.

They have an instinctive sense for the art of the possible.

CHAPTER 26

The Last Word

New occasions teach new duties.
Time makes ancient good uncouth.
~ JAMES RUSSELL LOWELL, *THE PRESENT CRISIS*, 1844

JR: If you could write a paragraph in the last chapter of someone's book, what would you say?

MLT: The person is greatly blessed to have loved, been loved, and to have lived close to the earth.

JT: The measure of a man is how much he will be missed!

MARY LOU AND JOHN LIVE THEIR LIVES IN A QUIET AND peaceful corner of the world. Their charitable efforts are offered without expectation or hope of personal gain. To empower others in the service of conservation fulfills their aspirations. A few onlookers have taken note, and these onlookers will be given the last word.

In recognition of Mary Lou's services as a pro-choice activist, Merle MacJannett wrote the following on June 25, 1970: "How satisfying to know that because YOU started the ball rolling in Michigan, women for generations will benefit."

The pro-choice movement was a hot topic on the national agenda in 1972. At the time, N. Thomas O'Keefe, M.D., commended Mary

Lou for her activism: "Your individual effort and dedication was fantastic. Thanks for doing your share and my share in the public eye. Your cool exterior when under attack is admirable, if not amazing. I'm very proud to know you."

In recommending Mary Lou for the Milliken Freedom Award, Linda Lumley, Northern Michigan Planned Parenthood director, said this: "Mary Lou has served on the board of directors of Northern Michigan Planned Parenthood from its founding in 1970 to the present. It is not an exaggeration to say that, without her continued commitment and involvement, the affiliate would not likely exist today—and certainly not in its current form. There is scarcely a role within the affiliate that she hasn't played. She has made countless presentations on Planned Parenthood or reproductive health issues to civic groups, written articles, extensively engaged in lobbying and educating legislators, organized and motivated others to write their legislators, engaged in public debate with the opposition, served as board president, vice president and secretary, and written fund-raising materials and proposals for funding. Because she is widely known and highly respected in the community by virtue of her other civic involvements, she has been able to cultivate many volunteers for the agency and has been able to open doors and ears that might otherwise have remained closed. Similarly, because of her contacts and standing in the community, she has been able to locate donors capable of contributing at the level necessary to allow the affiliate not only to survive, but to grow over the years. For many years, Mary Lou almost single-handedly raised the majority of private contributions to the affiliate."

In 1990, John received the Chevron Conservation Award in the Citizen Volunteer Category based on a nomination submitted by Colorado's former governor Richard Lamm. In his nomination, Governor Lamm stated: "Perhaps it was through watching a small, interdependent community of farmers, or maybe the religious teachings of the church which he attended as a youth, or the enduring commitments he saw within his own family, but John decided early on that he had an obligation to contribute to his community and his country. Fortunately, for all of us, he picked environmental conservation as the focus for his public interest endeavors."

Patrick Noonan, then president of The Conservation Fund and the former president of The Nature Conservancy, supported Governor Lamm's nomination by stating, "I have known Dr. Tanton for fifteen years and worked with him on several projects for the preservation of valuable open space. He had a true naturalist's intimate knowledge of the topography of the region, and an unfailing sense of what would be ideal and what was possible, and wisdom to distinguish between the two . . . In my many years at the helm of a major national conservation group, I had the good fortune of meeting many capable individuals, quite a few of them deserving of special recognition. Among these exceptional people, John Tanton stands out, not only for his natural leadership qualities and willingness to work hard personally, but because he never had any sense of himself as doing anything remarkable. For John, the opportunity to preserve a legacy for generations yet to come has been its own reward, adequate in every way. Should John be selected for this prestigious award, I am sure that he will be the most amazed of your winners—no doubt pleased but perplexed, protesting all the way that 'Really, it was nothing.'"

Edward G. Voss, curator of Vascular Plants and Professor of Botany at the University of Michigan, joined in the nomination by stating, "He (John) not only has the skill and experience to know how to accomplish things, but he also devotes an incredible amount of his time to using those skills and keeping up on his 'continuing education.' And he knows when it's time to turn an organization loose to thrive without his constant attention, while he goes on to revitalize another."

David H. Irish, John's co-plaintiff in the early Michigan Environmental Protection Act suits and a co-founder in the Little Traverse Conservancy, endorsed Lamm's nomination by sharing this view: "The pattern has been for John to come up with an idea of a project that would protect or preserve or better our environment and lives, to pick from among his many acquaintances several individuals who have an interest in that area, and then to educate those individuals in the subject . . . John then will have the information on how to proceed, will work the hardest to get started, and will then gradually withdraw as others come up to speed. He always seems to have another project in mind . . . The attention, interest, and stewardship have been unending on his part. We have seen others get a project started and then lose interest, but I believe John applies a perspective longer than his lifetime to his work. John is a leader who is always ready to step aside and let others lead but never turns his back on a project he inspired. He is thus vastly effective in leveraging his own efforts with those of others who volunteer to help."

Thomas L. Washington, the late executive director of the Michigan United Conservation Club (MUCC), supported Governor Lamm's nomination by stating the following: "It would be difficult to find someone who has a broader and more varied interest in natural resource conservation issues than Dr. Tanton . . . John Tanton has spent his entire adult life serving his fellow man. As a medical professional and as a lay conservationist, he is eminently qualified and deserving of a Chevron Conservation Award, and we urge your favorable consideration of him for this high honor."

M. Rupert Cutler, president of Defenders of Wildlife, also endorsed the nomination: "While on the MSU faculty and later as the assistant secretary of agriculture for Natural Resources and Environment, I have heard of many instances in which John was the essential catalyst in making good things happen for the environment through wise use of land and water in the Petoskey area. The people who live in that region today owe John Tanton a lot for his effective campaigns to save the quality of their lives. I hope you'll reward this unsung hero with a Chevron Award."

Kathy Bricker, the first executive director for the Little Traverse Conservancy, stated: "John brings out the best in people, encouraging and guiding gently, nudging one step at a time. He explained his philosophy to me once as 'Learn one, Do one, Teach one.' He learns constantly by tackling difficult issues, always making sure he is grounded in fact about endangered species, threatened habitat, etc."

Roger Conner, the executive director of FAIR, had this to say: "I am trying to think of a single word which characterizes John and the word is *generous*. The U.S. is full of conservation activists who have made a difference and then discovered they enjoy the limelight . . . By contrast, John is forever always pulling someone else on stage to enjoy that crush of public exposure and then slips off to one side while they get credit. He focuses on people and their interests as a genuine friend, not just as people who can help with his cause."

Tom Bailey, executive director of the Little Traverse Conservancy, spoke of LTC's accomplishments in northern Michigan and as a catalyst for other land conservation efforts nationally when he voiced his support of the Chevron Conservation Award nomination: "John's conservation work proceeds on a personal as well as an organizational level. He has taken hundreds of people on field trips on the Conservancy's behalf and on his own. He is a naturalist of considerable knowledge and is quite adept at interpreting the natural world for all people from outdoor neophytes to seasoned naturalists. John is a master storyteller and always creates a pleasant atmosphere on his trips. He arouses curiosity, he raises people's levels of consciousness and leads people to become not only interested in the outdoors, but active as well."

Biologist Gary Williams (the eye behind the cover photo) of Mackinaw City, Michigan, stated: "When we socialize, and I have the opportunity to observe him interact with his friends and patients, I am often reminded of the fact that John has never lost touch with his roots. His association and interchange with common people in northern Michigan or Kenya reminds one of his solid, rural, agricultural roots. His easy conversation about local concerns and international problems indicates a quick grasp of complex situations. There is no one in my circle who has done more for his fellow man in efforts at general conservation. He is a true inspiration to those who know him. It is his opinion that I seek first on complex problems of a biological or almost any other sort. I have often commented that there is no person I more admire than John Tanton. It should be no surprise, then, that I support him for this award in the strongest possible terms."

And finally, Glen Sheppard, editor of the *North Woods Call*, offered these words in support of Governor Lamm's nomination: "In 1970, Tanton was the first to use Michigan's then new Environmental Protection Act . . . With the lawsuit established as an effective conservation tool, Tanton shifted to the Conservancy to preserve land . . . I know of no other single individual who has made as great, or as lasting, a contribution to Michigan conservation . . . "

Epilogue

Random Events in a Safe Refuge for Civility

The unexamined life is not worth living.
~ Plato, Apology 38

The unlived life is not worth examining.
~ Attributed to Paul W. Sullivan, Ph.D.

History's pendulum continues its eternal sweep. On our edge of time, we glimpse only a snapshot of a moving target. As the conventional wisdom of one era fades, a new ideology will be ushered in by the forerunners of the next.

Ideas blossom and wither on the tangled vine of human history. By examining the causes founded by the Tantons, we can still derive unique insight into the issues germinating today. These issues bring us face to face with our forebears and our successors. They lead us to probe the scope of our responsibilities to the past and to the future. Examining these issues enables us to discern the shadow we cast upon the future by enabling us to define who we are and who we wish to become.

Someday we will become the ancients. The insights Mary Lou and John have provided will, in time, give us a glimpse of how the future might peer back on us when our time has become history. A view from the future becomes, momentarily, almost perceptible.

✦ ✦ ✦ ✦

As the Tantons' story can be told only to the present, it can only foreshadow a process. The measure of their "success," as it is commonly defined, will have to await another day. Their early experiments under the Environmental Protection Act were not well received in the courts. Their population advocacy notwithstanding, human numbers in underprivileged lands continue to soar daily. Despite their efforts to provide for planned and wanted children in receptive homes, a high percentage of births in the United States are to single parent households. Despite their advocacy on immigration issues since the early 1970s, the rate of immigration into the United States has steadily increased.

Success cannot be measured merely by increments, weighing a victory here against a loss there. Rather, it must be judged in the light of the role the Tantons have played as part of an ongoing process. Yesterday's heretics—Galileo, Lincoln, Jefferson, Susan B. Anthony, Mary Wollstonecraft, and Mendel—eventually claimed success, albeit posthumously. They were only part of a process in which their ideas eventually triumphed. Unexamined convictions of the day inhibit our perceptions, much as Galileo's oppressors remained resolutely unaffected by the evidence in his telescope.

As a tribute to the tireless spirit of the heretic-to-be-prophet, Galileo muttered this footnote to his full confession to the Inquisition: *Eppur si muove* ("But still, it moves"). In return for discontinuing his heretical experiments, he was spared the death sentence and remitted to house arrest for life.

Surely not all of the farsighted causes of the Tantons have been embraced by the nation. But the more fundamental question is whether they have advanced and, in some cases, initiated the process of debate and inquiry. This, after all, is the process from which consensus must, at last, emerge. How different might our prospects for a responsible legacy be had they not raised a voice in our day?

Epilogue

✦ ✦ ✦ ✦

By contemplating the future and acting on what they saw, the Tantons have made today a better time. In the process, they have contributed to the creation of a more civil society, and a safe refuge for compassion. These are the operational consequences of considering the interests for our successors.

By our actions, we can blindly disavow the future. The southwest building boom drains fossil aquifers. There is no known source for life's essential water resources, yet the boom persists. The Great Lakes comprise twenty percent of the world's surface fresh water. We have so burdened this great body of water that the fish are no longer safe for human consumption. Strained resources are a symptom of short-sighted actions, and few are poised to respond to these future concerns.

Scarcity prompts one of two human responses: either cooperation or competition. As the world drama continues to unfold, cooperation seems to prevail only among cohesive groups, not among the masses. Long-term prospects for civility are compromised by rising human numbers and congestion. By gazing through the Tantons' telescope today, we may still improve the prospects for civility tomorrow.

Concerns for the future fade into the sheltering vastness of market strategies. If we take the time to look, even here the Tantons will be found provoking a thought and prompting an insight. They give us the tools to assess our responsibility to the future. In the future they find security. The future domain is their home.

History's judgment awaits us.

✦ ✦ ✦ ✦

The pilot detecting a thunderhead on the radar screen has two choices: Navigate around inclement weather or fly directly into it. The second alternative affords the pilot the chance to be recognized for heroic aviation skills in battling the storm. Anticipating and avoiding the storm, however, seldom generate the same tribute from the passengers on board.

By anticipating future problems, today's prophets similarly hope for an uneventful journey. In their best case, the concerns, like the thunderhead, will be anticipated and averted.

When future consequences have been anticipated responsibly, the prophets become forgotten.

This is also true for the environmental movement. By anticipating problems and successfully advocating preventative measures, the movement, in a sense, has discredited itself. When the predictions have been successfully averted, the antagonist has a cynic's field day.

The United States experienced high fertility rates during the baby boom and the baby boom echo. Only by cautious planning and vigilant advocacy were fertility rates reduced. Mary Lou and John were on the front lines of this movement while domestic fertility rates were plummeting. When their adversaries point to gains in water and air quality, they seldom acknowledge the foresight having led to these gains.

The sheen of optimism invites the inference that population never really was a concern or that environmental regulations were unnecessary. The conservationist's vigilance and activism have often subdued imminent threats of environmental harm. When the threats of harm are removed by diligent and thoughtful efforts, the opposition is quick to minimize the averted harm.

Politicians are likewise quick to clamor for recognition when they clean a toxic site but are slow to recognize the forethought of others averting similar problems elsewhere. We continue to be enslaved by the rituals of consumption. A biography in conservation is intended to confer recognition upon the forgotten prophets of our day.

✦ ✦ ✦ ✦

The experience of the Tantons is unusual, but only by proportion. Others like them strive in many ways to leave a more civil place and to save a few pieces of the biological puzzle while we can still take an inventory. Their services are offered without regard to profit or praise. They do not expect recognition from the present, so long as their spirit succeeds in blazing a trail into a better future.

We might do ourselves, and our successors, a great favor by recognizing worthy recipients of our attention while there is still time.

✦ ✦ ✦ ✦

John's advocacy in the 1970s and early 1980s drew the attention of Kenneth Scheffel at the University of Michigan's Bentley Historical Library. Like other historical libraries in the nation, Bentley preserves the personal records of noteworthy individuals. Field representatives identify notable people with ties to the state of Michigan or to the University of Michigan who might be creating significant documents of historical value. On February 25, 1981, Ken Scheffel requested authority to preserve John's papers at the Bentley Historical Library. Many of John's writings are now safely cataloged and archived in the library, alongside many other original historical documents.

Mr. Scheffel started with Bentley Historical Library in 1967. He has encountered many of the policy makers and thinkers of our day. In his words, "John Tanton has to be the most brilliant man I have ever met in terms of the breadth of his interests and the depth of his knowledge." While, in other cases, such a wealth of knowledge has been exploited for personal gain, in John's case it has led to a life of charitable works.

✦ ✦ ✦ ✦

To dwell only in the present is to remain blissfully removed from the world awaiting our successors. The future presses upon those with foresight, placing them in close communion with our descendants.

Nature's fabric is unraveling around the planet. Fifty percent of the world's bird species, and one-third to two-thirds of *all* species, are doomed to extinction by 2050.[52]

A few gifted eyes apprehend the effects. For them, the loss is tangible. It is imprinted on their souls with an indelible mark tracing back to childhood. They look in disbelief upon the lack of awareness and disrespect for the future.

✦ ✦ ✦ ✦

The decision by Congress to increase our population and congestion by relaxing our borders ignores the Tantons' message. If the nation needs more people, then where is the water too pure? Where is the air too fresh? Where are the trees beckoning to be cleared? Where is there too little congestion? Not enough traffic? Too little urban sprawl? Where are there too few visitors in our national parks?

Our immigration laws must be governed by compassion and ethics. We have a responsibility to the less fortunate in foreign lands. We fail by limiting our compassion to those crossing the borders and positioned in our direct line of sight. We see only a thin veneer of the world's hardship.

✦ ✦ ✦ ✦

This Epilogue will end where the Preface began: by expressing concern over the devaluation of celebrity status.

Worthy mentors elude recognition. They are no longer accessible to us. At times we shroud them with numbing disdain. Perhaps they are drowned out by the clamor of self-absorbed glory-seekers. We have good reason to question motives, to criticize results, and to ridicule well-intentioned actions.

We have become a cynical people.

Where are our praiseworthy role models? Where have our mentors gone? Who can we hold up to our children as good citizens? Where are we to find folks worthy of emulation? Who is still selflessly engaged in the business of making this a better place? A more civil society? Is anyone undistracted by the trappings of a consumption-driven economy? Who still possesses the imagination and foresight to contemplate an undiminished legacy? Does anyone still rise above the quest for money and power?

Surely, but it runs against their grain to seek recognition. That's just not their style. They elude acclaim today, for they belong to the future, and the future will claim them. Yet, they might just be found residing up the hill from your home.

When the environmental history of the nation is written, from a resting place, they'll still be silently protesting: "Really, it was nothing." But future historians may find it was, really, everything.

Michigan, Home of the Tantons

A Scrapbook of Memories

Mary Lou and Keith Brown, horse Charlotte, pony Madelyn. October 19, 1943.

Tanton family (left to right): Tom, John F., Hannah, Elizabeth, John H., and "Laddie." August 1948.

Top: John and "Elsie." 1947.

Middle: Tom, Hannah, Elizabeth, and John H. 1948.

Bottom: Mary Lou's brother Keith Brown, holding percheron stallion "Black Hawk," and Mary Lou's mother, Marion Brown, at Brownson Farms (the family farm). 1985.

Top: John's childhood family farm in Sebewaing, Michigan.

Middle: The wedding. June 15, 1958.

Bottom: The wedding party. June 15, 1958.

Top: Garrett Hardin and John Tanton. October 1984.

Middle: John, U.S. Attorney General William French Smith, and Colorado Governor Richard Lamm. January 1986.

Bottom: Scenic Michigan display at Agriculture and Natural Resources Week, Kellogg Center, Michigan State University, East Lansing. March 1999.

Top left: John, Laurie, Jane, and Mary Lou Tanton. John receives Chevron Conservation Award. May 1990.

Top right: Mary Lou speaking at a Scenic Michigan Conference, Michigan State University, East Lansing, during Agriculture and Natural Resources Week. March 2000.

Middle: Mary Lou and Michigan Atttorney General Frank J. Kelley at a Scenic Michigan Conference. 2000.

Bottom: Mary Lou's poppies on a hillside overlooking Petoskey, Michigan. June 9, 1986.

Top (left to right): John Rohe, Debbie Rohe, Mary Lou and John Tanton. December 1999.

Middle: Mary Lou with 14 quarts of tomatoes, 28 jars of salsa she canned, and vegetables from the Tanton garden.

Bottom: John at his Burns Clinic desk on June 16, 1998, just before his retirement.

APPENDIX A

The Mitchell Prize: International Migration 1975

by John H. Tanton

In 1975 John Tanton's essay entitled "International Migration" placed third in the Mitchell Prize competition. The award was given during the Limits to Growth Conference in Woodlands, Texas. The conference was sponsored by the Club of Rome, the University of Houston, and Mitchell Energy & Development Corporation. The paper became the cover story for *The Ecologist* in July 1976. This essay is the earliest formal record of John's initiating thoughts on immigration reform. It planted the seed from which immigration reform germinated. The movement needed a readily reproducible handout. It now had one. While John's subsequent writings reveal a deeper insight, none is more prescient or pivotal.

Continued population growth is now widely recognized as a major component of the social, economic, and environmental problems facing mankind. The inevitability of some form of stationary state is gaining wider acceptance. In contemplating the possible forms of a stationary state, it seems certain that one of its attributes must be human populations of relatively stationary size. Further, the spatial distribution of human populations is importantly related to such phenomena as urban areas insufficiently dense for mass transit and the loss of prime agricultural land to development. Migration from the rural to the urban, and from the urban to the suburban, has many associated problems. Age structures in many regions result in high dependency ratios. The huge size of some population units, even if stationary, would make their management difficult. The environmental literature has extensively discussed these and other aspects of the population problem.

Conspicuous by its absence from the environmental literature, however, is the role international migration plays in the demographic and other problems facing mankind.

This omission is perhaps due in part to oversight. So much stress has been laid on the role of reducing births in controlling population growth that the role of international migration in perpetuating population growth has largely escaped notice. Agencies such as the U.S. Department of Health, Education and Welfare issue reports on births, deaths, and resultant natural increases as part of their vital statistics, but make no mention of the contribution of immigration to the country's population growth. Even the papers laying out the ground rules for the Mitchell Prize defined a population of constant size as one where the birth rate equals the death rate, ignoring the migration factor in regional or national population growth. Migration also proves to be a factor in global population growth, surprising as that may seem at first glance. International migration has also escaped attention because it has been the province of sociologists and economists, who have generally shown little concern about population and environmental problems. Conversely, those interested in environmental and population problems tend to be drawn from the physical and biological sciences, disciplines not traditionally touching the migration question.

Complexity of the topic is another barrier. The U.S. Immigration and Nationality Act runs to 179 pages and is said to be second in length in federal law only to the Internal Revenue Code.

Fear may well be another factor suppressing the discussion of international migration in environmental (and other) circles. I have often encountered otherwise thinking people who reject out of hand the consideration of immigration questions as being too sensitive or controversial. This visceral reaction is understandable, as most of us have immigrant roots and thus feel compromised. It is, however, no more inconsistent for the offspring of immigrants to consider the limitation of immigration than it is for the products of conception to plan to limit births or the beneficiaries of past economic growth to consider its limitation.

An aversion to discussing immigration is also understandable in light of the seamy history surrounding past efforts to limit immigration. These were marked by xenophobia and racism and gave rise to the likes of the Know-nothing political party and the Ku Klux Klan. Other -isms of past debates that we seldom hear today include jingoism and nativism. The subject was often highly emotional and divisive (2). Any person who attempts discussion of immigration policy will soon learn as has the author that the situation is unchanged in this regard.

These difficulties must be overcome. In the inevitable stationary state to which man is consigned by the finiteness of our globe, the growth of both human numbers and material consumption must eventually end. We can now see that the inevitable stationary state may actually be an improvement over our present one and perhaps should be actively sought, rather than postponed as long as possible.

Similarly, international migration on its current scale is destined to end in the near future, owing to the same finiteness of the globe. As the principal countries currently receiving immigrants—the United States, Canada, Australia—reach or surpass the limits of population that they can support, they will likely move to curtail immigration. As with the coming material equilibrium, we should ask whether this is a good or a bad thing. Is the end of significant international migration an evil to be deferred as long as possible, or could it be a benefit to be welcomed and encouraged with all deliberate speed?

It is time for environmentalists to deal with this important question. They will need to acquire knowledge in a field new to them, conquer its difficulties, and deal with controversy as they have so often in the past. Otherwise a whole new set of problems will catch us unaware, and the achievement of material equilibrium will be significantly delayed.

Historical Background and Demography

A short historical background is advisable to provide a common basis for considering the international migration question. These notes generally follow Davis (3).

As civilization advanced and cities developed, the dominant pattern of migration through the 1700s was from less developed to more developed areas, and from the rural to the urban. Nor was all of this migration free, for slavery was a common source of energy for developing civilizations.

These patterns persisted until the middle 1800s, when in Europe populations began to press hard upon the resource base and environment. Timber resources had become depleted and epidemic diseases such as the potato blight fed upon monocultures that had developed to support increasing populations. Grave difficulties were avoided as the less developed worlds of that day—North America, Latin America, and Australia—opened to comparatively easy migration at about the same time. Steamships came into use, lessening the difficulty and danger of the voyage (4). Excess population was exported and resources were imported, lessening pressures in Europe.

The twin factors of the "push" to leave home and the "pull" of opportunity abroad thus served to reverse the historic trend of migration. People began migrating from the then developed world to the less developed in massive numbers. Between 1840 and 1930 at least fifty million persons emigrated from Europe. In the past one hundred years, 25 million have emigrated from Italy alone, a huge movement when compared with its present day population of 55 million. This trend of migration continued in pulses of varying strength through 1950, with the recipient countries developing and in some cases surpassing the countries of origin in their stage of development.

Since the end of World War II, the flow of migrants from the developed countries of northern Europe has slowed, and the historic pattern of migration from the less to the more developed countries has returned. The poorer countries around the Mediterranean Sea and those of Latin America, Africa, and Asia are now supplying increasing numbers of migrants. Times have changed, however. This present-day migration must be viewed in the context of the massive populations and overpopulation of many of the sending and receiving countries. There are no remaining virgin continents waiting to be peopled or to have their resources exploited.

What is the current scale of international migration? There have been very large movements of people since World War II. More important than the current scale are the trends and causes of migration. These promise large increases in migration pressures in the future if conditions continue to deteriorate in the less developed countries.

In Europe, since the end of World War II, more than 10 million "guest workers" have migrated from southern Europe and the Mediterranean area into northern Europe, to participate in and facilitate the economic recovery and prosperity that followed World War II (5, 6). This phenomenon has reached its zenith in Switzerland, where migrants make up thirty percent of the work force (20).

In North America, the United States has a current population growth from natural increase of about 1.2 million persons per year, supplemented by about 400,000 legal immigrants. (Emigration is estimated at 37,000 yearly by the Bureau of the Census.) Legal immigration thus increases the U.S. rate of growth about one-third over what it would otherwise be. More than fifty-five percent of these legal migrants now come from the less developed countries (7). In addition, a new phenomenon of the last decade—large-scale illegal migration—adds an inaccurately known though apparently large number. Estimates range from 800,000 to one million or more yearly, most of whom come from a wide variety of less developed countries (8). Combining the lower estimate of 800,000 for illegal immigrants with 363,000 net legal immigrants, immigration accounts for about fifty percent of the current annual population growth of the United States. Continued to the turn of the century, these rates of immigration will account for the addition of an estimated 15 million (for legal) (9) and 40 million (for illegal) (10) persons to the United States. For comparison, natural increase at replacement level fertility will add 38 million by the year 2000 (11). Similar situations exist in other major industrial nations.

The situation in the United States may be contrasted with its developing neighbor to the south. Mexico has 59 million people and an annual growth rate of about 3.2 percent, which dictates a doubling time of twenty-two years. Forty-six percent of its population is under fifteen years of age (12), poised to enter a labor market in which unemployment/underemployment may be as high as forty percent (13,20). Mexico's natural increase is 1.8 million persons per year—fifty percent larger than that of the United States, which has nearly four times as large a population. Differentials in per capita GNP across the border are perhaps ten to one (14), a ratio of averages that doesn't take into account that income distribution is generally more unequal in less developed countries (15).

Mexico is one source of illegal migrants to the United States. The driving force behind the migration northward is the great disparity in employment opportunity and income between the two nations. This differential promises to increase with time, not so much from economic growth on the American side as from a lack of economic growth on the Mexican side, relative to its high rate of population growth.

Conditions similar to those in Mexico exist throughout the rest of Latin America, which as a whole had a 1974 population of about 325 million, a 2.7 percent annual growth rate, a doubling time of twenty-six years (12), and generally high underemployment/unemployment rates. Asia and Africa have similar situations. There is obviously a great storm brewing. Any scenario for the future should take into account these massive pressures to migrate from the less to the more developed countries, whether legally or illegally.

So much for the historic setting of the immigration dilemma and the numbers involved. The phenomenon of international migration touches many other aspects of human life and significantly affects the prospects for achieving material equilibrium. Let us look at some of these effects.

Effects on the Country of Emigration

The sociological and economic analysis of international migration has focused heavily on the effects of immigration on the recipient country and the immigrant as a person. Let's look at the largely neglected effects on the country of origin and those individuals who are left behind.

The damaging effects of the "brain drain" have long been argued. The term originally applied to the migration of highly skilled persons and students from the war-torn yet developed countries of Europe to North America. Concomitant with the recent shift to migration from the less developed nations of Asia, Latin America, and Africa, this transfer of highly skilled persons has continued and even accelerated (16).

This new form of the brain drain has a more profound impact. It is now the developing nations that lose not only some of their most talented citizens, but also the scarce capital which has gone into their rearing and training. They also lose the very persons on whom campaigns of social and economic development must be based; those with the highest expectations, the greatest initiative and intelligence; and those most dissatisfied with conditions at home. Educational systems continue to produce persons with skills inappropriate to the level of development of the country, often perpetuating patterns handed down from colonial times. Pressure to change the system is relieved as its products leave the country (17).

While there is widespread discussion in the developed countries about the effect on the less developed countries of exploitation of their material resources, there has been little concern in the same circles about the exploitation of their human resources. These are perhaps the scarcest and most valuable resources of all. The policies of the developed nations which perpetuate the brain drain, whether so intended or not, in effect are a new and subtle and highly effective form of colonialism. The brain drain helps ensure that the less developed nations will stay that way. Thus they will not become competitors of the more developed nations for raw materials and for markets for manufactured goods.

The loss of physicians and health workers in particular retards the development of birth control programs in the less developed countries (18). Resultant population growth further hampers their development efforts. Emigration also tends to remove persons of productive age, leaving behind the children and old people, aggravating the already high dependency ratios of the less developed countries (3).

The dollar value of the brain drain from the less developed nations to the United States has exceeded the United State's foreign aid to some of these same countries (17, 19).

This is a form of "reverse" foreign aid. It is another example of the poor of the world subsidizing the rich. It is one more reason that the disparity in incomes between the developed and less developed countries is so large. One of the most effective forms of aid that the developed nations could give to the less developed ones would be to stop appropriating their human resources.

The term "brain drain" should not blind us to the fact that most who emigrate, whether or not technically skilled or educated, have high motivation. These persons are an important key to develop at home if they are given the tools to work with.

Traditional analysis holds that these deleterious effects are in part balanced by remittances from migrant workers in the developed nations, and that this may be one of the more effective forms of foreign aid, instilled as it is at the bottom of a social structure. However, developing nations dependent on such payments are doubly vulnerable to the conditions in the developed countries. As rates of growth decline and employment falls, foreign workers are often discharged. The less developed country loses not only the foreign exchange, but often gets the unemployed worker back home as well. This is true whether the decline in the developed nation is unintended, as in Europe today, or planned, as in the transition to a stationary state. Stationary state planners in countries with large foreign worker populations will have to pay particular attention to these effects.

The value of remittances has been questioned by Jonathan Power in an excellent analysis of costs of migration to the country of origin (20). He contends that such monies are spent mainly on consumer goods, often imported, and not on financing development. In the end, trade deficits are increased and native agricultural systems are undermined. Sights are set on emigration, and enterprising families are lost to the economy of the less developed country.

Effects on the Countries of Immigration

Let us now take a look at brain drain and related migration phenomena from the standpoint of the developed country, and in the context of the quest for the stationary economic state.

Brain drain effects. In recent times the countries of immigration—the Statue of Liberty's pronouncement notwithstanding—have actively sought out the skilled persons of the world as immigrants. The clear purpose has been to stimulate and facilitate perpetual economic growth and development, a purpose only recently challenged as a social good. The 1952 McCarran-Walter Immigration Act set aside fifty percent of U.S. visas for those in the professions who would "substantially benefit prospectively the national economy, cultural interests or welfare of the U.S." (21). There is no mention of the effect on the country of origin. There is little doubt that the infusion of highly skilled persons has been an effective economic stimulant (19, 20), just as the ready supply of cheap labor provided by earlier immigrations was one of the essential factors in industrial growth.

At the same time that international migration is raising the dependency ratios of the developing nations, it reduces this ratio in the developed nation. The developed country gains highly motivated, ambitious, and hardworking persons whose goal is personal economic growth. All these factors stimulate growth.

On the pathway to stabilized world material consumption, the developed nations must not only consume absolutely or at least relatively less, but also some provision must be made for improving the living standards of the world's poor. The international migration of skilled persons has tended to increase the gap between the less and the more developed countries: Its cessation is one step which would move us toward a more stable and less disparate world.

Internally, the importation of skilled persons delays the modernization of educational systems in the more developed countries as well as those of the less developed country. For instance, doctors are imported, rather than trained. This denies opportunities for upward mobility to native citizens, particularly minorities. In the United States, there are more Filipino than black doctors (9).

The developed countries have promoted skilled migration because of a faulty analysis of where their interests lie. They have asked what is good for their own country, ignoring the effect on the country of origin and on the world as a whole. It is as if the analysis of purse snatching ended with a determination of what was good for the thief, and ignored the effects on the victim. We need a new, broader, and world view of what is good for the developed countries. It must look not only at short-term advantages, but also at the long-term price to be paid in world instability for further increases in their prosperity, especially if a portion of that increase comes at the expense of the world's poor.

Illegal immigration is at least a step-child of the brain drain, for it is increasing the economic disparity between nations that is the chief impetus behind this phenomenon. There is a measure of retribution about to be meted out, however, for some of the steps that will be required for the developed countries to control illegal migration promise to very directly affect some of their most cherished liberties and freedoms. These will likely include Orwellean measures ranging from considerable restrictions on movements across international borders to the carrying of identity cards to establish one's right to social benefits, a job, and to be in the country. Thus will the residents of the developed countries most directly experience the effects of rampant population growth and the dire economic straits of the less developed nations.

Resource effects should be considered. Immigration helps to perpetuate the population and economic growth of the developed nations that, in turn, will tend to increase their draw on the world's resources. Further population growth in the food-exporting countries will likely consume more agricultural land, decreasing their food production capacity. At the same time, their domestic food consumption will increase. These changes will decrease the amount of food available for export, deleterious changes for both the developed and the underdeveloped nations.

Demographic implications for the developed nations were outlined in the historical section using the United States as an example. To the extent that legal migrants from less developed countries bring their traditionally high fertility patterns with them, the estimates for their increase are understated, for the presented data assume replacement levels of fertility. The developed countries lose some of the benefits of their declining fertility to the extent that averted births are replaced by immigrants.

Because the mean age of migrants is in the early twenties (7) and because the bulk of the post-World War II children are just entering this same age range, immigration adds further to the existing distortion of age pyramids caused by the excessive births of that period. This is another move away from stability.

Socioeconomic problems should not be side-stepped, though mentioning them immediately opens one to charges of the various -isms. Migrants tend to concentrate in urban areas where jobs and their relatives are found. In the United States, with the resident population at replacement level fertility, immigrants will account for twenty-three percent of all urban growth between 1970 and 2000. They thus add to already massive urban problems. By concentrating in a few states and cities, they impact those areas in particular (9).

Illegal immigrants tend to take jobs at the bottom of the socioeconomic scale and thereby help to perpetuate some of the resource consumptive practices of the developed nations. Without this input of inexpensive labor, the developed society would have to choose between improving the pay and working conditions to have the job done or going without (20). The former course would tend to level incomes; the latter would decrease consumption. Either course is desirable en route to a stationary state. As Herman Daly has pointed out, "The rich only ride their horses—they do not clean, comb, curry, saddle and feed them, nor do they clean the stables" (22). Without someone to do the servile tasks, consumption is perforce limited by a lack of time, for the individual must do his own maintenance work. I judge this a more healthy situation both physically and ethically.

By taking jobs at the bottom of the socioeconomic scale, illegal migrants compete for jobs with the disadvantaged and highest unemployment sectors of society: minorities and teenagers, and minority teenagers in particular. This again helps to prevent leveling of incomes and frustrates their ambitions.

The achievement of material equilibrium, and many of the emerging qualitative environmental goals of the developed countries, will require a great unanimity of values and purposes among their populations. These are unlikely to be shared by the bulk of illegal immigrants who migrate looking for personal economic growth. As with the developed countries in their early stages and the developing countries today, the ethic of environmental quality will doubtless come a poor second to economic growth. Any language barriers will increase the difficulties. These factors will weigh against the achievement of a stationary state.

The World View

There is evidence that countries that traditionally export a large proportion of their excess population postpone necessary internal demographic changes which would make such emigration unnecessary (3). Thus emigration facilitates a segment of continued world population growth that might otherwise be avoided. In the special case of Italy, it is interesting to speculate upon possible changes that could have occurred in the Roman Catholic attitude on birth control-related matters if emigration had not relieved its population pressures. Such changes, if they had been brought about several decades ago, could have markedly ameliorated the population problems many nations face today.

Internal migration moves people from less consumptive lifestyles to more consumptive ones. Indeed, the chief reason behind migration is the hope of improving one's economic position. Migration thus contributes to increasing world consumption. The change needed in the world today is just the opposite: reduction of excessive and wasteful lifestyles. The resources required to support the migrant in his new, more affluent lifestyle could support many more of his former countrymen in their less consumptive lifestyle (23).

As we approach the stationary state, throughput must be minimized, for people as well as material goods. Demographically, this implies low birth and infant mortality rates and long life expectancies, with births equal to deaths. It also necessarily means minimal throughput from migration, with low levels of immigration equal to emigration.

The world population problem cannot be solved by mass international migration. If the developed nations took in the annual growth of the less developed nations, they would have to accommodate 53 million persons yearly. This would give them an annual growth rate of 6.3 percent and a doubling time of eleven years (3). In the face of this impossibility, the main avenue open for the developed nations to help the less developed ones is to restrict their own growth and to seek to apply the resources thus conserved to the solution of the problems of the less developed nations.

Conclusions

It is time to take a fresh look at international migration in the light of the need to slow the economic growth of the developed nations, rather than stimulate it, and in turn to promote the economic growth of the less developed countries, at least to some minimal acceptable standard. Current migration policy pushes both considerations in the wrong direction and stimulates overall population growth as well.

As certain portions of the globe deal with their problems more effectively than others, they will stabilize more quickly. This will doubtless increase their attractiveness, especially if other regions are not making progress or are even slipping backward. This will increase pressures for international migration that, if it is allowed, will tend to destabilize those regions otherwise approaching stability. Thus international migration will have to be stringently controlled, or no region will be able to stabilize ahead of another. If no region can stabilize ahead of another, then it is likely that no region whatsoever will be able to stabilize in an orderly and humane fashion. A more hopeful scenario calls for some regions stabilizing at an early date, and then helping others to do so.

Given the demographic and development situation of the world, the control of international migration will be one of the chief problems developed countries will face in approaching equilibrium conditions.

Immigration may be good for the vast majority of the migrants themselves. They find new economic opportunities and, in the special case of refugees, new freedoms. It emerges, however, that their migration in the main runs counter to the real interests of both the countries of origin and the recipient countries, and the world as a whole. This is true whether the analysis is conducted in the traditional growth framework or in the context of the stationary state. What first appears as a new area of conflict between the interests of the individual and those of society is really a conflict between the interests of the individuals who migrate and those who do not. It is time for the larger and longer-range interests of the latter to prevail. We need in particular to give more weight to the interests of the unseen countrymen of the immigrant who are left behind, to live with the conditions the migrant might have helped to change.

Future historians may well record such a broadened examination as one of the factors that led to the end of the age of international migration, one of the alterations that will necessarily accompany the transition to a stationary state.

The question we face is not whether immigration should be restricted, for it has been for decades in all countries. Rather, the question is, what restrictions are appropriate to today's world? Re-examination of this question is made easier by the realization that current limits are arbitrary in their origins. Many were set decades ago without consideration of population, resource, environmental, and other facts that can and should be taken into account today.

Happily, it is possible to envision a world in which international migration could become free and unfettered. Appropriately, it is the world of a stationary state, in which people in different regions are in equilibrium with resources and in which there is a reasonable chance in each region for self-fulfillment, matched with social equity. Under these conditions, international migration could be unfettered, because there would be little incentive to move. Contentment with conditions at home, coupled with man's strong attachment to things familiar, would serve to keep most people in place. While the freedom to migrate at will is incompatible with the physical realities of today's world, it is one of many things that can be restored as man achieves balance with his environment.

REFERENCES AND NOTES
1. *Declaration of U.S. Policy of Population Stabilization by Voluntary Means*, 1971. Hearings on S.J. Res. 108, special Sub-committee on Human Resources, Committee on Labor and Public Welfare, August 5; October 5, 8, 14; and November 3, 1971. Doc. No 68-976, p. 13.
2. See, in general, Higham, John, *Strangers in the Land*. New York: Atheneum, 1963.
3. Davis, Kingsley, "The Migrations of Human Populations." *Scientific American*, Vol. 231, No. 3, September 1974.
4. See, in general, Hansen, Marcus L., *The Atlantic Migration, 1607-1860*. New York: Harper-Row Torchbooks, 1961.
5. *International Migration Trends 1950-1970*. U.N. Secretariat Background Paper for the Bucharest World Population Conference. Document E/Conf. 60/CBP/18, 22 May 1974.
6. Hume, Ian M., "Migrant Workers in Europe." *Finance and Development*, Vol. 10, No. 1, March 1973.
7. *Annual Report, Immigration and Naturalization Service*. U.S. Government Printing Office, Washington, D.C., 1974. Available from the Superintendent of Documents, price $2.00.
8. "How Millions of Illegal Aliens Sneak into U.S." *U.S. News and World Report*, 22 July 1974.
9. *Population and the American Future*. Report of the Commission on Population Growth and the American Future. U.S. Government Printing Office, 1972. See Chapter 13. Available from the Superintendent of Documents, price $1.75.
10. McLellan, Andrew C., and Boggs, Michael D., "Illegal Aliens: A Story of Human Misery." *AFL-CIO Federationist*, August 1974.
11. *Current Population Reports, Population Estimates and Projections*. Series P-25, No. 493, December 1972. U.S. Bureau of the Census, Dept. of Commerce, See Series "X", p. 26. Available from the Superintendent of Documents, price 35¢.
12. *1975 World Population Data Sheet*. Population Reference Bureau, Washington, D.C. Available from the PRB, 1755 Massachusetts Avenue, Washington, D.C., 20036.
13. Ardman, Harvey, "Our Illegal Alien Problem." *American Legion Magazine*, December 1974. Hard data on rates of unemployment/underemployment in the developing countries are difficult to come by.
14. *1973 World Population Data Sheet*. Population Reference Bureau, Washington, D.C.
15. *The U.S. and World Development*. Overseas Development Council, New York: Praeger, 1975.
16. Keely, Charles B., "Immigration Composition and Population Policy." *Science*, Vol. 185, 16 August 1974, p. 587.
17. *Brain Drain: A Study of the Persistent Issue of International Scientific Mobility*. Sub-Committee on National Security Policy and Scientific Developments, Committee on Foreign Affairs, U.S. House of Representatives. September 1974. Doc. No. 35-962. Available from the Superintendent of Documents, price $2.15.
18. *U.S. Aid to Population/Family Planning in Asia*. Report to U.S. House of Representatives, Committee on Foreign Affairs, 25 February 1973. Doc. No. 89-939, p. 9. Available from the Superintendent of Documents.

19. Fortney, Judith, "Immigrant Professionals, a Brief Historical Survey." *International Migration Review*, Vol. VI, No. 1, Spring 1972.
20. Power, Jonathan, "The New Proletariat." *Encounter*, Vol. XLIII, No. 3, September 1974.
21. Immigration and Nationality Act, Sect. 203(a)(3). Copies of the entire act with amendments and major case decisions are available from the Superintendent of Documents, price $1.00.
22. Daly, Herman, "Toward a New Economics: Questioning Growth." *Yale Alumni Magazine*, May 1970.
23. Tanton, John H., "Immigration: An Illiberal Concern?" *Zero Population Growth National Reporter*, Vol. 7, No. 3, April 1975.
24. *Annual World Refugee Report*. U.S. Committee for Refugees, New York, 1974.
25. *Immigration Policy Perspectives*. A report of the Canadian Immigration and Population Study. Ottawa: Information Canada, 1974. Available from Information Canada, 171 Slater Street, Ottawa, Ontario, Canada. Price $1.50.
26. *International Migration, Proceedings of a Seminar on Demographic Research in Relation to International Migration*. Committee for International Coordination of National Research in Demography, Paris, 1974. Available free from CICRED, 27 rue du Commandeur - 75675 Paris - Cedex 14 France. See especially the summary statement, p. 17, and the final report, p. 284.
27. *Recommendations for a New Immigration Policy for the United States*. Zero Population Growth, 1975. Copies available on request.

APPENDIX B

End of the Migration Epoch?

by John H. Tanton

> It is hard to envision a win/win outcome to our migration dilemma . . . As the second millennium closes we find the "irresistible force" of growing migration pressure confronting the "immovable object" of escalating resistance to migration.
> ~ JOHN H. TANTON

John Tanton is editor and publisher of *The Social Contract* and a retired physician who has worked on population issues for thirty-five years and on immigration policy for twenty-five.[1] In this article, published in the spring of 1994, he summarizes the demographic view of international migration.

End of the Migration Epoch?
Time for a New Paradigm
by John H. Tanton

Prologue
Adage tells us that we often "don't see the forest for the trees." Nowhere is this more true than in immigration policy: The complexity of immigration law or the plight of individual migrants tends to narrow our focus and bog us down in minutiae.

201

This paper backs away from the details and examines the bigger picture—in the longer run. It explores the three "pillars" on which the contemporary migration edifice is built: population growth engendered by public and personal health measures, better transportation, and better communications. It closes with a new paradigm for understanding migration phenomena and with a new set of ethical principles to guide immigration policy in the twenty-first century.

In the Beginning

The human migration story begins with our earliest forebears. Divergent schools of thought on our origins nonetheless agree that humans were initially few in number and far between. From very modest beginnings we have gradually spread across the globe.

Our ancestors were apparently nomadic peoples. Hunters and gatherers, they moved when local stocks of animals and plants were exhausted or simply followed the seasons and the migrations of animals on which they preyed. Later, a more settled pattern developed with slash-and-burn or rotating agriculture. People moved on when nutrients ran low or weeds took over. Even after a more permanent agricultural system evolved, people pushed out from the historic population epicenters and resettled, if only locally.[2]

Demographers estimate that at the beginning of the Common Era world population was about 150 million. Although humans had by this time spread a considerable distance from their places of origin, the most dense populations remained in the Mideast, southeast Asia, and the Indian subcontinent. Figure 1 approximates the demographic situation in 1 A.D.[3]

Populations were relatively stable during the first millennium A.D. due to the historic demographic balance of a high birthrate matched by an equally high death rate. Together they dictated a short life expectancy—about twenty-five years at the height of the Roman Empire. There was only slow change until 1350 A.D.; demographers estimate that by then the population had doubled to about 300 million. Figure 2 roughly depicts this growth. Note that vast areas of the globe were very sparsely settled and that humans were only gradually spreading from their places of origin. The Americas were scantily

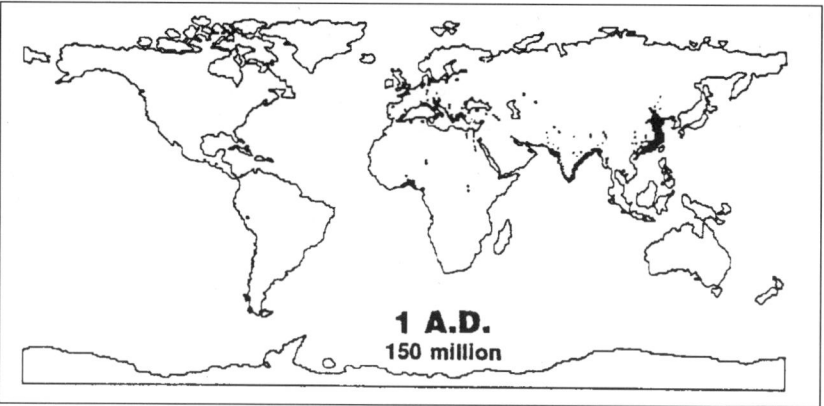

Figure 1
(Each dot represents one million people.)

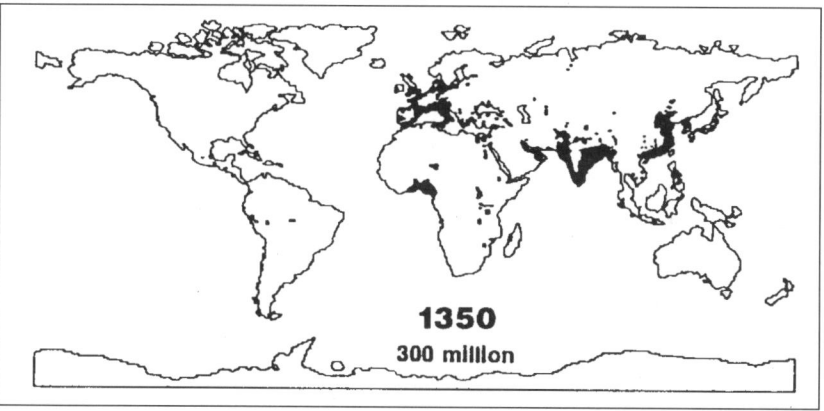

Figure 2

populated, even though the forerunners of the American Indians had crossed the Bering Strait some twenty-five thousand years before.

The plagues of 1350-1450 actually reduced population somewhat, but by 1600 human numbers had recovered and were beginning to grow more rapidly, reaching about 500 million—approximately three times that of 1 A.D.

I. The 1600s and Pillar One:
Public Health Measures, Pre-Modern Medicine, and the Beginnings of the Population Explosion.

During the seventeenth century, the foundations were laid for the first of three main pillars that account for the migration dilemmas we face three centuries later. Scientific and medical discoveries led eventually to the first public health practices and, much later, to modern individualized health care. These ultimately reduced death rates while disturbing high birth rates very little, leading to the unprecedented growth of human numbers we see today.

A quick survey of the medical highlights of the 1600s shows that Barelli[4] did pioneering work on human physiology, as did Santario Santario (sic). In 1626, the latter was the first to measure human temperature with a thermometer. In 1619, the Royal College of Physicians in London issued its first pharmacopoeia, presaging today's compilations on drugs. William Harvey announced his seminal discovery of the circulation of the blood in the same year. Quinine came into use in the 1640s, as did arsenic. The Dutch physician Isbrand de Diemerbrock published a book on the plague in 1649. Books on anatomy and surgery appeared. Thomas Willis described typhoid fever in 1659, midwifery forceps followed in 1665, and a description of diabetes appeared in 1670. The first medical treatise written in the Americas was published in 1678, discussing smallpox

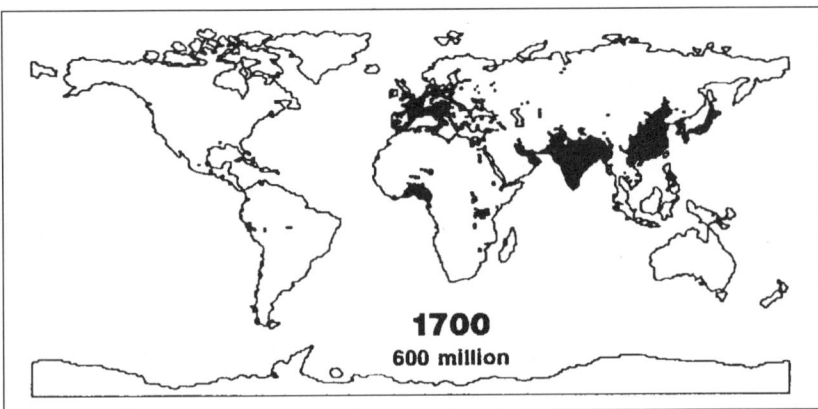

Figure 3

and measles. These were all forerunners of today's public health practices and powerful medical technology.

Perhaps most significantly, in 1674 the Dutchman Anthony van Leeuwenhoek first saw microbes with a microscope he had invented, paving the way for the germ theory of disease and the discovery of antibiotics. But the story of civilization is not one of uninterrupted progress; in 1697, Daniel Defoe first recommended the adoption of an income tax!

Figure 3 shows the demographic situation at the close of the 1600s: The human population was about 600 million, four times that of our starting point of 150 million.

II. The 1700s and Pillar Two: The Industrial and Transportation Revolutions.

The eighteenth century saw the early development of the second pillar on which modern-day migration problems rest: the self-reinforcing industrial and transportation revolutions. The central figure in these advances was surely James Watt, with his inventions relating to the steam engine.

Beginning in 1765, the twenty-eight-year-old Watt invented a condenser to recapture energy from waste steam and thus increase the energy efficiency of steam power. By 1769, he had patented his steam engine. In 1781, he invented the gears that converted the engine's reciprocal motion into the rotary motion of a shaft, highly important for applications to transportation.

In 1782, Watt constructed a more efficient double-acting engine, in which the piston was pushed from both sides. Then in 1784, he came up with what he considered his most ingenious invention, which he called "parallel motion." It was a new way for connecting a piston to a shaft. He followed up with his centrifugal governor in 1788, a pressure gauge in 1790, and then a counter, an indicator, and a throttle valve.

While Watt's engine powered the industrial revolution, it also revolutionized transportation. By 1783, Jouffroy d'Abbans had installed a steam engine in a paddle wheel boat. In 1804, Richard Trevithick built the first steam locomotive.

Overseas travel was further aided by Vitus Bering, Captain James Cook, Louis-Antoine Bougainville, and George Vancouver, who explored the globe and made maps. Navigators improved their instruments, allowing more accurate determination of latitude. The British Parliament in 1714 offered a £20,000 prize for the discovery of a method of calculating longitude within thirty miles during a sea voyage. The Englishman John Harrison solved this age-old problem and won the prize by inventing a highly accurate and durable chronometer, tested in 1761-1762. Lighthouses were built, improving safety on the seas.

The first cast iron bridge was built in 1773, foreshadowing bridging capabilities beyond those allowed by wood and stone. Extensive canal systems were dug in Europe (and started in the American colonies) to transport fuel, food, and fiber.

Heralding yet another transport revolution, the Montgolfier brothers flew the first lighter-than-air fire balloon in 1783.

Other industrial changes that I won't detail improved the living conditions of the populace, increasing health and life expectancy, and hence human numbers. The result when combined with better transportation: more people who were more mobile.

During the 1700s, the public health and medical fields continued to evolve, addressing chiefly infectious disease. A veterinary school opened in 1761, starting us toward control of animal-borne diseases, such as undulant fever and bovine tuberculosis. In 1776, Edward Jenner introduced the small pox vaccination, reducing the death rate. This ancient scourge had killed ten to twenty percent of those infected—which was nearly everyone, for it was an extremely virulent disease.

Advancing us along the road toward better individual health care, Gabriel Daniel Fahrenheit invented the mercury thermometer in 1714. Claudius Aymaud did the first surgery for appendicitis in 1731 (without anesthesia, probably just draining an abscess). Chest percussion (important for detecting tuberculosis) came along in 1761, the same year that Giovanni Morgagni launched the study of pathological anatomy.

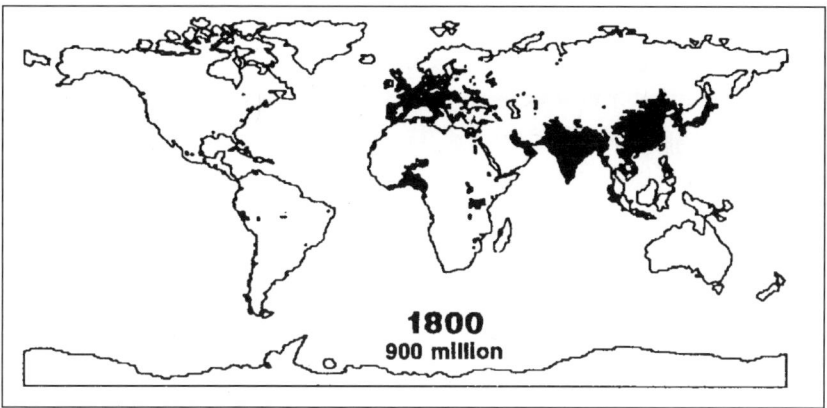

Figure 4

Figure 4 approximates the demographic situation at the close of this second century of major industrial, transportation, public health, and medical advances. Humans now numbered about 900 million—six times the population used as the starting point for this paper.

III. The 1800s and Pillar Three: Better Communications

By 1800, two of the three pillars undergirding today's migration problems were well in place and undergoing rapid development. First, public health improvements combined with better living conditions had started to cut the death rate and engender population growth—the principle "push" factor in human migration. Second, transportation improvements launched in the 1700s and advanced in the 1800s made it possible in the 1900s to move huge numbers of people long distances with greater speed, safety, and ease, at a moderate cost.

The 1800s witnessed the early development of the third pillar that supports today's mass international migration: improved communications. This century—the first electrical century—produced a virtual pantheon of electrical greats, like Michael Faraday, James Clerk Maxwell, Samuel Morse, and Gigliemo Marconi, who laid the foundations for the communications revolution.

André Ampére set down the laws of electrical dynamic action in 1820. Faraday described electromagnetic rotation in 1821, discovered electromagnetic induction in 1831, conceptualized electrical and magnetic lines of force in 1832, and in 1834 wrote the Law of Electrolysis (of great importance in chemistry). George Ohm formulated his Law of Potential and Resistance in 1827. Charles Wheatstone invented his bridge for electrical measurements in 1833. By 1834, Morse had installed a functioning telegraph between Baltimore and Washington and had developed his Morse code. A printing telegraph appeared in 1856. Lord Kelvin invented the galvanometer in 1858. Maxwell published his famous and fundamental equations in 1865. Edison improved the telegraph in 1872, and Alexander Graham Bell invented the telephone in 1876.

But then the limitation of the wire was broken! Heinrich Rudolph Hertz reported on the nature of radio waves in 1888, and the twenty-one-year-old Marconi announced the invention of the wireless telegraph in 1895; it utilized the Morse code. As the century closed, R. A. Fessenden transmitted human speech by radio waves for the first time.

The stage was now set for the inexpensive and nearly instantaneous transmission of information to the most remote corners of the globe, where it could stimulate interest in migration. (Some years ago, herdsmen in East Africa actually held up their annual migration for two weeks so they could watch the last episodes of the TV series *Dallas*!) Improvements in transportation enabled masses of people to migrate, either to fulfill their highest hopes or to escape their worst fears. And migrate they did, by the tens of millions.

Further Medical Advances

These movements will be reviewed shortly, but first let us note the continued evolution of the public health, medical, and transportation fields.

In 1827, James Simpson developed sand filters to purify the London water supply, of obvious benefit to the city's public health. Oliver Wendell Holmes Sr. wrote a paper on puerperal (childbirth) fever in 1843. The obstetrician Ignaz Semmelweiss discovered the contagious nature of puerperal fever, and as a preventative, advised his fellow physicians in 1874 to simply wash their hands between patients as they attended women in labor. He was driven mad when the medical establishment pilloried him for such radical advice. Louis Pasteur formulated the germ theory of fermentation (1861) and invented pasteurization (1864), a chicken cholera vaccine (1880), and a vaccine for the dreaded rabies (1885). After he died in 1895, the Pasteur Institute was established in Paris to perpetuate his work and memory.

One of the most significant public health measures of the century, however, was Englishman Thomas Crapper's invention of the flush toilet, which he demonstrated at the Health Exhibition in London in 1884. This device helped control water-borne diseases, no mean killer of people: Cholera epidemics around the middle of the nineteenth century killed thirty thousand people in London alone.[5]

Care for individual patients was still ineffectual, but some progress was being made. In 1816, René Laënnec invented the stethoscope—important for diagnosing and treating the ancient (and now recrudescent) scourge of tuberculosis. The British medical journal *The Lancet* first appeared in 1823, fostering the communication of medical ideas. William T. Morton gave the first ether anesthetic in 1846; the first appendectomy (now with anesthesia) followed in 1847.

In 1865, Sir Joseph Lister introduced the disinfectant carbolic acid and launched the concept of antiseptic surgery, tolling the end of the era of "laudable pus" in medicine. In 1871, G. A. Hansen discovered the leprosy bacillus.

Robert Koch identified the anthrax bacillus in 1876 and developed a method for staining and identifying bacteria in 1877. In 1882, he discovered the tubercle bacillus, developed an inoculation against anthrax (1883), and in 1887, formulated his seminal "Four Postulates" for proving the bacterial causation of a disease.[6] To round out his career, he traveled to India to discover the causative organism of cholera and while en route, identified the organisms that caused two varieties of Egyptian conjunctivitis (a severe eye inflammation). What a record!

Closing out the medical events of the nineteenth century: The malarial parasite was discovered in 1890, the plague bacillus in 1894, and the dysentery bacillus in 1898. Steam sterilization of surgical instruments started in 1886, rubber gloves were introduced in 1890, and Wilhelm Roentgen discovered X-rays in 1895. The translation of these advances into definitive, personal, and life-saving systems of patient care was to come in the next century.

As a result of public health measures and better living conditions fostered by the industrial revolution, death rates decreased, especially among the young. Children who formerly would have died survived to reproduce themselves, and human numbers expanded. By 1850, population approached 1.2 billion—approximately eight times our starting population of 150 million in 1 A.D.

Further Transportation Advances

Industrialization and transportation also evolved rapidly in the 1800s. Robert Fulton built a steam-powered paddle boat in 1803. Bell had a steamship running on the Clyde in Scotland by 1812. Augustin Jean Fresnel invented his prisms in 1822, greatly improving the efficiency of lighthouses and safety on the high seas. The first steamship crossed the Atlantic in 1827, reducing travel times by days and eventually weeks. A steam-powered, screw propeller ship first appeared in 1829, and could do six knots! In 1872, Lord Kelvin invented a machine that allowed ships to take accurate depth soundings at sea—another major advance in safety.

On the rail front, George Stephenson built the first practical locomotive in 1814. Trains first carried passengers in Britain in 1825, and in the United States in 1828. The first Swiss railroad opened in 1847, and three years later Robert Stephenson (George's son) constructed the first cast iron bridge capable of carrying a train. Rail lines were pushed through the Brenner Pass by 1867 and construction of the trans-Siberian railroad was begun in 1891 (and completed in 1917).

Transportation by car was not far behind. John Macadam developed a road-building process that still bears his name. An internal combustion engine was developed in 1860. Karl Benz built the first single-cylinder motor car engine in 1885 and followed up in 1893 with the first four-wheel car. Henry Ford's first "flivver" appeared in 1894.

Advancing the concept of air travel, Count Ferdinand von Zeppelin constructed his lighter-than-air ship in 1895.

We would be remiss if we failed to note the highly significant agricultural revolution that took place alongside the industrial one. New crops from the New World rounded out and enhanced the diet: potatoes in the north of Europe; tomatoes and maize (corn) in the south.[7] Cultivation of sugar beets started after the British blockaded ports and supplies of cane sugar during the Napoleonic wars.

Patent and Copyright Laws

Let us pause here to note the creation of two key social conventions that bridged these three centuries and facilitated much of this scientific innovation: patent and copyright laws.

An early patent law, the statute on monopolies, was adopted in England in 1623. As one of its first acts, the United States' Congress passed a comprehensive patent statute in 1790. So did France in 1791, as did numerous other countries in the 1800s. The International Convention for the Protection of Industrial Property was signed in Paris in 1883, initially by eleven countries.

The first copyright act, the Statute of Anne, passed in England in 1710. Denmark followed suit in 1741, the United States in 1790, and France in 1793. The Bern Convention, an international copyright accord, took effect in 1886 with fourteen signatories.

These social measures served the twin goals of financially protecting those who made scientific advances while assuring that the innovations were disclosed and eventually became public property. They were of more importance in the transportation and communications fields than in medicine, where a different ethic of freely sharing discoveries (at least among physicians) was and still remains in place.

The Situation at the Close of the Nineteenth Century

Having reviewed the three main lines of discovery and invention that both caused and enabled the mass migrations of the 1800s and

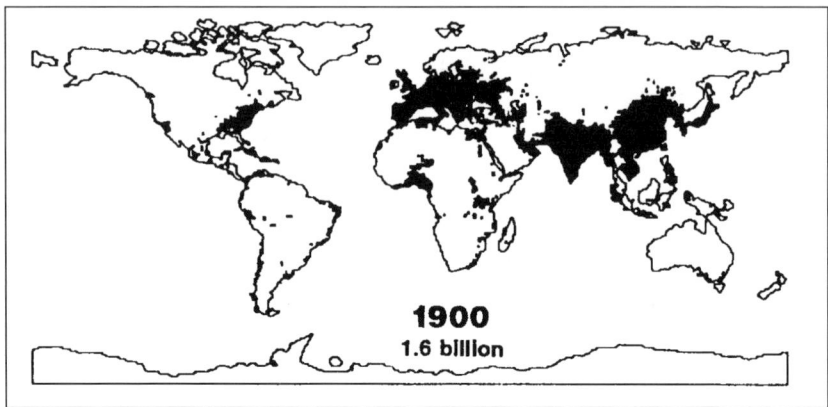

Figure 5

1900s, let us pause to sum up mankind's situation after three centuries of continuous scientific advancements. Figure 5 approximates the demographic situation in 1900, with a world population of about 1.6 billion, about ten times our starting point of 150 million.

The Reverend Thomas Robert Malthus published *On the Principle of Population* in 1798. It was no accident that his seminal essay appeared then. By the end of the 1700s, Europe's population had grown to the point where, given the then-available technology, it pressed hard upon its resource base. The Europeans were worried about supporting their increasing numbers.

As a practical matter, the space and resources of the Americas were not yet available to the Old World. It took months to cross the ocean in tiny ships—with frequent dismastings, sea sickness, and shipwreck in the bargain. The oft-cited (but little read and less understood) Malthus observed that while humans had great reproductive powers and often had many children, the human population increased much more slowly than high birth rates would seem to predict. In his view, numbers were held in check by "misery and vice," that is, the classic Four Horsemen of the Apocalypse: war, civil strife, hunger, and death. Shortages of food, clothing, and shelter, coupled with diseases, killed many people or kept them from marrying and reproducing. Malthus's chief concern was with food supplies and the slow rate at which they could be increased.

Then the unexpected happened. Thanks to improvements in transportation, the New World became more accessible. Surplus people poured out of Europe (perhaps 50 to 60 million between 1840 and 1930). Resources were imported by the Old World to supply its industries, and overseas markets opened up for the resulting manufactured goods.

As railroads reached the American Midwest, they were able to carry grain to Atlantic seaports where it could be shipped inexpensively to Europe. The flood of cheap imported food closed down farms all across England, Europe, and into Russia.[8]

Traveling east, ships were heavily laden with bulky raw materials; returning west, they were lightly loaded with more compact manufactured goods. Rather than carry ballast on the westward leg, the steamship companies decided instead to haul paying passengers. (The streets of Boston in the earlier years had been paved in part with stones from Europe—nonpaying ballast stones!) To that end, agents were sent to the interior of Europe to promote emigration, at which they proved very effective. The displaced farmers and others embarked on boats returning to America, where they took up farming and perpetuated the cycle of dislocation. My maternal great-grandfather was typical. Migrating at age twenty-seven after discharge in 1854 from one of the many German armies, he was eventually naturalized at Niagara Falls, New York, in 1868. He became a farmer, as are many of his descendants to this day.

Europe's incessant wars and such catastrophes as the potato blight of the 1840s and '50s (which also occurred on the Continent though with less severe consequences than in Ireland)[9] drove others to leave.

The net result of the opening up of the New World was that Malthus's cup of "misery and vice" was taken away for a while. Europeans pushed by straightened circumstances at home and pulled by the opportunities of the New World proceeded to colonize the newly opened lands and utilize their resources. I specify Europeans because this migration was largely a Europe-to-New World phenomenon, and was based on the European scientific advances outlined in this paper.

By contrast, in Africa (except for the slave trade), on the Indian subcontinent, and in Asia, population growth remained largely *in situ*. (It was also much less, due to the absence of most of the factors we've cited that engendered European population growth and migration.) Only the Europeans were in a position to export their excess population and use these expatriates to harvest and ship back home overseas resources. The colonists in turn provided a market for manufactured goods, further spurring the Industrial Revolution. Indeed, demographer Kingsley Davis calculates that had Europe not been able to export its surplus people, its population in 1970 would have been fifty percent larger than it was—1.08 billion rather than 650 million.[10]

Davis also notes that until the great trans-Atlantic migration of 1840-1930, the historic direction of migration had generally been from sparsely settled territories to thickly settled ones, and from less-advanced to more-advanced areas, i.e., from the rural to the urban. Then the direction of the flow reversed, with people leaving thickly settled and developed Europe for the sparsely populated and rugged overseas frontiers. Today, he notes, the historic pattern has returned, with flows now running toward the developed countries, though in some cases the donor countries are more thickly settled than the recipient ones.[11]

The Twentieth Century: Raising the Stakes

We now arrive at our own century, the population dynamics and scientific developments of which are well enough known that they need not be reported in detail. Suffice it to state that in the transportation and communication fields, innovation and advancement have gone apace, stimulating interest in and facilitating migration.

Medicine, however, has changed. While public health measures have continued to appear (vaccines for diphtheria, whooping cough, tetanus, polio), the age of potent, life-extending, *individualized* health care is upon us. This is now an increasingly important factor in the expansion of human numbers.

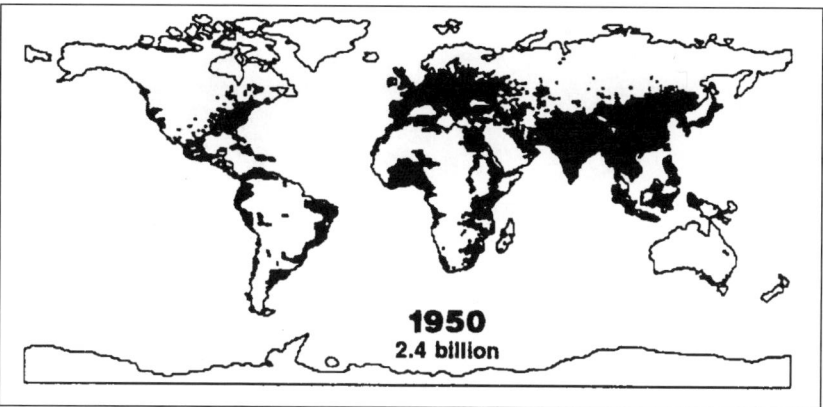

Figure 6

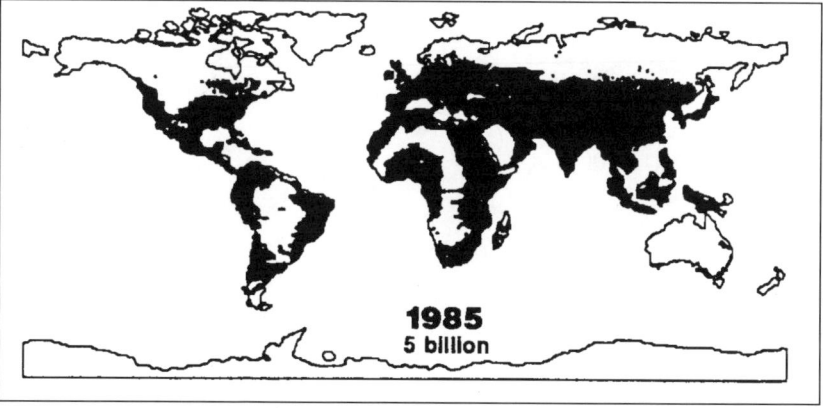

Figure 7

In addition, our scientists have given us pesticides to suppress plant and animal diseases, and fertilizers, herbicides, and the green revolution to produce more food. We humans have responded by increasing our numbers to match and test these new limits. Here is a summary of our situation at century's end.

Population Push Pressures

World population by 1950 had reached about 2.4 billion, sixteen times our base-year number of 150 million. By 1985—just thirty-five

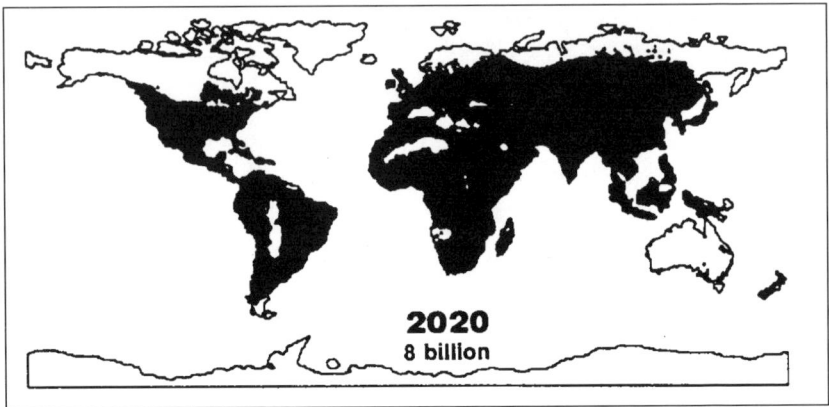

Figure 8

years later—it had doubled to approximately five billion. (See Figures 6 and 7.) As of the 1990s, the percentage *rate* of population growth may be down somewhat, but it now applies to a progressively larger base, so that today the net increase (births minus deaths) is 10,000 per hour, 250,000 per day, 90-plus million per year—the fastest numeric increase in world history. When India lost 30,000 people in an earthquake in 1993, it replaced that number *by itself* in just two eight-hour shifts; its population currently grows by 50,000 per day.

Making matters worse, demographic momentum now at work (and beyond reversal in the short term) will greatly swell world population over the next few decades, inevitably increasing human misery and therefore migration push pressures (Figure 8).

In the United States by 1990, our population had grown to 250 million, nearly sixty-four times the four million counted in the first census in 1790. The Census Bureau now projects that by 2050, our population will reach 392 million-a further sixty percent increase-due chiefly to the admission of large numbers of young and fertile immigrants.[12]

Beyond just human numbers, consider:

Employment Push Pressures

In March of 1994, the International Labor Organization reported that per capita income for the world's workers fell in 1993 for the fourth straight year. Thirty percent of the world's labor force—820 million people—were unemployed or underemployed at the beginning of 1994.[13]

Basing our prediction on the number of people *already born* (this is not a "guesstimate"), we can see that between 1990 and 2010 the work force of the less-developed countries will expand another 800 million, far more than the *entire* current work force of the more-developed countries (less than 600 million). Where will these people find work?

Social and Political Push Pressures

Freedom House, which reports annually on the status of freedom around the globe, states that as of 1993, only nineteen percent of the world's population lives under conditions it describes as "free." Those living under "partially free" conditions make up forty percent; the "not free" account for forty-one percent. Adding these last two figures together, we find that over eighty percent of the world's 5.4 billion people—some four billion souls—live under conditions less than "free." Most of these people could improve their lot in several ways by moving to a developed country. This reservoir of human discontent grows by about eighty million per year, as ninety percent of the world's annual population growth of 90 million occurs in less-developed and less-free countries.

Environmental and Natural Disaster Push Pressures

A nearly endless list could be cited: deforestation-exacerbated floods in Bangladesh,[14] the collapse of fisheries in the Black and Azov Seas resulting from the accidental introduction of the West Atlantic comb jelly fish,[15] pollution in the former USSR,[16] the desertification of Africa's Sub-Sahara, and so on.

Natural disasters such as earthquakes, volcanic eruptions, and floods now find many more people "in harm's way." Many of the people displaced by such acts of God are candidates for moving to higher and firmer ground.

But to Where Can Such Populations Move?

North America cannot accommodate huge additional numbers—

it is now quite *fully occupied*, with scarcely any virgin land or untapped resources awaiting settlers. Easily accessible resources have been substantially harnessed and, in many cases, run down. South America still has sparsely populated areas but is hardly in a position to resettle tens of millions of people with the attendant economic costs and social turmoil.

Europe is more densely populated than North America, and an even less likely candidate for resettling millions of migrants. For instance, reunited Germany has a surface area about equal to that of the combined states of Oregon and Washington, but it has a population one-third that of the *entire* United States. The Netherlands is twice as densely populated as Germany, with an average 1,300 people per square mile. How can either of these places receive millions of newcomers? The same is true of most of Europe and the habitable portions of Africa and Asia. The globe's hospitable lands are in the main already taken up.

Does outer space offer an answer? Regrettably not, at least in our time. We know of no other liveable planets. Even if we did, just to keep up with population growth, we would need to fire ten thousand people an hour into space—*never to return*. Anything less would be demographically ineffective. Any volunteers?

In Addition: Growing Resistance to Migrants

From the pool of four billion potential migrants, there are probably fewer than four million persons worldwide who are allowed to migrate *legally* each year—about one in one thousand, or 0.1 percent (Table 1). Of the 170-plus member countries of the United Nations, only a handful still *seek* immigrants. And in each of these countries, public opinion polls show strong opposition to both illegal and legal immigration. Serious reexamination of immigration policy is underway in all of these countries with sharp reductions as a possible outcome. The other U.N. members are in the market for newcomers only under the most stringent of conditions, and usually in very limited numbers.

In retrospect, it took only two hundred years—from 1790 to 1990 —to skim the cream of the Americas' resources and return mankind

TABLE 1

Legal Immigration to the Main Immigrant-Receiving Nations

Country and Year for which data is available	Number
Australia (1991-1992)	107,400
Canada (1991)	230,781
Fed. Rep. of German (1992)*	1,489,449
France (1990)	176,115
Israel (1992)	77,032
Italy (1992)**	11,350
Sweden (1989)	58,944
United Kingdom (1990)	51,960
United States (1990)***	1,536,483
TOTAL	**3,739,514**

* This includes 281,847 ethnic Germans from the former East Germany, Eastern Europe, and Russia.

** Italy doesn't consider itself a country of immigration and so does not keep relevant data. The 11,350 are family reunification visas and asylees (2,650), but do not include tens of thousands of people of Italian descent returning from places such as Argentina.

*** This includes 880,372 aliens granted permanent residence under the provisions of the 1986 Immigration Reform and Control Act.

SOURCES: Center for Migration Studies (Washington, D.C.); European Forum for Migration Studies, Bamberg, Germany.

to the conditions faced in Europe in 1798 when Malthus wrote his essay: millions of people in dire circumstances, with huge pools of under- or unemployed labor. But now the numbers are vastly larger, and no virgin continents await settlers.

End of the Migration Epoch?

It is hard to envision a win/win outcome to our migration dilemma. In sum, as the second millennium closes, we find the "irresistible force" of growing migration pressure confronting the "immovable object" of escalating resistance to migration.

How Will It All Turn Out?

If the developed countries cannot or will not control their borders, they will quickly be swamped in the remaining years of this century or the opening ones of the next. It seems unlikely that their welfare systems can provide benefits to any and all who can afford the price of a ticket, or that their social, political, and economic systems can cope with the resultant plethora of languages, religions, races, and ethnicities. Even if the developed countries take in tens of millions, it will have little effect on the growing numbers of people left behind. In this hapless scenario, migration would stop only when it is no longer worth moving—only when abject poverty prevails everywhere. I cannot believe the developed countries would allow this to happen.

If the developed countries do muster the will and the very considerable resources required to control their borders, we will be the subject of "Isle-of-Prosperity-in-a-Sea-of-Misery" TV shows—shows that vividly portray the chaos and anarchy that many envision for the Third World.[17] Given that many of the developed countries' resources come from the less-developed regions (the United States, for instance, imports more than fifty percent of its oil), the developed world's future is far from assured in this scenario.

In contrast, let us assume some outpouring of compassion. Say eight million legal migrants were accepted worldwide in one year, twice the present annual number. That would accommodate only one months' world population increase and do nothing to decrease the ranks of the discontented. What happens the next year? Do we accept another eight million, while falling further behind?

My estimate is that as these alternate futures become known, the forces working worldwide to secure borders and decrease immigration will prevail. By the turn of the century, both illegal and legal migration will be severely curtailed. Transborder migration of impoverished tens of millions, as occurred between 1840-1930, is simply impossible to envision; this would be viewed everywhere as an invasion. It is now and would then be vigorously resisted by whatever means necessary.

Toward a New Paradigm

I have chosen my words carefully. I write of the virtual end of migration of people who will be *welcome*, wherever in the world they may settle. Doubtless, some clandestine migration will continue, but most migrants will increasingly be resented by the majority of the populace in the target countries.

The world is not *full*, but is *fully occupied*, and by those who for reasons lamented by some and lauded by others do not wish to divide their patrimony into smaller pieces by admitting more people. Unfortunately, we can offer no encore analogous to the occupation in the 1800s and 1900s of the Americas and Australia/New Zealand. There are no new continental land masses to be discovered, and few remaining unclaimed virgin resources. We have finally done it—we have spread completely across the *habitable* surfaces of the globe and fulfilled at least one Biblical injunction—to be fruitful, multiply, and subdue the earth.

The three scientific revolutions that made migration a solution in the *fin de siècle* times of the 1890s have now made it a difficult problem in the *fin de millénaire* times of the 1990s. To review:

1. Medical and public health science are relentlessly saving lives and, by postponing death beyond the fertile years, pushing human populations to ever higher levels.
2. Communication technology is constantly evolving and ever cheaper, informing people of bad conditions at home and greener grass elsewhere.
3. Transportation improvements are making it ever more possible for huge numbers of people to move at relatively small expense anywhere on the globe in a matter of hours.

I predict that future historians, looking back on the end of the second millennium, will report that just as mankind went through Ages characterized as Stone, Bronze, and Iron, so it went through an Immigration Epoch that bridged all of those ages, and came to a close about the year 2000. Movement of people continued just as did use of stone, bronze, and iron, but the human race had to find ways other than migration to address its problems. There was no alternative.

An important chapter in human history, these historians will say, had closed.

Needed: A Paradigm Shift

The world has changed since our Republic was formed two hundred years ago. Our mental image of it must change to keep pace. Thomas Kuhn calls such readjustments "paradigm shifts" and defined them in his 1962 book *The Structure of Scientific Revolutions* as "a set of assumptions about reality—an accepted model or pattern that explains the world better than any other set of assumptions."[18]

The next section lays out side by side some of the paradigm shifts needed to align our view of international migration with new realities.

A Proposed Shift in the Immigration Paradigm

The Old Dogma	The New Understanding
1. There is enough for all, regardless of numbers. Selfishness and greed are the problem. Just distribution is the solution.	1. Resources and livable conditions are scarce. Manna does not fall from heaven. Scarcity is the rule and requires a degree of self-interest.
2. The population problems and pressures can be solved by moving people to sparsely populated countries.	2. Population problems are beyond solution by migration. No habitable, unclaimed lands remain. Most people will never be able to leave the country of their birth.
3. Large-scale migration can continue indefinitely.	3. The large-scale migration of the past two hundred years is an aberration enabled by conditions that cannot be replicated. In a limited world, it must necessarily come to an end.
4. National boundaries are arbitrary and illegitimate. We should transfer our allegiance upward to world government. Robert Frost was right: "Something there is that doesn't love a wall."	4. The nation-state is one of the essential levels of human government. Modern life is impossible without it; most people will transfer their loyalties down to the clan or tribe, not upward

5. We are a nation of immigrants. The Statue of Liberty stands for open immigration.	to world government. Robert Frost's neighbor had it right: "Good fences make good neighbors."
	5. All nations are nations of immigrants at some point in their history. The United States is not special in this regard. The Statue of Liberty stands not for immigration but for the rule of law and "Liberty Enlightening the World."
6. Immigration is primarily a civil liberties problem to be dealt with by specialists: lawyers, judiciary committees, courts.	6. Immigration is primarily a population and resource problem. Policy should be set by demographers, resource committees, and biologists, in consultation with the citizenry.
7. The proper focus of our attention is on those who migrate—the less than 0.1 percent.	7. The proper focus is on the 99.9 percent of people who remain at home to contend with the conditions that migrants leave behind. They are the ones who most need and deserve our support.
8. Those who migrate are to be celebrated as heroes.	8. Those who stay and struggle to change things for the better—the Lech Walesas of the world—are the real heroes.
9. Limiting immigration is selfish or worse.	9. Limiting immigration and hence population growth is our duty if we are to pass our national estate on to our successors in livable condition. Migrants are usually selfish in their motivation.
10. Diversity is good and more diversity is better-without limit.	10. Commonality is also good and essential to workable social arrangements. Too much diversity leads to divisiveness and conflict.

But what about ethics and morals? What is the *right* thing to do?

Many great human questions are at bottom ethical and moral, rather than economic or political. Elimination of the age-old practice of slavery was not based on cost/benefit analysis. Philosophers and their governments have long sought to define the "just" war. Volunteer associations by the hundreds are actuated by high-minded concepts of right and wrong, even in this secular era.

Down through the years, many codes of conduct have appeared to guide mankind in wrestling with ethical or moral decisions. Without such common, agreed-to benchmarks, resolution of disputes and probably even civilized life would not be possible.

Control of migration is one of the great and age-old human questions. Based on the new paradigm presented above, we need to develop a new set of principles to guide the formulation of immigration policy. These are the ones that seem to be evolving:

A New Decalogue for an Increasingly Crowded World

Principle I: World population growth of 10,000 per hour, 250,000 per day, 90-plus million per year, dwarfs the absorptive capacity of the few countries still willing to receive legal (and certainly illegal) immigrants. The stresses caused by population growth cannot be solved by international migration. They must be confronted by and within each individual nation.

Principle II: The nation-state remains an *essential* unit of human governance. Sovereignty is the guarantee of a nation's and its citizens' right to exist. Sovereignty includes the right to regulate entry into one's territory. The United Nations' *Universal Declaration of Human Rights*[19] recognizes this by enumerating a right of emigration, but not of immigration. The alternative to delineating and controlling borders is anarchy.

Principle III: *Each nation* has a solemn responsibility to provide for the health, education, employment, and security of its own citizens. No nation can expect to solve deficiencies in these areas by exporting its surplus people. Fundamental to the concept of national rights and responsibilities is the duty of each nation to match its population with its political, social, and environmental resources, in both the short and the long term. No nation should exceed what the biologists call its "carrying capacity."

Principle IV: In setting its immigration policy, any nation must *first* look after the *interests of its own citizens*, including those at the bottom of the socioeconomic ladder. The long-term consequences of any actions, including the need to ensure social cohesion, and the long-range management of social, political, and environmental resources must be considered. Passing these on in healthy condition to future generations must be a fundamental objective of public policy. This is not selfish; it is a requirement of social responsibility.

Principle V: *Each nation* should *train* its own technical and professional personnel, matching supply to demand. The developed countries in particular should not continue to encourage a brain drain from the less-developed countries, luring their talented people, and thus benefitting from the scarce capital that went into their education. On their part, the less-developed countries should educate their citizens in fields appropriate to their own country's needs, and not for some personnel export market.

Principle VI: *Each nation* should arrange to *do its own drudgery work*, even if this means extra expense to improve the wages and conditions of service workers. Communities within the developed countries that have few or no immigrants have long demonstrated their ability to maintain themselves without outside help. In the long course of human history, there have always been those who wanted to harvest the product of another's labor. This was the underlying theme of slavery. It is time we closed this chapter of human history.

Principle VII: *Illegal immigration* is unacceptable, both for the individual migrant and for the recipient nation. Newcomers should arrive legally, indicating their respect for the laws and customs of their prospective new land. If workers have legal status, it will reduce the temptation of potential employers and others to exploit newcomers because of their illegal status. Illegal immigration should be held to the irreducible minimum.

Principle VIII: *Legal immigration* should come under the discipline of a "budget" concept, one that specifies an all-inclusive ceiling. If more in one category are to be admitted, balancing cuts must be made elsewhere.

The three fundamental questions that must be answered to set a policy on legal immigration are:

1. *How many* people shall we admit, and *what factors* should be taken into account in setting this limit?
2. *Who* should be chosen to immigrate, and *what criteria* should be used for choosing among candidates?
3. *How* can we humanely enforce the rules we decide upon?

To be taken seriously, any proposed legal immigration policy must set out specific answers to this "How-Who-How" trilogy.

To underscore the value of citizenship, legal immigrants should enjoy a lesser "bundle of rights" than citizens during their trial period of legal resident alien status. When they become eligible for naturalization, they should either commit themselves fully to their new country by becoming citizens and receiving full rights and accepting full responsibilities or, if they choose not to make this commitment, they should return home, making room for someone else. Both dual citizenship and permanent, lifelong resident alien status are ethically unacceptable. People should commit themselves to one polity or another and participate fully in efforts to improve its social, political, and economic life.

Principle IX: Concerning *asylees* and *refugees*, the emphasis should be on *temporary* succor with eventual repatriation, rather than permanent settlement. The U.N. High Commissioner for Refugees states that repatriation must be the solution for most refugee problems, given the numbers involved.[20] The limited refugee funds available are better spent on the relatively inexpensive per capita maintenance of many refugees in their region of origin, rather than on expensive permanent resettlement of a few in the developed countries. Refugees should not be introduced to the developed countries if there is to be any hope of repatriation.

Principle X: The *epoch of international migration* as a solution to human problems is over for the overwhelming majority of mankind. Most people will never be able to move from their place of birth; there are simply too many people and too few places left to go. Instead, individuals will have to work to change conditions they find unacceptable.

Acknowledging the realities underlying these principles could usher in a whole new epoch in human history, one in which support will flow toward individuals attempting to deal with their problems, rather than to those who simply take flight from them.

The astute reader will note that we have not placed heavy emphasis on a plethora of "immigrants' rights." Rather, we emphasize the rights (and responsibilities) of the citizens in both the receiving and sending countries.

Many axioms and corollaries to this basic set of ten principles could and need to be enunciated. However, these broad guidelines can provide an overall framework for policy making.

In Summary: End of the Migration Epoch!

It is now time to remove the question mark from the title of this essay and replace it with an exclamation point to assert that the convergence of events and data show that we are fast approaching the end of the migration epoch. *Welcoming* international migration—legal, and especially illegal—is no longer a practical option for almost all of the world's people. Rather, they will have to bloom where they are planted if they are to bloom at all. They will have to work to change conditions they don't like rather than just move away from them. Helping make it possible for them to stay rather than leave is the proper focus for our efforts.

Rampant twentieth-century population growth has brought sobering new realities. We must adjust our immigration paradigm and its derivative ethical system accordingly.

NOTES

1 In pursuit of his demographic and immigration policy interests, Tanton has served as organizer and president of Northern Michigan Planned Parenthood (1965-1971), as chair of the national Sierra Club Population Committee (1971-1974), as a member of the national Zero Population Growth board (1973-1978), as chair of its Immigration Study Committee (1973-1975), as its national president (1975-1977), as organizer (1979) and chair (1979-1987) of the Federation for American Immigration Reform (FAIR), and as a board member of Population/Environment Balance (1980-1990).

2 For an excellent overview of these early human movements, see Davis, Kingsley, "The Migration of Human Populations," *Scientific American*, Vol. 231, No. 3, September 1974, p. 93-105. In my view, this article is one of the classics in immigration literature.

3 The main resource used to construct these population growth maps was *The Atlas of World Population History* by C. McEvedy and R. Jones (New York: Penguin Books, 1978) plus data published by the Population Reference Bureau, Inc., 1875 Connecticut Avenue, N.W., #520, Washington, D.C., 20009, 202-483-1100.

4 The dates for the historical events mentioned throughout this paper are taken from *The Timetables of History* by Bernard Grun (New York: Touchstone Books/Simon & Schuster, 1982). This book was originally published in German as Werner Stein's *Kulturfahrplan*—an excellent addition to the library of anyone with an interest in history.

5 Ecenbarger, William, "Flushed With Success." *Chicago Tribune Magazine*, 4 April 1993, p. 23.

6 Koch's Postulates:
1. Obtain an organism from a diseased individual.
2. Grow it in pure culture.
3. Inoculate a healthy individual with the organism and precipitate the original disease.
4. Successfully reculture the same organism from this newly infected individual.
Koch held that this sequence proved that the organism was the cause of the disease.

7 McNeill, William, in *Seeds of Change: A Quincentennial*. Herman Viola and Carolyn Margolis, eds. Washington, D.C.: Smithsonian Institution, 1991.

8 Moynihan, Daniel P., *Pandaemonium: Ethnicity in International Politics*. New York: Oxford University, 1993, p. 137-138.

9 Waldheim-Smith, Cecil, *The Great Hunger*. New York: Harper & Row, 1962; McNeill, op. cit.

10 Davis, op. cit, p. 99.

11 Davis, op. cit., p. 95, 100, 102.

12 Blonston, Gary, "Census Forecast for 2050 Gives Minorities Big Gains." *Detroit Free Press*, 4 December 1992, p. 3A.

13 Sands, David R., "1 in 3 Worldwide Can't Find a Job or Living Wage." *Washington Times*, 7 March 1994.

14 Homer-Dixon, Thomas F., Boutwell, Jeffrey H., and Rathjens, George W., "Environmental Change and Violent Conflict." *Scientific American*, February 1993, p. 38-45.

15 Travis, John, "Invader Threatens Black, Azov Seas." *Science*, Vol. 262, 26 November 1993, p. 1366-1367.

16 Thompson, Jon, "East Europe's Dark Dawn; The Iron Curtain Rises to Reveal a Land Tarnished by Pollution." *National Geographic*, June 1991, p. 36-69.

17 Kaplan, Robert D., "The Coming Anarchy." *Atlantic Monthly*, February 1994, p. 44-76; Raspail, Jean, *The Camp of the Saints*. New York: Charles Scribner's Sons, 1975; Homer-Dixon, op. cit.

18 Osborne, David, "The Power of Outdated Ideas." *Chicago Tribune*, 12 January 1992, p. 13.

19 *Universal Declaration of Human Rights*, Article 13, No. 2, 10 December 1948.

20 See, in general, "The State of World Population 1993." United Nations Fund for Family Planning.

Editorial Note: John invited the response of six people likely to object to this thesis. Their comments and his response can be found on *The Social Contract* website at www.TheSocialContract.com in the Archives Section, Volume V, No. 1. The above article is in Vol. IV, No. 3. A reprint of this material is available from *The Social Contract* Bookstore, located on the website.

APPENDIX C

Mary Lou Tanton's Viewpoint on Abortion

The following *Viewpoint* by Mary Lou was published on Wednesday, July 2, 1969, in the *Charlevoix Courier*. The law at the time allowed for an abortion only to save the life of the mother.

If no abortions were being done, critics of abortion law reform might have a point. The fact of the matter is that abortions *are* being done. A 1968 questionnaire sent to Michigan physicians indicates fifteen thousand women requested abortions. It is not known how many of these women resorted to self-induced or criminal abortions. It is known that criminal abortions are the leading cause of maternal death in our nation. An estimated one out of every five American women will have an "out-of-the-hospital" abortion by age forty-five. Only one-third of these will have the services of a medical doctor; the remaining 650 thousand will risk death or crippling at the hands of the criminal abortionist.

The present abortion law in Michigan accomplishes two things: It forces women to have children they don't want or to have an illegal abortion. It does not prevent them from having an abortion. What strange satisfaction derives from forcing a mother to the haunts of the criminal abortionist? Or from promoting compulsory pregnancy? To quote Dr. James Lieberman, Chief, Center for Studies of Child and Family Mental Health at the National Institute of Mental Health, "Pregnancy as punishment for sex has not been notably effective."

It has been suggested your readers "look at the places where such laws have been enacted and see what is happening . . ."

In June 1967 the California Legislature passed what was hailed in some quarters (and damned in others) as a "liberal" reform of the laws governing abortion. Yet under the new laws a couple of modest means, the parents of two idiot children, sought and were refused a hospital abortion to terminate the wife's accidental pregnancy. She bore a third idiot child.

A seventeen-year-old girl was seduced by an older man who was driving her home from a babysitting job. Her request for an abortion was denied. In an effort to abort the child, she leaped off the roof of her family garage and died in the fall.

A married woman was raped and became pregnant. Medical authorities approved an abortion, but the district attorney vetoed it on the grounds that her husband might really be the father of the child. The child was born, deeply resented by its "parents."

During 1968 nearly five thousand legal abortions were reported in California, a sevenfold increase above the estimated rate of therapeutic abortions before the new law. Yet these figures don't begin to make a dent in the estimated one hundred thousand dangerous illegal abortions performed in California each year. The "abortion mill" in that state remains in the "office" of the criminal abortionist! The total effect of that law has been so far from what its boosters had envisioned that some of the men and women who pressed for its passage are now trying to get an initiative on the ballot to have this, and the 1872 abortion law itself, repealed.

It must be borne in mind that contraceptives are not available to more than a fraction of the five million underprivileged women of childbearing age who need and in most cases want them. An estimated 4,500,000 have not practical access to contraceptives at all. Must these women be subject to "compulsory pregnancy" and "unwanted, unloved, uncared for" children? Certainly a prime birthright of every human being is to be wanted and loved . . . would we wish it otherwise?

The public in Michigan has developed an increasing awareness of the problems of public health. We have mustered our public and private health forces in a concerted attack on venereal disease. We no longer pretend V.D. doesn't exist, nor do we refuse to treat it. But in the abortion field where we deal primarily with the married (eighty-five to ninety percent), we ignore the problem and create what credible statisticians estimate is the third most extensive illegal and criminal apparatus in the nation.

"In a democratic secular society, those who oppose abortion should not deny medical protection to those who do not oppose it . . ." The foregoing is from a statement of beliefs of the Michigan women for Medical Control of Abortion. The following groups are among those urging reform or repeal of existing abortion laws:

Michigan State Medical Society, American Medical Association, American Public Health Association, American College of Obstetricians and Gynecologists, Florence Crittenton Association of America, Metropolitan Detroit Council of Churches, National YWCA, Detroit YWCA, Protestant Episcopal Church-Diocese of Michigan, Detroit Annual Conference of the Methodist Church, Unitarian Universalist Association, American Baptist Convention, American Friends Service Committee, American Civil Liberties Union, Planned Parenthood-World Population. Furthermore, in Michigan ninety-five percent of non-Catholic physicians and fifty-six percent of Catholic physicians have indicated they favor reform or repeal of Michigan's abortion law.

Some segments of our society are not exhibiting the same love and concern for existing children in need as for the unborn! Katherine Finseth, M.D., states: "There is a distinction between the unborn fetus, and the infant viable outside the uterus, in terms of the role that our social and medical institutions can play in its support . . . In a society in which there are current problems of child neglect, maternal misery, and considerable numbers of illegitimate pregnancies, these distinctions must be considered. In a world with prospects of overcrowding and major famines before the end of this century, these distinctions must be considered."

Appendix D
Social Contract Themes during John H. Tanton's Editorship

While John served as editor of *The Social Contract*, he selected the following themes for the quarterly journal. The themes were selected to prompt an interest in issues of emerging national significance.

The Uses and Misuses of History, Winter 1990-1991. John built this theme around the logical fallacy known as "False Analogy." Just because something worked in the past does not necessarily mean it will work again today. For example, just because high levels of immigration were assimilated during the first two decades of the century does not necessarily suggest the same is true today. When is it permissible to rely on history as precedent? When is it not?

A World Without Borders, Spring 1991. Music knows no borders. It is a universal language. On the other hand, the cells in our body, from the vantage of John's medical training, require semi-permeable borders. Without a membrane, the cell would be exposed to a host of complications. Impermeable membranes, on the other hand, would cause the cell to suffocate. This edition of *The Social Contract* assembled articles evaluating the applicability of history to the immigration debate. Might principles in the musician's world without borders be applicable to our world experiencing a daily net population gain of 230,000 people?

Politically Correct on Immigration, Summer 1991. John's editorial comments reviewed the three stages through which the United States was likely to progress as it reached the goal of a full and rational discussion of immigration policy:

1. The Emma Lazarus/Statue of Liberty Phase. In this phase, Emma Lazarus's poem on the Statue of Liberty is quoted in response to all questions on immigration policy: "Give me your tired, your poor, your huddled masses yearning to breathe free . . ." End of discussion.

2. The Caveat Phase. In this stage, thoughtful people would begin entertaining questions about immigration. Accordingly, the conversation would open apologetically: "I want you to know I'm not a racist, but I've been wondering about the wisdom of this aspect of the immigration policy . . . "

3. The Mature Phase. In this stage, the ethics of a rational immigration policy for the world and for our successors could be rationally discussed. In the summer of 1991, John expressed the belief that "we have been in the Caveat Phase for several years and seem to be arrested there."

Immigration and Free Trade with Mexico, Fall 1991. People instinctively favoring *inter*national "free" trade under various trade treaties would not favor *intra*national "free" trade if that would return us to the era before child labor laws, OSHA, Social Security Insurance, Workers Compensation, unemployment insurance, health plans, environmental controls, retirement plans, employee stock ownership plans, profit sharing, anti-trust regulations, etc. The protections established to confer dignity upon the work force and safety in our environment resulted from long, hard-fought battles. These reforms are undermined when our workers and our surroundings are placed in direct global competition under free trade treaties with other countries not affording similar protections.

Getting Past the Immigration Taboo, Winter 1991-1992. The U.N. High Commissioner for Refugees lists 18 million refugees worldwide. Additionally, 20 million people in Africa are displaced by natural or political causes. On the other hand, of the 160-plus countries belonging to the United Nations, only three openly admit appreciable numbers of legal immigrants. Of the world's population, approximately 3 billion people live under conditions that are either "not free" or "partially free." In China, the poverty level was set at thirty-eight dollars per year, and 50 million Chinese qualify.

The migration pressures are steadily increasing. Approximately 3 billion people worldwide could improve their circumstance by migrating to the few immigrant-receiving countries. And the potential pool of migrants is increasing by about 80 million per year. But worldwide, only about 3 million people are willingly received as immigrants each year. On the other hand, there are 3 billion potential migrants. That means only .1 percent are willingly received as immigrants.

Conclusion: The vast majority of people, 99.9 percent, according to John, will have to "bloom where they are planted." They will never be able to solve their personal or societal problems by moving away from them . . . The age of migration is at an end for all but the tiniest fraction of the human race. Sadly, the few who are able to pack up and leave are often the very ones on whom their fellow citizens most need to rely for social change—those with some education and a view of a better future, those whose dissatisfaction can energize them to help bring about the changes that could make life more acceptable at home. If these people leave, how will change ever come? Should we pat ourselves on the back for facilitating their exodus? The United States accepts approximately one million immigrants per year (including a low estimate for illegal alien flow), Canada receives about 150,000, and Australia accepts approximately 125,000.

Words, Symbols and Roadblocks in the Immigration Debate, Spring 1992. This edition of *The Social Contract* focused on the symbolism of the Statue of Liberty. Emma Lazarus's poem is, according to John, "arguably one of the most politically potent documents ever written in North America."

Twenty Years Later: A Lost Opportunity (remembering the 1972 report of the Commission on Population Growth and the American Future), Summer 1992. This *Social Contract* commemorated the twentieth anniversary of the first attempt to articulate a national population policy. As chair of the Sierra Club Population

Committee, John had testified before President Nixon's Commission on Population Growth and the American Future. The central message of the commission's report, as submitted to President Nixon in 1972 by John D. Rockefeller III, stated this: "After two years of concentrated effort, we have concluded that, in the long run, no substantial benefits will result from further growth of the Nation's population, rather that the gradual stabilization of our population would contribute significantly to the Nation's ability to solve its problems."

Insights from the 1972 report included quality of life gains, freedom of choice, the risks of just "coping," population as the amplifier of environmental decline, social consequences of population growth, the effect of further regulations to cope with population pressures, political overpopulation, population and national security, the fears of an aging population, and smaller families tending to liberate women and to foster women's rights. Twenty years later, John found a nation eagerly responding to the message by reducing its fertility but still unable to meaningfully discuss the effect of immigration at home and abroad.

Revealing the Costs of Immigration, Fall 1992. Since he began working on the immigration issue in the late 1960s, John professed that if reasonable people did not take up the issue and deal with it while moderate and socially acceptable measures would suffice, then it was likely the issue would end up in the streets. In this edition of *The Social Contract* the theme demonstrated that reasonable people in fact did not take up the issue, and it has ended up in the streets. The findings of a 1992 study revealed that more than fifty percent of the 1,933 defendants in a Los Angeles County study were identified as deportable, criminal aliens. This edition also featured studies on the costs of immigration on the welfare system.

The Role of Churches in Population Growth, Immigration and the Environment, Winter 1992-1993. John pointed out that the adherents of many faiths have often worked for high immigration levels, sometimes for noble reasons, and sometimes for less exalted reasons. Sincere ideas about the "brotherhood of man" or the "universalism that disdains national borders" leads some to argue for the unimpeded movement of people. On the other hand, some groups see immigration as the way to increase their numbers and to guarantee the continuance of their influence, political power, and existence. Roy Beck, international traveling correspondent for the national United Methodist Reporter, penned the lead story on religion and the environment.

A Land of Opportunity: Crime and Immigration, Spring 1993. Looking at the war on drugs, the Nigerian crime network, and Asian gangs, ethnic gangs, and the associated costs led to these cover stories. In his editorial comments, John stated, "If one has a problem, the first line of defense should be to limit its size, especially if the same actions will help address other difficulties such as unemployment, social discord, and population-induced environmental decline."

What Makes a Nation? Summer 1993. "'The land of the free and the home of the brave,'" according to John, "has enjoyed the attributes of a nation without thinking much about 'What makes a nation?'" There has been a reasonable degree of cohesiveness, though the 1992 Los Angeles race riots pitted the black against the Mexican against the Korean. Diversity is essential to a nation. It provides resourcefulness and the opportunity for new ideas to flourish. In asking "What makes a nation," this cover theme asks what it takes to make a functional political unit on the national level. What politics are needed to maintain (or reclaim) civility?

NAFTA and Immigration, Fall 1993. This was the second *Social Contract* in as many years resisting the drift toward globalism under free trade agreements. Money has the ability to scour the planet, at the speed of light, for the weakest child labor laws, the lowest worker safety standards, and the poorest environmental protections. As free trade agreements open the nation's borders to trade, they also freely undermine the protections developed during two hundred years of industrialization. As more goods cross the borders, more people follow. John also questions the effect of foreign economic growth on indigenous cultures and lifestyles. Free trade can become a form of imperialism. Moving U.S. jobs to Mexico is not equivalent to moving Mexicans into U.S. jobs, but they are two sides of the same economic coin. Both discriminate against America's poor. John's early concerns over surrendering national sovereignty to a multi-national trade tribunal are beginning to materialize. Even water from the Great Lakes might be considered a "commodity" under NAFTA, and thus subject to its control. Under Article VI of the U.S. Constitution, treaties such as NAFTA become the "supreme Law of the Land." Will the public trust in water resources yield to the quest for profits under international trade treaties?

An International Perspective on Migration, Winter 1993-1994. In this edition, John turned to international affairs. During his October 1993 Writer's Workshop in Washington, D.C., he scheduled people from Australia, New Zealand, the United Kingdom, and Germany to join writers from the United States. He reflected on the worldwide nature of the migration dilemma as he observed that this is not just an American concern. The lead article was authored by Ranginui Walker, a New Zealander of Maori descent. Walker presented the native peoples' view on immigration in New Zealand. "The reduction of the Maori to a position as one of many minorities," according to Dr. Walker, "negates their status as people of the land." John expressed the hope that, "Despite the dire prospects, those bold souls who cannot or will not give up will find in these pages some of the knowledge, ideas, and encouragement they need to press on in the quest for a more sane immigration policy."

End of the Migration Epoch, Spring 1994. The lead story in this edition of *The Social Contract* will likely be recognized as John's opus. It was entitled "End of the Migration Epoch? Time for a New Paradigm." The first section in this Appendix is dedicated to this essay. In his editorial comment in the Spring 1994 journal, John congratulated the *Atlantic Monthly* for having published articles on immigration every three to four months. The *Atlantic Monthly* is one of our nation's earliest magazines. In 1992, the *Atlantic Monthly* published articles on the U.S.-Mexican border and an article on the divisive relationships among ethnic groups in Los Angeles.

The U.S. Congress and U.S. Population Growth, Summer 1994. John's editorial comment focused on new and novel arguments for claiming refugee status. A Norwegian sailor claimed refugee status in Australia because his home country had not banned whaling. This was coupled with a backup claim that his nation of origin had jailed men for refusing compulsory military service.

If everyone is a refugee, then no one is a refugee. New bases for claiming refugee status include sexual orientation, Chinese objectors to the one-child policy, Seventh Day Adventists and Jews in Russia, athletes and musicians, those subject to tribal unrest, women in Islamic or other countries not attaining equal rights (approximately one billion would qualify here), people in Islamic countries wanting to use alcohol, Christians and Jews in fundamentalist Islam countries, smokers in countries opposing tobacco, and users of hallucinogenic drugs as a religious practice.

John suggests these problems—real in most cases—could never be solved just by moving people away from them. The numbers are far too great. The issues must be confronted on home ground. When the catalysts for change leave, the prospects for change are diminished.

Irredentism and the American Southwest, Fall 1994. Irredentism refers to the desire to regain a lost territory. Along the Mexican border, what might be seen as a separatist movement by Hispanic groups might actually be part of a Mexican irredentism movement. This is explored at length in this edition of *The Social Contract*. The edition was printed just days before California passed Proposition 187, in which voters decided to terminate social services to illegal residents in California. The financial burdens strained the system. John predicted the proposition would pass (as it did) and that the new idea would pass through four stages: first, wild enthusiasm when it was adopted; second, bitter disappointment if it were not implemented; third, a search for the guilty; and fourth, punishment of the innocent.

Camp of the Saints Revisited, Winter 1994-1995. *The Social Contract* brought Jean Raspail's *The Camp of the Saints* back into print. Remarkably, *The Camp of the Saints* became the cover story of the December 1994 *Atlantic Monthly*. In Raspail's work (first translated and released for U.S. publication in 1975), the overpopulated masses from the East converge upon the shores of Western nations. The West struggles with its compassion. The issue is taken to the streets.

Raspail foreshadows a world in which reasonable people are unable to responsibly address population and immigration issues in a timely manner.

Religious Lobbies and the Immigration Debate, Spring 1995. The cover asked whether individual churchgoers knew what religious groups were saying on their behalf. The lead story was written by Roy Beck. He focused on what major religious denominations had to say about immigration, while also exposing what Washington lobbying offices were actually doing. The two do not always coincide. John began to show the strains of attempting to enable reasonable people to discuss reasonable solutions to the immigration dilemma: "One needs courage and an optimistic nature to wade through such a collage of reports and essays and come up still willing to fight on! But we need the facts and clear-eyed assessments."

Blacks and Immigration, Summer 1995. In *The Social Contract,* John recognized the centennial anniversary of Booker T. Washington's Atlanta Exposition speech. While black leadership has never been particularly active on immigration policy questions, people of color continue to be jostled to the back of the bus by U.S. immigration policy.

One hundred years ago, on September 18, 1895, Booker T. Washington offered his "Cast Down Your Bucket Where You Are" speech. Washington pled for the hiring of blacks, rather than the importation of foreign workers. In his speech, Washington drew on a metaphor: "A ship lost at sea for many days suddenly sighted a friendly vessel. From the mast of the distressed vessel was seen a signal, 'Water, water; we die of thirst!' The answer from the other vessel at once came back: 'Cast down your bucket where you are.' A second time the signal: 'Water, water; send us water!' ran up from the distressed vessel. And the answer was the same: 'Cast down your bucket where you are.' The captain of the distressed vessel, at heeding the injunction, cast down his bucket. It surprisingly came up full of fresh, sparkling water from the mouth of the Amazon River. To those of my race who depend on bettering their condition in a foreign land or who underestimate the importance of cultivating friendly relations with the Southern white man, who is their next-door neighbor, I would say: 'Cast down your bucket where you are'—cast it down in making friends in every manly way of the people of all races by whom we are surrounded."

Weighing the Arguments, Fall 1995. This edition of *The Social Contract* attempted to again strike a balance. John's editorial comment acknowledged the noteworthy contributions of many immigrants, including Albert Einstein, Henry Kissinger, Sidney Poitier, and others. But before the score card was put away, he noted, the score card of others should also be considered. Noting that not all newcomers were Albert Einsteins, the lead story by James S. Robb included information on Guiseppe Esposito, father of the Mafia in America; Donovan Ellis, the man with twenty-six aliases who was arrested at least fifty times for a variety of crimes including firearms, drugs, armed robbery, and others; Sirhan Sirhan, Robert Kennedy's slayer; Michael Flannery, financier of the Irish Republican Army; Rosario Ames, active in Soviet espionage; Vyacheslav Kirillovich Ivankov, the highest ranking Russian mobster in America; and the Marielitos Boatlift in which Fidel Castro emptied his prisons of hardened criminals, sending them to the United States. Partially because of the Marielitos Boatlift, twenty-five percent of all federal prisoners in this country are foreign-born.

Other criminals include Meyer Lanski, kingpin of American crime, who immigrated to the United States from native Poland, Charles Ponzi, affable inventor of pyramid schemes; Colin Ferguson, mad executioner of the Long Island Railroad, and Sheik Omar Abdel-Rahman, the blind Islamic clerk from Sudan who organized fanatical followers into planting a massive bomb beneath the World Trade Center in 1993.

The objective in this *Social Contract* was not to diminish the positive benefits of immigration but rather to suggest that a rational discussion should acknowledge a balanced assessment of the pluses and minuses of international migration. John's editorial comment also noted Pope John Paul II's visit to the United States calling for an open-ended U.S. immigration policy. In response, John suggested charity should start at home, with the Vatican leading through example and opening its doors to immigrants without limit. The Vatican retains a formidable border and is perhaps the most rigorous border patrol in the world.

Affirmative Action for Immigrants, Winter 1995-1996. In his second lead story in as many editions, James S. Robb pointed to faculty hiring preferences, American university enrollment, government contracts, and affirmative action favoring the foreign born to the U.S. citizen. Other essays in this journal included a collage of material on population, immigration, language, and national unity.

Help in Analyzing the Debates, Spring 1996. Having recently completed a course on logic conducted by David G. Payne, Ph.D., John directed this edition of *The Social Contract* to evaluate logical fallacies in the immigration debate. Dr. Payne authored the lead story. Typical fallacies were exposed, such as ad hominem fallacies, ad populum fallacies, and causal fallacies. Logical fallacies can proceed in both directions. As an example of the causal fallacy, just because the federal deficit has been growing substantially since the adoption of the 1965 immigration bill does not, necessarily, suggest immigrants are solely responsible for the federal deficit.

The Battle for Official English, Summer 1996. In the Letter from the Editor, John focused upon language as the tie that binds a nation. Correspondingly, language differences divide people even when they are not physically distinguishable (for example, as in Sri Lanka). This edition of *The Social Contract* coincided with the efforts to bring an English language case from Arizona to the U.S. Supreme Court. With the assistance of U.S. Foundation, Arizona passed a constitutional amendment making English the official language of state government. It passed by a vote of 51.5 percent to 49.5 percent. This constitutional amendment was challenged as violating the right of free speech (presumably to speak in the language of choice while in the course of government duties and on the government payroll). The case drew national attention. Supporters of the constitutional amendment prevailed in a unanimous decision of the U.S. Supreme Court, but the decision was based exclusively on procedural issues. In a subsequent case involving substantive First Amendment issues, the constitutional amendment became emasculated.

Anchor Babies, the Citizen-Child Loophole, Fall 1996. This edition of *The Social Contract* analyzed the practice of granting citizenship to children born to illegal alien parents on U.S. soil. In 1992, nearly 96,000 babies were born to illegal aliens in California. Perhaps as many as 200,000 citizen-children were added to the population that year. John's editorial note compared this number with the average total annual migration to the United States. Between 1925 and 1965, the average annual total was 178,000! Anchor babies might exceed many other immigrant categories.

Looking Back on the 1996 Elections, Winter 1996-1997. John's editorial comment recognized then-Senator Spencer Abraham, of John's home state, becoming chair of the Immigration Subcommittee of the Senate Judiciary Committee. In making his announcement, Senator Abraham traveled not to his home state of Michigan but rather to California. There he appeared with a number of computer executives to deliver the message that Americans weren't good enough for the jobs they had to offer, so they were offering the jobs to low-paid workers from overseas.

Restraining the American Brain, Spring 1997. John's Letter from the Editor was entitled "The Reverse Brain Drain." Earlier editions of the journal had discussed the effects of placing American workers in front-line competition with the under-employed or unemployed of the world. In short, the wages, household incomes, and working conditions of America's neediest were declining. In this issue of *The Social Contract*, the effects of skilled migration were evaluated, resulting in not only a brain drain in foreign lands but also a brain restrain in the United States. The preferences in medical research fields for foreign-born scientists caused physician Mark Godec to profess, "Any nation that believes it can hire people from other countries to do its thinking is in serious trouble."

In reviewing the Rand Report on Higher Education, David Simcox of the Center for Immigration Studies highlighted the tensions and contradictions resulting from affirmative action in favor of foreigners on our campuses.

The Spring 1997 journal also included an excerpt from a 1928 book showing there is nothing new about the request by business and agriculture for cheap foreign labor. John reported he has continually heard from highly trained Americans complaining of *unfair* competition from foreigners. "It is time" according to John, "to address their very real employment concerns."

The Abuse of Asylum and Refuge, Summer 1997. As of 1997, approximately 20 million persons were registered as refugees with the United Nations High Commissioner for Refugees. By definition, refugees are persons living outside their country of origin, and hoping for admission to a third country (not the one they are currently in). The U.N. indicated another 4 million persons were internally displaced within their own countries, technically not refugees. Additionally, there were asylees: persons who had left (often illegally) their country of origin and fled into another nation where they were applying for residence. By U.N. definition, a "refugee" is someone fleeing because of "persecution or a well-founded fear of persecution on account of race, religion, nationality, or membership in a particular social group, or political opinion."

John pointed out there was no concept in the legislation that the social, political, economic, or environmental disruptions causing the refugee to flee might be only temporary, after which they could return home. Moreover, there was no notion that in returning home, the former refugee might help to resolve the disruptive conditions. There was also no concern about those left behind to live with the conditions the refugee might have helped to change. John recognized that a number of reforms were possible, but one of the most effective would be this: make asylum and refugee status temporary and not convertible to permanent status. This would be based on the understanding from the outset that when the home front settled sufficiently for a safe return, the asylee or refugee would return home to help their countries and societies make progress. "In the bigger picture and in the longer run," John said, "we need to think of Lech Walesa and Vacla Havel as examples. Either of them would have been readily accepted as an asylee or refugee and perhaps even feted with a tickertape parade to congratulate ourselves on our magnanimity. But they chose to stay and fight for what they believed in and made a better life for themselves and their countrymen in this and future generations. They should be our role models."

Carrying Capacity & Caring Capacity: Are They at Odds? Fall 1997. John offered the guest editorship of this journal to Lawrence Harrison, visiting scholar at the Center for International Affairs at Harvard University, and director of five missions in Latin America for U.S. AID between 1965 and 1981. Mr. Harrison has authored several books on cultural values and economic/political success. His letter from the (guest) editor stated: "when we try to apply ethical considerations to migration and immigration issues, the result is murky in the extreme. Ethics collide with one another. Those whose first allegiance is to humankind everywhere are likely to advocate less restrictive immigration policies. Those whose first allegiance is to human beings in their own society are likely to advocate a more restrictive approach, because open policies inevitably lead to costs for the receiving society, and, in the case of the United States at least, costs are often paid by the less affluent."

Dr. Harrison asked which position was more ethical? While he could not answer the question to his satisfaction, he clearly falls into the latter group. This is based on a practical, pragmatic approach to life, rather than more universal concerns. Because he might order his priorities differently, does that make him more right? More moral?

Dr. Harrison also expressed concerns about the division in our society along racial and ethnic fault lines, concerns that have been intensified by recent immigration volume. He wondered whether we can find our way out of the disagreement by debate of moral considerations? This led to his conclusion that we should let the people decide on the levels. "Let democracy work."

Australia's Identity Crisis, Winter 1997-1998. This issue of the journal spotlighted ten essays on the effects of immigration in Australia. John recognized an "astonishing correlation" of issues and concerns between North America and Australia. In case there is any doubt that demography is destiny, John reminded the reader of Malaysian prime minister Dr. Bin Mohamad Mahathir's threat to use the surging populations of developing nations as the ultimate weapon against the West.

Malthus Revisited, Spring 1998. The letter from the editor's desk was entitled "The Durable Rev. Malthus." John posed the following question: "Which of us expects our writings to still be under discussion two hundred years from now?" Thomas Robert Malthus achieved this distinction with his *Essay on the Principle of Population*, published anonymously on June 7, 1798. Irrespective of our personal views on the ethics of explosive demographics in certain nations and the migratory pressures on others, all participants in the debate will acknowledge that this essay is the foundation upon which other population studies exist.

As this edition of *The Social Contract* went to press, the *Detroit News* pronounced Malthus "thoroughly discredited" by the economic advances of the Industrial Revolution. Notwithstanding, the writings of Thomas Robert Malthus remain a durable building block in the evolution of Western thought. He held the first chair in economics in the West. He observed limits to growth in all biological systems. He found excess reproduction by all species—all would reproduce beyond the carrying capacity provided by their niche in the ecosystem. Thus, scenes of misery and vice would be visited upon the surplus population of all species.

The terms misery and vice were carefully selected. Vice refers to human intervention to excess population, such as war and infanticide. Misery, on the other hand, refers to involuntary intervention, such as famine and disease.

Efforts to discredit Malthus essentially reduce to an abiding belief in the intellect of the human species to rise above universal biological laws. John's editorial comment began to draw attention to the effect of prolonged, voluntary subreplacement level fertility in many of the developed nations.

Europhobia: The Hostility Toward European-Descended Americans, Summer 1998. This edition of *The Social Contract* rounded out eight full years of John's service as editor and publisher. In the summer of 1998, John retired as an ophthalmologist at the Burns Clinic in Petoskey and surrendered the editor's post at *The Social Contract* to Wayne Lutton.

Wayne has a Ph.D. in modern history, had served as associate editor of *The Social Contract* for six years, and had participated in the immigration debate for decades. John looked forward to concentrating on different aspects of the immigration question, chiefly fundraising and, outside of the structure of the U.S. Foundation, attempting to touch off the political phase of the immigration reform movement. John remained publisher of the journal after he resigned editorship.

In the opening remarks of this issue, John realistically conceded that a color line separates Americans. What started as a concern over a surging population's assault on the natural integrity of the land led to increasing recognition of cultural implications, culminating in the aptly titled theme "Europhobia."

Phobias are irrational fears. John looked at the demographic destiny of the United States and asked, "How might affirmative action work when there is no majority against whom claims can be made?"

APPENDIX E

Nothing More Can Be Done
. . . A Fable for Our Times

by John H. Tanton

Editorial note: This essay was written during John's five-year tenure as chair of the American Academy of Ophthalmology Low Vision Rehabilitation Committee in the early 1990s. It reveals his sensitivity and philosophy about the practice of medicine. The essay was distributed to all ophthalmologists in the United States and was also published in *Ophthalmology Clinics of North America*, Vol. 7, No. 2, June 1994.

Once upon a time there was a trial lawyer who was also a juvenile diabetic. Despite taking reasonably good care of his diabetes, he developed peripheral vascular complications and gangrene of one foot. A below-knee amputation was required. The attorney was concerned that with the leg removed, he might not be able to return to his usual promenading around the courtroom and an otherwise active lifestyle.

"Not to worry," his orthopedic surgeon reassured him. "Even though it is necessary to remove your lower leg, we have learned many ways through the years to replace the function with one sort of prosthesis or another. With a little luck and *some* work on your part, we should be able to get you back to nearly normal function."

The rehabilitation process started soon after surgery. Initially, the patient got up in a wheel chair to provide some mobility. When the edema and reaction of the operation began to subside and the patient could tolerate having the leg dependent, he was referred to physical therapy for long-arm crutches. The therapist made sure that they were of the right length and gave him some instruction in their use. He soon learned that it was easier to use two crutches than one, for this allowed a swing-through gait, and that if only one crutch were used it should be on the side opposite to the operated leg. These were minor points, but it made a big difference to the patient to have them explained.

After he was out of the hospital and back in his law office, he began to note that the long-arm crutches rumpled his suits and made his armpits sore. In addition, he was unable to carry papers very well. The physical therapist, who had stayed in touch with him during his rehabilitation process, suggested that he switch to the short Canadian crutches, which were much more convenient to use, left his hands free without setting the crutches aside, and made it easier for him to carry papers in a shoulder bag, which the physical therapist also suggested.

When the stump was finally healed, the orthopedic surgeon referred his patient to the prosthetist. When the artificial leg was ready, it was back to the physical therapist for gait training. Adjustments along the way were needed to the socket, after which a final leg was made, complete with an articulating ankle and a flesh-colored "skin."

In the end, the attorney was delighted: The focus of his care had been not just fixing the leg, but fixing the patient. The plan for his rehabilitation had been outlined beforehand, had been started early, and had been adjusted to his particular needs along the way. He had received encouragement and emotional support. His disease had led to a disability but, thanks to the care he had received, very little ultimate handicap.

Time passed, and our attorney developed diabetic maculopathy. His ophthalmologist went right to work, but despite the best that modern diabetic management, angiography, and laser treatment could offer, the patient ended up with 20/100 vision in his better eye, and with peripheral and central field defects to boot. The retinal specialist, who could no longer be bothered with such mundane things as refracting patients, announced in magisterial tones that the treatment was complete and that . . .

"Nothing more can be done."

He gave the attorney an appointment for a three-month follow-up examination, with the pupils to be dilated on arrival so the doctor could complete his examination with a minimum of time.

Our attorney went into a profound funk. He could no longer read well enough to keep up his legal practice and so was faced with unemployment and loss of income. He had difficulty measuring his insulin dosages, trouble getting around in dim lighting, and was unsure of himself crossing the street. His fellow pedestrians seemed to resent his awkward mobility and gave him no quarter. Since our patient's vision was impaired, he had lost the prime means of gathering information that might have led him to some rehabilitative measures for his new handicap.

Fortunately, a relative came to his rescue. She had read of an ophthalmologist who was actually interested in rehabilitating not only the eye, *but the whole patient*! The patient was kindly received at this doctor's office and was scheduled for a full one and a half hour examination. The ophthalmologist participated in the workup, but much of it was done by others who had been specifically trained in the rehabilitation of the visually impaired.

Our attorney was shown a range of *optical* aids such as high add bifocals, base-in prism reading half eyes, and a lighted pocket magnifier that once again allowed him to read the menu at business lunches in dimly lit restaurants. A theater buff, he was given a head-borne telescope that allowed him to follow the action on the stage.

Then he was introduced to a series of *nonoptical* aids, such as a white support cane, valuable not so much for support, but because it announced to his fellow pedestrians that he had some visual difficulties, to which they might defer. He was shown devices for measuring his insulin dosage and was given absorptive lenses to help out with glare problems. He was surprised to learn how much yellow lenses could improve visibility under marginal conditions. A closed-circuit TV (CCTV) also proved to be a big help for his legal work.

Finally, he was told about some *social service* items that were available. For instance, although he was no longer able to see well enough to qualify for a driver's license, he was able to obtain the non-driver's card issued by many driver's license bureaus to serve as an identification document. He was introduced to a low vision support group, where similarly affected patients exchanged ideas on what had worked best for them, and where they gained confidence and discharged some of their frustrations.

In the end, it turned out that there was indeed a great deal more that could be done, if not for the eye, at least *for the patient as a whole*. Our disabled attorney was rehabilitated to the point where he could resume his law practice on a satisfactory, if somewhat less intense, level.

But his pleasure with the low vision rehabilitation services he had received was balanced by his anger at the doctor who had treated only his eye and then dumped him back on the street. At his next follow-up visit, he confronted his surgeon with the contrast in rehabilitation care that he had received from ophthalmology as compared with orthopedics. The ophthalmologist stammered a bit, saying something about being a highly trained specialist, about being very busy, that there was no money to be made in low vision rehabilitation work, and that ophthalmology was a fairly narrow field whose practitioners couldn't be expected to know very much about the whole patient in which the eye rides around.

The attorney took into account that the medical care had been first rate. He settled out of court for just his economic loss between the time his ophthalmic care was completed and when he had finally found rehabilitation services on his own.

The Morals of the Story
 I. Even though it may be true that nothing more can be done for the eye, it is *almost never true* that nothing more can be done for the *patient*.
 II. Providing rehabilitation services for their visually impaired patients is the medical and moral—and will likely soon become the legal responsibility of all ophthalmologists. It is no

more acceptable for an ophthalmologist to abandon a patient once the medical treatment is completed, but before needed rehabilitation services have been provided, than it would be for an orthopedic surgeon to abandon an amputee to hopping around on one leg. The difference is that common public knowledge would condemn an orthopedist who acted in this way, whereas a similar deficiency in the ophthalmic field is not yet so apparent to the layman. The ophthalmologist must *either provide* these services or *refer* the patient to someone who does.

III. Low vision rehabilitation services should start *early*, as soon as the patient's disease proves disabling, and long before a handicap is well established. The mild measures needed in the early stages of visual decline are often simple, inexpensive, and relatively easy to provide. They should be available as part of the routine care offered by every ophthalmologist.

APPENDIX F

Mary Lou Tanton's Twenty-Five Most Influential Books

The following list has been prepared by Mary Lou.

Childhood
1. *Holy Bible*
   Old and new testaments were studied and verses memorized.
2. *Girls' Stories of Great Women* by Elsie Egermeier
   This book gives inspiring accounts of women's achievements.
3. *A Child's Garden of Verses* by Robert Louis Stevenson
   This is a favorite book with timeless illustrations by Jessie Willcox Smith.
4. *Heidi* by Johanna Spyri
   Heidi exemplifies respect for elders as well as empathy, grit, and determination.
5. *Folk Tales Children Love* published by Platt & Munk Co and edited by Watty Piper
   These are stories with morals, a favorite folk reading.
6. *The Good Master* by Kate Seredy
   This book provides memorable lessons in human kindness.
7. *Complete Works of James Whitcomb Riley*
   These volumes were a gift from my Grandfather DeGraff and foster love and respect for rural family living.
8. *Junior Scholastic* and *Weekly Reader*
   These cover current events—specifically economics, geography, and politics.
9. *Huckleberry Finn* by Mark Twain
   This is enjoyable reading for its personal loyalties and unique literary style.
10. *The Little Prince* by Antoine de Saint Exupéry
    The Little Prince is a tale of hidden truths and of what really matters.

257

Adult Life

11. *Nineteen Eighty-Four* by George Orwell
    A futuristic book, revealing of human interactions.
12. *Brave New World* by Aldous Huxley
    The first of several Huxley creations read and yet to be reread.
13. *The Prophet* by Kahil Gibran
    A book of heartening joys and truths.
14. *The Power of Myth* by Joseph Campbell
    Describes important links with past beliefs and practices.
15. *Heroes and Hero Worship*
    Presents the hero as divinity, prophet, poet, priest, man of letters, king.
16. *A Touch of Greatness* by Harold Kohn
    Gives examples that lives of great men remind us we can make our lives sublime.
17. *Uncle Tom's Cabin* by Harriet Beecher Stowe
    A story of slavery and race relations in the United States.
18. *Silent Spring* by Rachel Carson
    This book sounded the alarm for stewardship of our planet Earth.
19. *North with the Spring* by Edwin Way Teale
    Records the seventeen-thousand-mile journey with North American spring.
20. *The Population Bomb* by Paul Ehrlich
    This book heralded efforts to control the U.S. birth rate.
21. *Babies by Choice or By Chance* by Alan F. Guttmacher
    Discusses the importance of birth control for effective family planning.
22. *A Sand County Almanac* by Aldo Leopold
    This beautiful work links the human spirit with wild things and wilderness.
23. *Desert Solitaire* by Edward Abbey
    An autobiographical melding of sensitive human and desert life.
24. *Human Options* by Norman Cousins
    Demonstrates that humans determine and guide attitudes in life and health crises.
25. *Pioneer of the Future* by Margaret Sanger and Emily Taft Douglas
    Chronicles Sanger's pioneering birth control and social conscience.

APPENDIX G

John H. Tanton's Twenty-Five Most Influential Books

The following list has been prepared by John. It is roughly in the order of priority.

Childhood
1. *Bible* (King James version)
   I read it all the way through two times ("begats" and all). I learned many quotes and precepts from it, which show up even today in such items as "The Jonah Syndrome" paper; the English is also fine, as in Psalm 90:10: "The days of our years are threescore years and ten; and if by reason of strength four score."
2. *Webster's Unabridged Dictionary*
   This was a regular dinner table companion, thanks to my wordsmith father.
3. *Compton's Encyclopedia*
   This was the encyclopedia my folks bought for us.
4. *National Geographic*
   Provided basic sex education and travel.
5. *Life/Post* Magazines
   For photos and jokes.
6. *Michigan Farmer* newspaper
   Covered progressive farming.
7. *Organic Farmer Journal*
   Covered even more progressive farming.
8. *Sebewaing Blade*
   Provided the weekly gossip/news sheet.
9. *Bay City Times*
   Our daily newspaper.

Adult Life

10. *Bartlett's Familiar Quotations*
    Consulted almost daily—sometimes several times a day.
11. *American Heritage Dictionary*
    Consulted almost daily and copiously underlined.
12. *Encyclopedia Britannica* (1975 Edition)
    Consulted weekly or more frequently.
13. *A Conflict of Visions* by Thomas Sowell
    See especially Chapter 2—a sensible world view ("weltanschauung").
14. *Voyage of the Beagle* and *Origin of Species* by Charles Darwin
    Exciting travel and basic evolutionary biology.
15. "The Migration of Human Populations" by Kingsley Davis, *Scientific American*, September, 1994, Vol. 231, No. 3, pp. 93-105.
    The seminal human migration article.
16. *Population Bomb* by Paul Ehrlich
    This had a big influence on me. I bought copies by the case and handed them out. I became friends with Ehrlich, and we hosted the Hardin Festschrift together.
17. Population Reference Bureau *Bulletins*
    About the only source of demographic information in the late '50s when I got started.
18. *The Living Wilderness*
    This is a journal of the Wilderness Society; I read each issue cover to cover. It fueled my interest in wilderness and natural areas preservation.
19. *A Sand County Almanac* by Aldo Leopold
    Classic on a land ethic.
20. *Lonely Land* by Sigurd F. Olson
    A classic book on backcountry canoe travel.
21. *Report of the Commission on Population Growth and the American Future* (1972)
    A basic set of documents on population.
22. *Limits to Growth* by Donella Meadows
    This is the foundational text on this topic, which led to the Mitchell Conferences and my paper on immigration that launched FAIR.
23. *Costs of Economic Growth* by Ezra Mishan
    A skeptic's view of the benefits of economic growth by a British economist.
24. *Decline and Fall of the Roman Empire* by Edward Gibbon
    First among many readings on history.
25. *Life of Dr. Johnson* by James Boswell
    Great language, quotes, and sayings.

APPENDIX H

"Cast Down Your Bucket Where You Are"

by John H. Tanton

In the following comments written on April 10, 2000, John offers thoughts on Booker T. Washington's essay regarding employment opportunities for the underprivileged in the United States.

At the Atlanta and Cotton States and International Exposition held in 1895, Booker T. Washington, the founder of the Tuskegee Institute, gave a famous speech that has come to be known by the phrase at the head of this article.

Thirty years after the close of our Civil War, Washington was looking for a way "Up from Slavery" (as he titled his autobiography) for those so recently freed from bondage. He thought he saw a good avenue in the expanding industrialization coming to our nation, if only the captains of industry would offer jobs to blacks, rather than import workers from overseas. Here in part is what he wrote:

> *A ship lost at sea for many days suddenly sighted a friendly vessel. From the mast of the distressed vessel was seen a signal, "Water, water, we die of thirst!" The answer from the other vessel at once came back: "Cast down your bucket where you are." A second time the signal: "Water, water; send us water!" ran up from the distressed vessel. And the answer was the same: "Cast down your bucket where you are." The captain*

of the distressed vessel, at heeding the injunction, cast down his bucket. It surprisingly came up full of fresh, sparkling water from the mouth of the Amazon River.

To those of my race who depend on bettering their condition in a foreign land or who underestimate the importance of cultivating friendly relations with the Southern white man, who is their next-door neighbor, I would say: "Cast down you bucket where you are"—cast it down in making friends in every manly way of the people of all races by whom we are surrounded.

To those of the white race who look to the incoming of those of foreign birth and strange tongue and habits for the prosperity of the South, were I permitted I would repeat what I say to my own race, "Cast down your bucket where you are."

Washington went on to urge that blacks be given jobs as the industrial economy developed. For the most part, the employers looked overseas instead.

Another contemporary of Washington's shared his views. Frederick Douglass wrote in his biography *My Bondage and My Freedom* that "The old employments by which we have heretofore gained our livelihood are gradually, and it may seem inevitably, passing into other hands. Every hour sees the black man elbowed out of employment by some newly arrived immigrant whose hunger and whose color are thought to give him a better title to the place."

Today's low unemployment rate still leaves blacks with twice the level of unemployment of whites. But it gives us the best opportunity of a generation to realize Washington's dream for advancement of all the folks at the bottom of the socioeconomic pile. This is not through some government redistribution or welfare program; it is through the workings of a free labor market. A tight labor market is the working man's best friend, for it will improve wages and conditions, will help level the income disparity that has been growing in recent years, and sends strong signals as to where the opportunities are . . . and aren't. The tight labor market has been the key factor in enabling us to reduce welfare roles. So let's celebrate it, rather than make it into bad news.

Journalist Ben Wattenberg in his book *The Good News Is the Bad News Is Wrong* contends there are three maxims in the news business: Bad News is Good News; Good News is No News; and finally Good News is Bad News. We can apply this to the treatment of the unemployment rate. Back when it was high, that was Bad News (and hence good copy); when the rate fell, that was good news, and hence not worthy of much reporting; and now that the rate is at record lows, that has become Bad News, for employers supposedly can't find workers (at the wages and conditions they'd like to offer.

Let's join Booker Washington in calling on American business to "Cast Down Your Bucket Where You Are" by letting the much-admired free market work its magic via the Smithian "Invisible Hand."

Editorial Note: Booker T. Washington's speech can be found at www.TheSocialContract.com by searching for his name.

Endnotes

1. 1999 World Population Data Sheet. Population Reference Bureau.
2. Population Reference Bureau, P.O. Box 96152, Washington, DC 20090-6152. Web site: www.prb.org/.
3. Hardin, Garrett, Living within Limits. Oxford University Press, 1993, p. 161.
4. Philanthropic is derived Greek, late Latin, and French, meaning love of mankind. Barnhart, Robert K., The Barnhart Concise Dictionary of Etymology. Harper Collins, 1995.
5. See Statistics maintained by the United Nations High Commissioner for Refugees at www.unhcr.ch/.
6. *2000 World Population Data Sheet*. Population Reference Bureau.
7. Hardin, Garrett, *Living within Limits*. Oxford University Press, 1993.
8. Meadows, Donella H., Meadows, Dennis L., Randers, Jorgen, and Behrens, William W. III, *The Limits to Growth*. Potomac Associates, New American Library, 1972.
9. Tanton, John H., "International Migration As an Obstacle to Achieving World Stability." *The Economist*, July 1976, p. 221-227.
10. Brown, Mary Elizabeth, *Shapers of the Great Debate on Immigration, a Biographical Sketch*. Greenwood Press, 1999.
11. Starch, Roper, *Attitudes toward U.S. Population Size and Growth*. Prepared for Negative Population Growth, March 1996.
12. Tanton, John H., "International Migration As an Obstacle to Achieving World Stability." *The Economist*, July 1976, p. 221-227.
13. A summary of the legislative activity on the Simpson-Mazzoli Bill can be found in Graham, Otis L. Jr., "Uses and Misuses of History in the Debate over Immigration Reform." *The Social Contract*, Winter 1990-1991, p. 45. This article can also be retrieved from www.TheSocialContract.com.
14. Reimers, David M., *Unwelcome Strangers, American Identity and the Turn against Immigration*. Columbia University Press, 1998, p. 116.
15. Replacement level fertility refers to the total fertility rate (TFR). Demographers tell us a TFR of 2.1 children per women is "replacement level." The ".1" accounts for early mortality.
16. Bouvier, Leon F., and Bertrand, Jane T., World Population, *Challenges for the 21st Century*. Seven Locks Press, 1999, p. 3.
17. Cooper, Mary H., "Population and the Environment." *CQ Researcher*, Congressional Quarterly, Vol. 8, No. 26, 17 July 1998, p. 618, quoting from "New Perspectives on Population: Lessons from Cairo," *Population Bulletin*, Natural Resources Defense Council, March 1995. See also "Global Issues, Selections from the *CQ Researcher*," Congressional Quarterly, 2001.

18. Beck, Roy, and Kolankiewicz, Leon, "The Environmental Movement's Retreat from Advocating U.S. Population Stabilization (1970-1998): A First Draft of History." *Journal of Policy History*, Pennsylvania State University, Vol. 12, No. 1, 2000. Also found at www.NumbersUSA.com, scroll to Issues, Environment.

19. Brown, Lester R., and Kane, Hal, *Full House*. W. W. Norton, 1994.

20. Tanton, John H., "International Migration As an Obstacle to Achieving World Stability." *The Economist*, July 1976, p. 227.

21. According to the Population Reference Bureau Glossary found at www.prb.org, the Total Fertility Rate (TFR) means: "The average number of children that would be born alive to a woman (or group of women) during her lifetime if she were to pass through her childbearing years conforming to the age-specific fertility rates of a given year. This rate is sometimes stated as the number of children women are having today."

22. U.S. Census Bureau, "Population Profile of the United States: 1997." *Current Population Reports*, Series P23-194, U.S. Government Printing Office, Washington, D.C., 1998, p. 9.

23. Lytwak, Ed, A Tale of Two Futures: *Changing Shares of U.S. Population Growth*. NPG Forum, March 1999, p. 5.

24. A FAIR Plan: An Immigration Reform Agenda for the 106th Congress. The Federation of American Immigration Reform, 1999.

25. See, for example, Wilson, Edward O., *The Diversity of Life*. Harvard University Press, 1992.

26. Sowell, Thomas, *A Conflict of Visions*. William Morrow, 1988.

27. *Skirmish in a Wider War* became the title of John H. Tanton's oral history conducted by Otis L. Graham Jr., Ph.D., on April 20 and 21, 1989. A copy of the oral history can be found with John's preserved papers at the University of Michigan Bentley Historical Library.

28. The reflections can be found in John H. Tanton's oral history, *Skirmish in a Wider War*, conducted by Otis L. Graham Jr., Ph.D., on April 20 and 21, 1989. A copy of the oral history can be found with John's preserved papers at the University of Michigan Bentley Historical Library.

29. U.S. Bureau of the Census, Document CPH-133, "1990 Census: Languages Spoken at Home and Ability to Speak English for Persons 5 Years and Over." Reprinted in *The Social Contract*, Vol. VI, No. 2, Winter 1995-1996.

30. In an officer safety bulletin released by the U.S. Department of Justice on October 25, 2000, FAIR was listed with several other organizations as an "anti-immigration and hate crime organization." Shortly after the study was released, FAIR was removed from the list. Nevertheless, this experience demonstrates how hate crimes legislation can be used to chill legitimate debate.

31. Mark Landler, et al, "What Happened to Advertising?" *Business Week*, 23 September 1991; Alan Durning, *How Much Is Enough?* W. W. Norton, 1992.

32. Miller, John, *Egotopia*. The University of Alabama Press, 1997, p. 42.

33. United States Supreme Court Justice Potter Stewart relied upon this oft-quoted phrase in defining "obscenity" under the First Amendment in *Jacobillis v Ohio*, 378 U.S. 184; 84 S. Ct. 1676; 12 L. Ed. 2d 793 (1964).

34. Personal correspondence from Mary Lou Tanton.
35. "Patterns on the Land: Our Choice—Our Future." *Michigan's Trend Future*, Michigan Society of Planning Officials, 1995, p. 4.
36. Kunstler, James Howard. *The Geography of Nowhere*. Simon & Schuster, 1993, p. 131.
37. Taxpayers for Common Sense, *Road to Ruin*. ISBN 1-888-415-12-6, 1999.
38. Wilson, Edward O., *Consilience, the Unity of Knowledge*. Alfred A. Knopf, 1998.
39. Hepworth, James R., and McNamee, Gregory, *Resist Much Obey Little, Remembering Ed Abbey*. Sierra Club Books, 1996.
40. Tennyson, Lord Alfred, *The Princess*. 1847.
41. May, Heather, "'English Only' the Only Way, Advocate Says." *Salt Lake Tribune*, 15 October 2000.
42. Lutton, Wayne, and Tanton, John H., *The Immigration Invasion*. The Social Contract Press, 1994.
43. Leading essays from the first five years of *The Social Contract* have been set forth in *Immigration and the Social Contract, The Implosion of Western Societies*. Edited by John H. Tanton, Denis McCormack, and Joseph Wayne Smith, Ashgate Publishing Limited, 1996.
44. Cooper, Mary H., "Population and the Environment." *CQ Researcher*, Congressional Quarterly, Vol. 8, No. 26, 17 July 1998, p. 618, quoting from "New Perspectives on Population: Lessons from Cairo," *Population Bulletin*, Natural Resources Defense Council, March 1995. See also "Global Issues, Selections from *The CQ Researcher*," Congressional Quarterly, 2001.
45. Ellis, Joseph J., *American Sphinx, the Character of Thomas Jefferson*. Alfred A. Knopf, 1997, p. 69.
46. The Thomas Jefferson quotes were derived from the following sources: http://etext.lib.virginia.edu/jefferson/quotations/jeffcont.htm and from *Thomas Jefferson Writings*, Merrill D. Peterson, ed., The Library of America, 1984.
47. Durant, Will and Ariel, *The Lessons of History*. MJF Books, 1968, p. 20.
48. *1999 World Population Data Sheet*. Population Reference Bureau.
49. *Replacement Migration: Is It a Solution to Declining and Ageing Populations?* United Nations, Population Division, Department of Economic and Social Affairs, United Nations Secretariat, 2000, p. 7. A copy of this study can be found at www.un.org/esa/population/unpop/htm.
50. *Replacement Migration: Is It a Solution to Declining and Ageing Populations?* United Nations, Population Division, Department of Economic and Social Affairs, United Nations Secretariat, 2000, p. 135. A copy of this study can be found at www.un.org/esa/population/unpop/htm.
51. Bouvier, Leon F., *Fifty Million Californians*. Center for Immigration Studies, 1991.
52. Quammen, David, "Planet of Weeds." *Harper's*, October 1998.

Index

A
AARR, 110, 140
Abbey, Edward, 130, 258
Abraham, Spencer, 245
Affirmative Action, 244-245, 249
AICF, 83
Alcohol and Drug Awareness Hour, 110, 162
alfalfa, 21-22
American Alliance for Rights and Responsibilities, 110, 140
American Cancer Society, 14
American Heritage Dictionary, 260
American Immigration Control Foundation, 83
American Sphinx, 267
Ames, 243
amnesty, 82
Anchor Babies, 244-245
Ann Arbor, Michigan, 25, 57
Anthony, Susan B., 2, 172
aplastic anemia, 25
Arizona, 109, 135, 137, 244
arsenic, 204
art of the possible, 30, 164
Artesian Street, 18
asylee, 246
Atlantic Monthly, 88, 145, 229, 240-241

Atlas of World Population History, The, 228
Audubon Society, 58-59
Australia, 162, 187-188, 219, 221, 237, 240, 247

B
Bailey, Tom, 169, 278
Baltimore, 208
Bangladesh, 217
Barnes, Sherry, 70-71, 278
Bartholdi, 67
Bartlett's Familiar Quotations, 260
basketball, 23
Bates, Nancy Bell, 57
Bay City Times, 259
Bear River, 58
Bear River Commission, 58
Beck, Roy, 31, 88-89, 92, 99, 101, 111, 239, 242
Beckley, Jean, 58
bees, 12, 21, 28, 53, 118, 157-158
Behrens, William W. III, 265
Bell, Alexander Graham, 57, 208
Bering, Vitus, 203, 206
Bern Convention, 211
Bertrand, Jane T., 265
Bible, 257, 259
Bikales, Gerda, 63, 69, 135, 138, 278
Birchwood Farms, 47
Blonston, 228

Boston, 213
Boswell, James, 260
Boutwell, Jeffrey H., 228
Bouvier, Leon, 265, 267
Bricker, Kathryn, 108, 277
Bringing out the Best in Ourselves, 110
British Parliament, 206
Brown, Keith, 13-14, 179-180
Buck, Israel, 13
Burns Clinic, 28, 46, 79, 107-108, 184, 248
Business Week, 266
bypass, 124-127, 130

C
California, 49, 70-72, 123, 160, 232, 241, 245
Calloway, Niki, 111, 277
Cambridge University, 141
Camp of the Saints, 229, 241
Canada, 18, 60, 134, 187, 200, 219, 237
Canadian Expeditionary Forces, 18
cataract surgery, 28
Census Bureau, 66, 89, 91, 97, 99-101, 116, 216, 266
Center for International Affairs, 247
chain, 35, 39, 88
Charlevoix, 46, 53, 231
Cheboygan, 53

269

Index

Chevron Conservation Award, 166, 168-169, 183
Chicago, 24, 61-62, 146, 228
Club of Rome, 62, 185
Clyde, 210
CNS, 111
Colorado, xi, 109, 135, 137, 166, 182
Coming Anarchy, 229
Compton's Encyclopedia, 259
Conflict of Visions, 114, 260, 266
Conner, Roger, 61, 68, 73, 84, 168
conservation ethic, 8, 29, 68, 160, 163
Conservation Fund, 167
Conservation News Service, 111
conservationist, 22, 52, 137, 168, 174
contraceptive, 57, 59
Cook, James, 206
Cooke, Alistair, 135
Cooper, Mary H., 265, 267
copyright, 143, 211
corn, 15, 21, 211
Costs of Economic Growth, 260
Cowell Foundation, 89
cows, 16, 20-22
Cronkite, Walter, 135
Current Population Reports, 199, 266
Cutler, M. Rupert, 168

D
Dammann, Tom, 144
Darwin, Charles, 2, 260
Davis, Bob, 124
Davis, Kingsley, 214, 260
Decline and Fall of the Roman Empire, 260
Defenders of Wildlife, 168

Defoe, Daniel, 205
DeGraff, Martin M., 13
deism, 19
Delta Upsilon, 6-7, 24, 59
democracy, 1, 68, 79, 116, 134, 247
Democracy in America, 77, 79
Denver, 24, 35, 43, 56
deOlazarra, Laura (Tanton), 56-57, 79, 278
Department of Natural Resources (*also see DNR*), 46, 52
desertification, 217
DeTocqueville, Alexis, 77
Detroit, 18, 24, 46, 228, 233, 248
Devon, 16-17
Diamond, Stanley, 133, 135
dictatorship, 1
Diemerbrock, 204
diphtheria, 214
DNR, 46-47
Donner Pass, 54
Douglas, Emily Taft, 258
Douglas Lake, 162
Douglas, William O., 117
Douglass, Frederick, 262
Durant, Wil and Ariel, 149, 267
Durning, Alan, 266
Duroc, 14

E
E Pluribus Unum, 110
Earth Day, 58, 60-62, 69, 89
Ecenbarger, William, 228
Ecologist, The, 62-63, 72, 185
Egotopia, 118, 266

Ehrlich, Paul, 58, 61-62, 69, 89, 258, 260
Einstein, Albert, 66, 243
Ellis, Donovan, 243
Emergency Committee on Puerto Rican Statehood, 110
emergency fund, 71
Emmet County Planning Commission, 56
employer sanctions, 93
End of the Migration Epoch, viii, 78, 201
English Language Advocates, 32, 110
Environmental Fund, 71, 80
Environmental Protection Act, 8, 43, 45, 167, 170, 172
environmentalist, 22
equality, 143-145, 147-150
Essay on the Principle of Population, 248
Ethnicity in International Politics, 228
Evangelical United Brethren Church, 19
exchange dessert, 6

F
Fahrenheit, 206
FAIR,32, 61, 63, 69-74, 80, 82-85, 93, 96, 108, 135, 140, 168, 227, 260, 266
Faraday, 207-208
Fenlon, Ned, 48
Ferguson, Colin, 243
Fessenden, 208
Fischer, John, 52
Flagler, Henry M., 71
Flannery, Michael, 243
Florida, 71-72, 109, 135, 137
Flushed With Success, 228

Index

Ford, Henry, 66, 211
Foresight, 27, 29, 55, 74, 111, 124, 174-176
Forest Service, 42
Four Horsemen of the Apocalypse, 212
France, xii, 79, 200, 211, 219
fraternity, 6, 24, 46, 59
freedom 12, 94, 97, 104, 119, 143-147, 149-151, 166, 198, 217, 238
Freedom House, 217
Friends of Oregon, 125
Fulton, 210

G
Galens, 24
Galileo, 2, 172
Gibbon, Edward, 260
Gleason, Gale, 46-47
Goldsmith, Teddy, 62
Graham, Otis, 70
Grandma Denning, 15
Great Books Foundation, 109, 277
Great Lakes, 8, 84, 109, 173, 240
Growth & Development Forum, 110, 124-125

H
Hampshire sheep, 14 8, 179-1806, 161-162
Hansen, Marcus L., 199
Harbor Springs, 47-48
Hardin, Garrett, 35, 39, 61-62, 71, 113, 139-140, 151, 182
Harris, Jay, 71
Harrison, John, 206
Harrison, Lawrence, 247
Hart, Senator Philip A., 42, 74
Hartwick Pines, 58
Harvard University, 24, 247, 266

Harvey, Ardman, 199
Hayakawa, Senator, 133, 135
heretics, ix, 1-3, 160, 172
Hertz, 208
Hillsdale, 13, 15
Hillsdale County, 13-14
Holmes, Oliver Wendell, 208
Holstein cattle, 14
How Much Is Enough?, 266
Huddleston, Senator, 72
Humphrey, Hubert, 62

I
identification, 93, 254
Imhoff, Gary, 69, 72
Immigration Reform Political Action Committee, 63
Irish, David, 277
Irish Hills, 8
Irish Republican Army, 243
Irredentism, 241
Isle Royale, 41
Ivankov, Kirillovich, 243

J
Jefferson, Thomas, 2, 19, 65-66, 147-149, 267
Jenner, 206
Jonesville, 14

K
Kane, Hal, 266
Kant, Immanuel, 133
Kaplan, Robert D., 229
Kappa Alpha Theta, 5-7
Keene, Private Investigator, 15
Kelvin, Lord, 55, 208, 210
Kennedy, Edward M., 66
Kennedy, John F., 52
Kennedy, Robert, 243

King, Martin Luther, xiii, 66, 115
Knoxville, Tennessee, 42
Koch, 17, 21, 209, 228
Koch, Grandfather, 17, 21
Kolankiewicz, Leon, 31, 92, 101, 266
Koury, Dorothy, 111
Kyser, Rev. Roert, 111, 277-278

L
Lady Liberty, 67
LaGraff, 13
Lake Huron, 84
Lake Superior, 41
Lake Tahoe, 54
Lamm, Richard D., ix
Landler, Mark, 266
Lanski, Meyer, 243
Lao-Tse, 85
Larson, Earl, 52
Lazarus, Emma, 66-68, 75, 236-237
League of Conservation Voters, 58
Learned Hand, 103
Leeuwenhoek, 205
legumes, 21
Leopold, Aldo, 42, 160, 258, 260
Lessons of History, 149, 267
Liberty Enlightening the World, 67, 223
Life of Dr. Johnson, 260
Limits to Growth, 62, 185, 248, 260, 265
Limits to Growth Conference, 62, 185
Lincoln, Abraham, 2, 66
Lintz, Carolyn, 7
Little Traverse Conservancy, 32, 43, 51-53, 108, 167-169
Living within Limits, 265
Locke, John, 2, 66

Lodge, Henry Cabot, 66
Lodgson, Gene, 11, 123
London, xi, 24, 204, 208-209
Lonely Land, 260
low vision, 28, 251, 254-255
Lowell, James Russell, 165
Lumley, Linda, 166
Lutheran Church, 18, 88
Lutton, Wayne Ph.D., 111, 248, 278
Lytwak, Ed, 266

M
Macadam, 210
MacJannett, Merle, 165
Mackinac, 53
Mafia, 243
Malthus, Thomas Robert, 212, 248
Marconi, 207-208
Mariel Boat Lift, 73
Maxwell, 207-208
Mazzoli, Romano, 72, 74
McAlpin, K.C., 83, 278
McNamee, Gregory, 267
McNeill, William, 228
Meadows, Daniel, 265
Meadows, Donella H., 260
Michigan Natural Areas Council, 25, 42
Michigan Society of Planning Officials, 267
Michigan State University, 5, 16, 21, 23-25, 182-183
Michigan United Conservation Club, 168
Migration Epoch, 201, 219, 227, 240
Milliken, Governor William, 51, 68, 166
Mishan, Ezra, 260

Mitchell Prize, x, 72, 96, 185-186
momentum, 91, 124, 152, 216
Monroe Creek, 46-48
Montgolfier, 206
Morgagni, 206
Morse, 207-208
Morton, William T., 62, 209
Moscow Township, 13-14
Moynihan, Daniel P., 228
MUCC, 168
multiplier, 20, 55, 58

N
NAFTA, 239-240
National Geographic, 228, 259
National Parks and Conservation Association, 69
nation-state, 222, 224
Native American, 27, 53, 92
Nature Conservancy, 43, 51-53, 167
navy beans, 21
Negative Population Growth, 73, 265
New Colossus, 67
New York Times, 31
Newsweek, 137
Niagara Falls, 17, 213
nitrogen-bearing, 21
nitrogen-fixing, 20-22
Nixon, Richard, 141, 238
Noonan, Pat, 167
North Adams, 15
North Channel, 84
North Fox Island, 47
Northwoods Call, 46
NumbersUSA.com, 31, 88, 101, 266

O
Oberlin, 68
Ohm, 208
O'Keefe, Thomas, M.D., 165
Old Dogma, 222
Olson, Sigurd F., 260
Omar Abdel-Rahman, 243
ophthalmology, 25, 57, 77, 79, 107, 251, 254
Organic Farmer Journal, 259
Origin of Species, 260
orthodoxy, 2-3
Osborne, David, 229
Oxford University, 228, 265

P
Paddock, William, 70-71
Pandaemonium, 228
Paradigm Shift, 222
Pasteur, Louis, 209
patent, 95, 143, 211
patriotism, 160
Patterns on the Land, 267
Payne, David, Ph.D., 244, 278
Percheron horses, 14
Peruzzi, Faidy, 111
Peterson, Merrill D., 267
Petoskey, 28, 46, 57-58, 68, 80, 101, 121, 124-127, 168, 183, 248, 277
Phi Chi, 24
Pierce, Frank, 52
Pikur, Donna, 108
Planned Parenthood, 31, 35, 56-59, 70, 77, 166, 227, 233
Poitier, Sidney, 243
Polio, 14, 214
Ponzi, 243
Pope, Alexander, 23, 162
Pope John Paul II, 243

Population Bomb, The, 58, 62, 258
population momentum, 91
Population Reference Bureau, 35, 39, 81, 92, 199, 228, 260, 265-266
Population-Environmental Balance, 71
Postupalsky, Sergei, 109
PRB, 35, 199
Present Crisis, 165
Presley, Elvis, 7
Pro-English, 32, 83, 110, 138
Prophets, 1-3, 174
PROWILD, 109

Q
Quammen, David, 267
Quinine, 204

R
racist, 75, 103-104, 137, 236
Randers, Jorgen, 265
Raptor Research, 109
Raspail, Jean, 241
Rathjens, George W., 228
Re-Charting America's Future, 89, 99
Recycle North, 109
Recycling, 16, 109
Red Cross, 14
Regrants Program, 109
replacement level fertility, 89, 91, 189, 195, 265
Resist Much Obey Little, 267
Rhodes, 24, 67
Richmond, Henry, 125
Road to Ruin, 123, 126, 267
Robb, Jim, 243-244

Rockefeller, John D., 71, 141, 238
Roentgen, 210
Roman Empire, 202, 260
Roosevelt, Theodore, 66
root cause, 38, 58, 116
Royal College of Physicians, 204
Russia, xii, 149, 213, 219, 241

S
Sand County Almanac, 258, 260
Sandberg, Donna, 7
Santa Barbara, 70
Santario, 204
Schopenhauer, Arthur, 2
Science, 62, 140, 199, 228
Science magazine, 62
Sebewaing, 13, 17-19, 181
Sebewaing Blade, 259
Seeds of Change, 228
self-evident truths, 3, 148, 161
Semmelweiss, 208
Seneca Falls, 2
Shapers of the Great Debate on Immigration, 65, 265
Shaw, George Bernard, ix, 1
Sheldon, Bill, 59
Sheppard, Glen, 46, 169, 278
shivaree, 17
Sierra Club, 31-32, 54, 59-60, 62-63, 227, 237
Simcox, David, 245
Simon, Julian, 115
Simpson-Rodino Bill, 73
Sirhan, Sirhan, 243
snow, 33, 141
Snyder, George, 7, 46

Social Contract, 32, 88, 110, 139-141, 201, 229, 235, 237-245, 248, 265-267
Social Contract Press, 89, 110, 267
soil science, 23-24
Sorenson, Leo, 135, 138
Sowell, Thomas, 1114, 260
Spudnut Shop, 7
Stacey, Palmer, 83
Starch, 265
Statue of Liberty, 67, 75, 193, 223, 236-237
Statute of Anne, 211
Stein, Dan, 73
Steketee, Peter, 46
Stephenson, Robert, 210
Stewart, Justice Potter, 119, 266
Story of Civilization, 149, 205
Structure of Scientific Revolutions, 222
Stuckey, Paul, 6
sugar beets, 20, 211
Sullivan, Paul, 171
sunset, 67, 78, 93
sweet clover, 21
Swensrud, Sydney, 70

T
Taxpayers for Common Sense, 126, 267
Tennyson, Lord Alfred, 136, 267
tetanus, 214
Thompson, John, 228
tiles, drain, 20
town meeting, 124-125
traffic, 124-125, 176
traffic congestion, 124
Tragedy of the Commons, 140
Travis, John, 228
Treichel, George, 62

Trout Unlimited, 47
Two Cultures, 141

U
U.S. Census Bureau, 66, 89, 91, 97, 99-101, 116, 266
U.S. English, 32, 109, 135-137
U.S. Foundation, 32, 89, 108-111, 124, 134, 138-139, 244, 249, 277
Udall, Stewart, 62
United Nations, 38, 154, 218, 224, 229, 236, 246, 265, 267
Universal Declaration of Human Rights, 229
University of Michigan, 8, 24, 47, 57, 62, 162, 167, 175, 266, 277
University of Toronto, 18
Unwelcome Strangers, 265

V
VanBuren, President, 14
Van Every, Timothy M.D., 79
Vancouver, 206
Vatican, 243
venture capitalist, 52
Vern, 14
Voss, Edward G., 167
Voyage of the Beagle, 260

W
Waldheim-Smith, 228
Wall Street Journal, 83
Walloon Lake, 58
Washington, Booker, T., 66, 141, 242, 261, 263
Washington, George, 66
Washington Post, 137
Washington, D.C., 69, 80, 88, 199
water shortages, 38, 160
Watt, James, 205
Wattenberg, Ben, 115, 263
Wausau, 88
West Michigan Environmental Action Council, 68
Wheatstone, 208
Whittier, John Greenleaf, 5
whooping cough, 214
Wilcox, Joe, 47
Wilderness Act of 1964, 42, 93
Wilderness Society, 42, 260
Wilderness State Park, 60
Williams, Gary, 169
Wilson, Edward O., 87, 129-130
Wilson, William Julius, 146
Winter wheat, 21
Wirtz, Willard, 61
Wollstonecraft, Mary, 2, 172
Wordsworth, 107
World War I, 13, 17-18
World War II, xii, 18, 125, 188-189, 195

Y
Yale, 24, 200

Z
Zall, Barnaby, 69
Zeppelin, Count, 211
Zero Population Growth (*also see* ZPG), 32, 60, 200, 227
ZPG, 60, 62-63, 68-71, 100

About the Author

JOHN F. ROHE PRACTICES LAW IN THE TANTONS' HOMETOWN of Petoskey, Michigan, where he resides with his wife, Debbie, son, Karl, and loyal canine companion, Kassie. He has a degree in mechanical engineering, is a former Peace Corps Volunteer, and is active in a number of land conservation projects. He is the author of two prior books and numerous articles on conservation.

Acknowledgments

HIS GUIDANCE HAS ALWAYS BEEN VALUED. IN 1978, WHEN we moved to Petoskey, Michigan, he urged us to get to know our new neighbors the Tantons. First and foremost, the author's father is thanked for that bit of sage advice.

Living a life is distinct from evoking it. Mary Lou and John Tanton have maintained a respectable distance from the manuscript prior to publication. Disclosure of the information in this biography is neither specifically authorized nor unauthorized by the Tantons. To know them is to become familiar with their overriding humility. They are drawn to issues but will not draw attention to themselves. This biography consists of the author's personal observations and reflections as a friend and co-worker on many projects.

The facts in this biography have been derived principally from a personal relationship spanning several decades, including insights drawn from activities and observations as a member of the board of John's charitable foundation, known as U.S. Foundation. We also have participated regularly in several discussion groups over the years. In one, we reviewed the complete works assembled by the Great Books Foundation. Few secrets survive open discussions of history's great writings.

The Tantons have chosen how to live their lives. History will judge whether they merit credit or criticism. On the other hand, responsibility for shortcomings or inaccuracies in how their lives have been evoked rests exclusively with the biographer.

This work includes the observations and insights of the Tantons' family, friends, and colleagues. Thank you Kenneth Scheffel, field representative at the University of Michigan Bentley Historical Library, David Irish, Kathryn Bricker, Niki Calloway, Rev. Robert Kyser,

Wayne Lutton, Ph.D., Laura (Tanton) deOlazarra, Jane (Tanton) Thomson, Sherry Barnes, Glen Sheppard, Max Thelan, Tom Bailey, Gerda Bikales, K.C. McAlpin, David G. Payne, Ph.D., Otis L. Graham Jr., Ph.D., and Don Ward.

Particular gratitude is expressed to several other individuals. Thank you Donna L. Theriault. Our mutual career as co-workers spans several decades. And thank you Fred Baker. A valued and enduring friendship has oddly resulted from your willingness to freely offer a brutally harsh, albeit truthful, critique. Particular gratitude is thus extended for your dispassionate editorial invectives as well as for the insights of Bob Kyser. I also wish to thank Jennifer Denson; Rebecca Chown, for her invaluable editorial and proofreading expertise; as well as Mareesa Orth at the Jenkins Group, who maintained the timely pace of production.

This publication has been made possible by a generous grant from the Hardin-Swensrud Fund.